D0948803

Personal Relationships. 3:

Personal Relationships in Disorder

Personal Relationships. 3:

Personal Relationships in Disorder

Editors

STEVE DUCK and
ROBIN GILMOUR

Department of Psychology
University of Lancaster, England

1981

ACADEMIC PRESS
A subsidiary of Harcourt Brace Jovanovich, Publishers
London New York Toronto Sydney San Francisco

ACADEMIC PRESS INC. (LONDON) LTD.
24/28 Oval Road,
London NW1

United States Edition published by
ACADEMIC PRESS INC.
111 Fifth Avenue
New York, New York 10003

British Library Cataloguing in Publication Data

Personal relationships.
    Vol. 3
    1. Interpersonal relationships
    I. Duck, Steven W.
    II. Gilmour, Robin
    302   HM132   80–41360
    ISBN 0–12–222803–0

Set in Times by
Book Economy Services, Cuckfield, Sussex

Printed in Great Britain by
John Wright & Sons (Printing) Ltd, at the Stonebridge Press, Bristol

Contributors

PETER M. BENTLER, Department of Psychology, University of California at Los Angeles, Los Angeles, California 90024, USA.

WINDY DRYDEN, Department of Educational Enquiry, University of Aston, Gosta Green, Birmingham B4 7ET, England.

STEVE DUCK, Department of Psychology, Fylde College, University of Lancaster, Lancaster LA1 4YF, England.

JOAN HERRMANN, Department of Psychology, University of Edinburgh, 1-7 Roxburgh Street, Edinburgh EH8 9TA, Scotland.

KEVIN HOWELLS, Department of Psychology, The University of Leicester, Leicester LE1 7RH, England.

JOHN J. LA GAIPA, Department of Psychology, University of Windsor, Windsor, Ontario, Canada.

MARGARET MANNING, Department of Psychology, University of Edinburgh, 1-7 Roxburgh Street, Edinburgh EH8 9TA, Scotland.

MICHAEL D. NEWCOMB, Department of Psychology, University of California at Los Angeles, Los Angeles, 90024, USA.

PAUL O'REILLY, Department of Clinical Psychology, Exe Vale Hospital, Woodwater Lane, Digby, Exeter EX2 7EY, England.

JIM ORFORD, Department of Psychology, Washington Singer Laboratories, University of Exeter, Exeter, England.

LETITIA ANNE PEPLAU, Department of Psychology, University of California at Los Angeles, 405 Hilgard, Los Angeles, California 90024, USA.

DANIEL PERLMAN, Department of Psychology, University of Manitoba, Winnipeg, Canada.

PETER TROWER, Department of Psychology, Hollymoor Hospital, Northfield, Birmingham B31 5EX, England.

H. DIANE WOOD, Department of Psychology, University of Windsor, Windsor, Ontario, Canada.

MAURICE YAFFÉ, Department of Psychological Medicine, Guy's Hospital, St. Thomas Street, London SE1 9RT, England.

Preface

Disorder and dissolution of personal relationships do not merely cause unhappiness but they can also have devastating psychological effects which spill into people's lives in complex ways that are only just beginning to be understood. As the clinical significance of disturbed personal relationships becomes more clearly recognized in therapeutic settings, so the growth in theoretical understanding of personal relationships assumes a greater urgency. At the same time recent developments in the social psychologist's approach to personal relationships have begun to turn towards explanations of the disruption of relationships. This convergence of interests is a timely one and suggests that cross-fertilization of ideas will produce considerable benefits — practical and theoretical — for both social and clinical psychology.

The recent development of clinical psychology has been marked by an increasing emphasis on the importance of social — i.e. relational — setting for the understanding and treatment of individual pathology. Indeed some clinicians (e.g. family therapists) would take the view that there is hardly an individual pathology as such, but that disturbance essentially takes place in a network of relationships and cannot simply be located within a given individual. Even if we do adopt an individual focus the importance of interpersonal relationships is indisputable; we derive crucial information about our world (and ourselves) in our interactions with others so that the maintenance of satisfactory relationships is essential through the whole developmental sequence from infancy (e.g. Pawlby, 1981) to old age (Chown, 1981). Conversely, appreciable disturbance in relationships affects the well-being of the individual just as it can also be regarded in some contexts as symptomatic of individual disorder; research, for instance, demonstrates that relationship breakdown can produce severe stress (Bloom *et al.*, 1978), can cause depression (Brown and Harris, 1978; Dryden see Chapter 9) and can also produce *physical* disorders (Lynch, 1977). The significance of this point is well reflected in the use of social adjustment as one of the main criteria for mental health.

It is surprising that such notions are relatively recent, given the long-standing recognition of the powerful punishing effects of social isolation. It has been used as disciplinary action both formally, in the isolation blocks or solitary confinement cells of military and civil prisons, and informally in the British sanction of "sending to

Coventry" (i.e. where a group jointly agrees to exclude one of its members from social intercourse). The crucial point here, however, is that these are examples of the exclusion (of an individual from social interaction) not only *intentionally* but, more importantly, *by other people*. For psychologists and professional helpers the consequences of such occurrences are naturally interesting, but the really key cases are precisely those where the relevant individuals create the conditions of exclusion *unintentionally or unconsciously* — and do it *for, or to themselves*. Whilst formal isolation is a clear example of separation from friends, for some types of socially incompetent individuals the isolation blocks are built unknowingly by the persons around themselves, and, in some forms of relationship disorder, the solitary confinement is effectively created by the person's unsatisfactory processes of social interaction. As readers of the present volume will find for themselves, the disturbed interpersonal context of the lives of many sorts of persons can be a crucial influence on their tendency to commit violent crime, to experience clinical depression, or to resort to abuse of alcohol or drugs. It is for such reasons that workers from many disciplines are showing an increasing interest in personal relationships, since the "root problem" may be poor relating, rather than the more obvious presented symptoms (e.g. violence or depression).

From a theoretical perspective an adequate science of personal relationship thus requires that we work towards an understanding of disturbance and breakdown in a wide variety of relationships. Such an understanding is important in itself, but it is also essential to a proper conception of satisfactory relationships — here, as elsewhere, the "pathological" illuminates the "normal". Most of the research on personal relationships has concentrated on non-disturbed relationships (and a limited range at that) so that the explanations and derived theories have only limited scope. Only by considering a full range of relationships and the full development of specific relationships from inception through growth, to decay and dissolution will researchers be able to devise theoretical structures appropriate to a truly general science of personal relationships.

It is for such reasons that our planning of the series of books about personal relationships, in which the present volume appears, began with the view that books on personal relationships in disorder and dissolution would be essential parts of the series. Disorders of relationships seemed to be the central concern from which some (therapeutic) work followed and to which other (research) work is ultimately directed. Thus, it seemed to us, those who study "normal" relationships can best justify their work in applied terms by reference to the light that their efforts can cast upon disruption or dissolution of those normal relationships. Clearly, also, disorders and dissolution of relationships had to be set in the context of what was known about their normal state, their normal manifestations, their growth and their development. In this way, then, it became clear that, although disorder or dissolution of personal relationships was our main starting point, the series of books would, paradoxically, need to lead up to that point rather than start with it! Accordingly, the four volumes in the series are arranged to start with *Personal Relationships 1: Studying Personal Relationships* (Duck and Gilmour, 1981a), which provides the discussion of the nature of personal relationships and exemplifies some types that have received intensive study; whilst *Personal Relationships 2: Developing Personal Relationships* (Duck and Gilmour, 1981b), considers the ways in which relationships grow between people and the ways in which attitudes to, and about, relationships, change over the life cycle. These volumes lead up to the present volume *Personal Relationships 3: Personal Relationships in Disorder*, in which we attempt to understand the disorders that occur in relationships of people in general, in relationships of specific types, and in the development or early beginnings of relationships, as well as the relationships of individuals at particularly stressful times of life. Consideration of the ending of relationships, its prediction and prevention is reserved for *Personal Relationships 4: Dissolving Personal Relationships* (Duck, in press, b).

Despite the strengths offered by such a group of texts, they are not claimed individually or collectively to provide anything approaching an exhaustive coverage of the field. Our intentions, as indicated in the Preface to the first volume, were "to accelerate the emergence of personal relationships as an interdisciplinary research perspective; to show its coherence as a body of knowledge; to map out the kind of terrain that the subject holds — and to encourage the fullest possible exploration and creative practical development of that territory". That last aim is particularly pertinent to this volume with its clinical and applied emphasis, where, as we shall see, the general perspective offers valuable gains in our understanding of clinical problems and in turn leads to real benefits in terms of practical implications for treatment. The interdisciplinary approach too, is well represented here with contributions from social psychologists, developmental psychologists, family therapists, clinical psychologists and sex therapists amongst others.

The present volume, *Personal Relationships 3: Personal Relationships in Disorder* explores personal relationships in disorder from three points of view, which are reflected in the three sections into which it is divided. The first section (*Relationship Breakdown*) deals with the disordering of relationships and their breakdown; and here, interestingly enough, the major input is from social psychologists who demonstrate the value of the theoretical approaches that they bring to the subject as well as the importance of the area to them. Thus Duck argues for the need to extend work on the general nature of personal relationships to include explanation of breakdown and dissolution, going on to provide the basis for such an extension by mapping out issues which need to be embodied in a research framework or programme. Secondly, Perlman and Peplau propose a new theoretical framework for understanding loneliness and review relevant literature to support their model. Thirdly, Newcomb and Bentler take a more specific focus on marital breakdown and demonstrate the kind of contribution that social psychologists can make both in terms of the information yielded by their research and the theoretical perspectives generated.

The second section (*Disordered Relationships*) takes as its focus the disordering of certain kinds of relationship and the disruptive impact of various factors on "normal" relationships. Trower starts with a view of clinical disorder in terms of deficits in social performance skills and shows how certain cognitive and behavioural strategies operate to maintain these deficits and work against therapeutic improvement. Subsequent chapters by Yaffé, and Orford and O'Reilly map disorders of sexual relationships, and look at the need for a satisfactory framework to encompass the complexity of disorders within the family system.

In the final section (*Relationships of Disordered People*) contributors consider the relationships occuring in different populations of disordered people, and here, as in the previous sections, one point worth bringing out is the range of backgrounds and perspectives represented. Thus Manning and Herrmann, both developmental psychologists, take a nursery school population and examine the importance of relationships in the disturbance of "problem children", the way their relationships differ from well-adjusted children, and how such disturbed relationships develop. La Gaipa and Wood, from a sociological tradition in social psychology, describe the different patterns of friendship found among disturbed adolescents; while Dryden, a clinician, surveys the empirical and theoretical literature that reflects the importance of relationships in the process of depression and its treatment. Finally, Howells, a clinicial psychologist with experience of work in forensic settings, reviews a number of studies which focus on the part played by interpersonal relationships and inter-actions in producing the violent behaviour of certain kinds of violent offender.

One distinct contribution of the present volume, in general terms, is its emphasis on the important causal forces of disturbed relationships upon *other* features of human life where the influence has hitherto been inadequately explored. Another of its features is the demonstration that many different disciplines have a focal interest in personal relationships and their disorder. Our authors include social psychologists, sociologists, clinical psychologists, family therapists, developmental psychologists, sex therapists, marital therapists, criminological psychologists, and counsellors. Their differences of training and perspective are evident from the styles and contents of their chapters. However, readers will also note one consistency, namely the frequency with which the different authors illustrate the *hidden* effects when "normal personal relationships" turn into "personal relationships in disorder". Common themes that emerge from a number of the chapters underline the need for better research that recognizes and does justice to the complexity of a personal relationships approach; and for the development of guiding theoretical frameworks that do likewise. The practical importance, too, of this approach is amply reflected in the extensive list of implications for therapeutic procedure emerging from most of the chapters. As we indicated earlier, one of our general concerns with the field of personal relationships is to show its practical value as well as theoretical value, which can be most easily seen in the clinical context, so that it is in the treatment of personal relationships in disorder that the considerable practical benefits of the field will be felt most strongly.

Naturally, in compiling and editing this book we have been assisted by the effort, tolerance and goodwill of many people who compose our own interpersonal context. In particular we record our gratitude to our colleagues, friends and "supporters", especially Charles Antaki and Phil Levy, and to our most capable secretarial assistants Jane Dickinson, Margaret Gill, Helen Lea, Anne Parker, Hazel Satterthwaite and Sylvia Sumner. Although work on this volume was jointly completed by the editors, we retained alphabetical order of editors' names and hence sign off the Preface thus:

University of Lancaster   Steve Duck
April, 1981   Robin Gilmour
                                                          (but not necessarily in that order)

Contents

Section I

Relationship Breakdown

Section II

Disordered Relationships

CHAPTER 4

Social Skill Disorder   97

PETER TROWER

CHAPTER 5

Disordered Sexual Relationships   111

MAURICE YAFFÉ

For Jane
in contradiction of the title

Section I
Relationship Breakdown

CHAPTER 1

Toward a Research Map for the Study of Relationship Breakdown

Steve Duck

One large and surprising omission in the present literature on personal relationships is a strongly developed approach to their breakdown. In this chapter I shall consider why this is so and I will discuss some of the traps that may await researchers when they begin to correct the omission, particularly problems of inclarity (both through lack of consistent definition and through failure to make many necessary distinctions) that hinder empirical and theoretical work. One major distinction here will be between *breakdown* of relationships (i.e., a decline in the attractiveness of the relationship, turbulence in feelings about the relationship, disturbance in its conduct, and so on) and *dissolution* of relationships (the ending or dismemberment of the partnership). Clearly, relationships can break down without dissolution necessarily following, and the research problems associated with the two phenomena are quite different. Yet theorists (e.g. Levinger, 1979c) have so far provided inadequate accounts of this difference, at one time assuming the relationship has gone sour without accounting for the occurrence of the sourness; and at other times assuming that a desire to dissolve is equivalent to "going sour". In my view this involves giving unsatisfactory accounts of

1

the origins of the desire to dissolve a relationship and moving too hastily to a consideration of the *consequences* of that desire in social terms (e.g. the social and network forces that prevent people carrying out the desire to end the relationship). Because the issues surrounding dissolution are so different from those concerning breakdown, I will reserve them for discussion elsewhere (Duck, in press, a) and will limit the present discussion to consideration of breakdown of relationships, decline of affect and intimacy, and other related issues, in an attempt to differentiate and map out the research terrain.

The literature that exists to guide such a task is limited in several ways, most importantly because it is composed almost entirely of work on marital and courtship decline or disruption (see Newcomb and Bentler, this volume, for an excellent review) and it has not always been recognized that such literature offers a very unsafe grounding from which to make general statements about relationships. In particular, marriage and courtship are special and nonparadigmatic relationships that have many features which make them unreliable guides in a search for general principles of relationship breakdown. I shall therefore draw on literature in the general field of interpersonal attraction and relationship growth (see companion volumes by Duck and Gilmour, 1981a; 1981b). This will lead me to consider the question that is inevitably pushed forward: is relationship breakdown merely the reverse of relationship growth? I hope to show merely by analysis that such a question cannot be answered affirmatively since to do so would be to place too much emphasis on the ill-defined "cognitive" concepts of affect and intimacy whilst ignoring the social management of relationships and the very real (but, of course, under-researched) attempts that are made to repair relationships in decline. Furthermore I will reject the notion that relationship decline is a steady, smooth and uni-directional decline of commitment, just as one must also reject the prevailing but simpleminded idea that growth of relationships is likewise steady, smooth and uni-directional (Duck, 1977c).

Some Features of the Terrain

Such objectives require a set of criteria through which phenomena are to be included or excluded from the field. However, it will take the whole chapter to create these, and I propose to take the first step towards them with a simple illustration drawn from work on adolescents. Adolescent relationships are sometimes thought to be inherently unstable and liable to breakdown vicariously. Can one, then, usefully begin by wondering whether certain types of relationship *do* break down more often than others? When comparative data are gathered, then we shall know the answer, but I suspect that psychologists will not be satisfied merely to classify relationships by reference to different liabilities to breakdown (itself a difficult taxonomic task) and they will want answers to the question of why such liabilities might exist. However, three studies of adolescents by Horrocks and co-workers illustrate the maze that we are entering, even if one limits attention to this one very special type of population and this very special problem of alleged liability to vicarious breakdown. Horrocks and Thompson (1946) identified the degree of fluctuation in adolescent friendship and found a trend towards greater stability in friendship with increasing chronological age, whilst Horrocks and Baker (1951) extended similar studies to younger children, with similar results. Whilst these studies identify an interesting and specific phenomenon they also raise some questions of general principles about relationship decline: whether, for example, "relationships" are actually different in style at different ages and hence more stable as a result of their own dynamic properties rather than as a result primarily of the properties or feelings of the partners involved. No mention is made of the possible effects of personality growth upon the development of style of approach to relationships although other, more recent, work suggests that this is a primary feature of adolescent relationship development (Duck, 1975).

From these studies, then, one might conclude that certain sorts of relational turbulence are mere consequences of an individual's ontogeny, development and growth. However, Skorepa *et al.* (1963) found greater fluctuation in college students' friendships than in adolescents' and they speculated that factors such as recency of arrival at college, diversity of sources for potential friends and separation from friends at home may be influential factors here. This, of course, is to introduce another, competing, reason why age may affect relational breakdown: a circumstantial consequence of position in the life cycle.

There are thus three possible features to the alleged correlation between adolescence and relationship breakdown: first, adolescence produces cognitive change and this may (adversely) affect an individual's relationships; second, adolescence produces extraneous experiences such as moving to college, or leaving home and these may create a special (or unfavourable) relational climate; third, adolescence presents the individual with a variety of new relational possibilities and these need to be handled and managed in unfamiliar, adult ways and this occurs with greater or lesser success. All three possibilities are plausible and not altogether mutually exclusive. Yet we do not know how far they represent generalities about relationship decline. Do they, *mutatis mutandis*, exist as possible features of adult relating and relationship dissolution at other stages of the life cycle (cf.

Dickens and Perlman, 1981; Reisman, 1981; Chown, 1981), where such things as changes in cognitive style, life events and adjustment to different social behavioural requirements can probably exert powerful effects on the relationships that are maintained or established? It seems *prima facie* plausible that for example, career development, birth of children, children leaving home, and death of spouse will influence adults' relating; but helpful data are scarce.

Similar localized issues that point to more general ones are found in the case of studies of courtship breakdown and marital dissolution, but since Newcomb and Bentler (this volume) review these studies comprehensively, I shall cover this only briefly and only insofar as it illustrates the general points I wish to make. In each of these two areas work is varied and tackles several operationally distinct conceptual issues. Work on marital dissolution has been descriptive, demographic and theoretical (Kerckhoff, 1976; Levinger, 1979) and has also focussed on a range of problems from exchange and equity in marriage (Levinger, 1979c; Hatfield and Traupmann, 1981) to detailed behavioural observation of marital conflict (Gottman *et al.*, 1977; Markman, 1979). There have also been studies of the causal attributions of couples whose relationships have declined (Orvis *et al.*, 1976; Harvey *et al.*, 1978) and a number of studies into courtship decline or the ending of premarital affairs (e.g. Hill *et al.*, 1976; Rubin *et al.*, in press). Some studies therefore explore possible *processual* inadequacies in relationship conduct whilst others explore the *experience* of those whose relationships have dissolved — an important difference in level of analysis whose significance is sometimes overlooked. The retrospective attributional studies, however, do indicate certain replicable patterns of response by males as opposed to females (for example, the tendency for females to be responsible for more breakups than males; the tendency for females to focus more on the path of the relationship). Such work seems to some workers to justify quite confident speculations and theoretical conceptions of the general area of relationship decline (Levinger, 1979c). For example, the work illustrates the importance of social pressures on the dyad to remain together over and above the affectional ties that bind them. Borrowing Lewin's term, Levinger (1979c) discusses these "Barrier Forces" which influence the willingness of a pair to dissolve once affection has declined and in some cases couples stay married because they otherwise fear social sanctions, kinship pressures, and so on, even though liking for one another has become minimal. Nevertheless, even if such barriers can be shown to be influential also in the case of friendships rather than marriage they are likely to be less numerous and less powerful but, most important, are *certain* to be quite different in form. It is an unresolved question, therefore, whether and to what extent the concept can be applied to other relationships.

Furthermore, even the comparison of courtship research with marriage/divorce research is problematic, given that courtship and cohabiting are crucially different relationships from marriage in a number of ways (see Newcomb, 1981, for a fuller discussion). For instance, marriage is a socially acknowledged, socially sanctioned relationship with legal (and tax) implications whilst cohabitation has not been so and courtship is so only in certain (different) ways. A marriage is expected to be permanent and the only one that the partners will experience in their life, whilst courtship carries no such expectations. Critical differences in psychological response to breakdown (or threatened breakdown) of the two relationships can therefore be expected. Finally, courtship and cohabitation are both relationships in themselves *and* possible stages on a pathway towards another form of relationship (marriage) such that they have the character of a trial or experimental relationship over and above their other features (indeed, Huston *et al.*, 1981, have used changes in "confidence of eventual marriage" as an indicator of courtship progress). Thus the nature of the relationship itself may contribute to its own instability.

For these local and general reasons, therefore, one is alerted to the need for caution in declaring that the decline of relationships may be a general area worthy of study. Indeed the above analysis provides us with at least eight observations about relationship decline that indicate a need for differentiation of features that probably require separate exploration. These eight are:

(1) a distinction between the *causes* of relationship breakdown and the *experience* of it;
(2) a distinction between decline in intimacy/affect and the desire to dissolve the relationship;
(3) a suggestion that circumstantial factors such as position in the life cycle can affect relationship decline (and formation);
(4) the fact that certain individuals may have pre-existing or developmentally-generated cognitive or behavioural disabilities in relationship conduct;
(5) the observation that relationship conduct or "process" (rather than affect decline) can cause relationship breakdown;
(6) the observed influence of social or barrier forces on relationships even after breakdown;
(7) the possible ways in which the nature of the relationship itself defines the instability of the relationship;
(8) the point that different sorts of relationship probably decline in at least partly different ways.

Reducing Involvement in a Relationship

Such distinctions are only part of the necessary features of a desired research map and terminological agreements are also required before we can do useful work about reducing involvement in relationships. Whilst Denzin (1970) noted that relationships may be analysed by their duration, location and partners' mutual involvement, most workers do indeed focus on the last. Yet involvement is itself a complex notion involving partners' greater knowledge of one another (acquaintance), greater commitment, greater intimacy and a more developed and personalized relationship. Further, one thing that has been given scant attention is the influence of changes in personal responsibility that are taken for a relationship as involvement develops. Thus, whilst "friendly relations" are often based on role ascription, their development into friendship is accompanied not solely by increased affective commitment but also by greater individual responsibility for their outcomes (Kurth, 1970). Workers focussing on "mutual involvement" need then, to study a wide range of components which maximize the likelihood of incomparability between studies and it needs to be clearly recognized that studies of, for example, equity in relationship conduct (Hatfield and Traupmann, 1981) are not necessarily studying the same features of involvement as are studies of resistance to the influence of external competitive attractions (Levinger, 1979c).

Such differences in style of approach to the issues are significantly misleading only if they are ignored, but in the area of interpersonal attraction in the past more forgettable papers were generated by such heedlessness than by any other cause. In the present case there is the additional danger that potentially significant differences between researchers are obscured by the general failure to negotiate or prescribe a shared terminology. This is a familiar problem in social psychology and one that workers in this field must surely greet with cordial remembrance given its affliction of attraction research for some ten years after Marlowe and Gergen (1969) first pointed out its significance. For instance, in the research on marital disturbance some workers talk of "marital disruption", some of "marriage breakdown", whilst Hicks and Platt (1970) distinguish "marital (in)stability" from "marital (un)happiness". In other contexts, some workers talk of "relationship collapse", and some simply of "ending" or "relationship failure". Until the component parts of the general problem are delineated, there is the difficulty that the significance of differences in terminology is hard to evaluate and there remains the possibility that investigators are blindly exploring different parts of the elephant without so realizing.

In the present paper, the term "decline" of relationships or of intimacy will be used to refer to the disaffection that precedes the ending of the relationship; "collapse" will refer to the ending of a relationship through incidental means such as relocation or through cataclysms like the death of a partner; whilst "breakdown" will refer to both intended and unintended disruption or failures of process or mechanism in relationships which may not be subsequently mended or re-established (since, of course, not all decline leads to the ending of the relationship); and the term "dissolution" will refer to the permanent dismembering of the relationship.

Reducing intimacy

Even with agreed terminology about the ending of relationships, one cannot conclude that theoretical issues are thereby resolved. It is only a first step towards the research horizon. It is clear that researchers in this field will need to follow that first step with a sharper attention to the very different problems of describing what happens when a relationship breaks down and what happens when intimacy or affect declines, but since the natural theoretical and historical pressure on workers in this field is to take the latter idea first, I will do so. It seems very likely that a decline in intimacy or affect is at least a clear protagonist for the role of main villain in the process of relationship breakdown.

It is, nonetheless, also clear that intimacy is not defined uniformly in social psychology. Much research acts as if a growth in relationship is defined by, and co-extensive with, growth in intimacy: thus Altman and Taylor (1973), Jourard (1964), Derlega and Chaikin (1976), Morton and Douglas (1981), and Huston *et al.* (1981) either offer theoretical accounts of relationship growth in such terms or use empirical criteria for intimacy growth as a measure of relationship state. For obvious reasons this is much more satis-factory than the previous crude method that equated time-in-relationship with relationship depth. Alternatively, intimacy growth is often treated from these and other perspectives as consequent upon growth in *knowledge* about partner (Levinger, 1974; Duck, 1977a; Crockett and Friedman, 1980), a treatment with many advantages, some empirical justification, some consequent oversimplification and some serious omissions (Berger, 1980). Other workers treat intimacy growth from a completely different perspective, in terms of the relaxation of formality in the rules governing interaction (Denzin, 1970), and yet others employ measures of commitment to partner as indications of depth of relationship (McCall, 1970).

Implicit in all these formulations, however, is the view that increased liking is an essential ingredient in the growth of relationship. One might then hope to explain breakdown or decline of relationships in terms of reducing intimacy, but the other features of relationships may each be differently affected by reduced liking and may change independently of it. Since each

feature may grow differently, so it may contribute differently to the occurrence of decline, and it is ultimately for research studies to clarify if and how
this may be true.

How does decline relate to growth?

Georg Simmel (1950, p. 123) noted that "a dyad depends on each of its two
elements alone — in its death though not in its life: for its life, it needs *both*,
but for its death, only one". Whilst growth of relationships depends on
*inter*action, decline can result from the action of one partner alone. Furthermore, as Kurth (1970) has observed the growth of relationships and the
increase of intimacy have a tentative, propositional and experimental
quality, with partners often making their "moves" ambiguously in order to
protect themselves against the consequences of their partner's refusal to
accept growth which also (and therefore) can be done subtly and without
affront. However, in the case of relationship breakdown one probable
feature is a progressive disambiguation of moves as the decline proceeds
and, indeed, such disambiguation is often reported to hasten decline
because it causes offence. The parallels between growth and decline of
relationships will not therefore be exact, and it is precisely the nature of such
differences that stands in need of clarification both from the "individual
psychological" perspective and from a systematic/network sociological
point of view.

   The theoretical explanation of relationship decline or breakdown must,
given all the above, include more than the mere decline of liking although it
remains to be seen whether the broader concepts of decline in intimacy,
involvement or commitment will suffice either. Such a view casts up the
theoretical unpreparedness of workers in the "parent area" of interpersonal
attraction to provide a satisfactory explanation of relationship breakdown.
Some reasons for this shall now be expanded to indicate useful threads in
previous research. However, the general point is a simple one: a theory of
relationship decline will presuppose the existence of a relationship and thus
assumes the existence of something that has had a complex evolution and
only *may* decline in a fashion that is a reflection of its evolution.

   Developmental theories in interpersonal attraction have focussed on the
development of intimacy rather than of relationship and this has so far been
seen in crude and limited terms, primarily affective ones (cf. companion
Volume 2, Duck and Gilmour, 1981b). The emphasis falls upon increments
in the intensity of affect, although there is also work on the changes in nature
or in expression of affect. Just as love can develop in intensity, so too can it
take new forms, say after marriage, and it can be shown to arise from or be
expressed by new activities. Even so the theoretical stress presently falls on

cognitive or strategic components of behaviour, such as the interaction between two cognitive systems, self disclosure, strategic information processing and so on. To an undesirable extent this neglects the important inputs of social processes, effects of membership of other groups and dyads, and social context (Andreyeva and Gozman, 1981; La Gaipa, 1981a). Growth of intimacy is *not* a simple incrementation of liking, but a processual change through which such increments are expressed or indicated. The emphasis on affect diverts us from this critical and fundamental distinction which would have helped us to see the inadequacy in this context of defining the stages of relationship growth analogously with stages on a bus route. It is more likely to be a more satisfactory analogy if one were to treat such stages as if they were stages in the metamorphosis of an extremely large and long-lived insect: in many cases the next stage is dependent upon but completely different in form from the previous one and requires quite different sorts of sustenance and input for it to survive at all, let alone proceed to the next stage. Without such a view of relationship growth one is left without much hope that existing intimacy growth theories will be useful to explain relationship breakdown even to a limited extent and it is a cause for optimism that previous theoretical assumptions, inconsistent with a sound explanation for relationship decline, have recently been attacked or reformulated.

Although work in interpersonal attraction (IPA) is evolving both methodologically and theoretically (Duck and Gilmour, 1981c; Hinde, 1981; McCarthy, 1981), many years of research work into it were completed in exploring the pre-existing properties of individuals which were thought to render them as inevitably attractive to one another as common sense supposes (e.g., as in the case of physical attractiveness). As work improved in theoretical style it began to focus more clearly on the ways in which these properties actually exerted influence on the perceiver; on the processes of social encounter when the properties were displayed; on the emitted social behaviours that were presumably consequent on these pre-existing personal properties; and on the influence of the process of communicating the properties. For example, some very early work in IPA (interpersonal attraction) concerned the rated general attractiveness of physical properties of individuals (Perrin, 1921) but it was not until recently that a satisfactory proposal was made to explain the psychological processes *in the perceiver* that could explain the influence of such outward properties: Dion *et al.* (1972) found that perceivers made detailed personality judgements about physically attractive people in directions that could account for the rated liking. Equally, work on personality similarity as a factor in acquaintance, all too often made the simplistic assumptions, firstly, that "personality similarity" was an elemental and atomic thing incapable of division to types or parts (in the same way that relationships are now treated); and, secondly, that the sorts of similarity detected by a research psychologist would be communicated and detected in real life encounters so as to influence liking directly. It is only recently that a proposal has been made to distinguish the types, the hierarchical structure and the communication of such similarity, thus clarifying the relationship between similarity and the serial growth of acquaintance (Duck, 1973a, b; 1977a, b; Duck and Craig, 1978; a suggestion made subsequently and independently by Huston and Levinger, 1978).

As argued elsewhere (Duck, 1980), these developments are to be welcomed as long as people are not misled into assuming that "properties are out, and process is in": both properties and process exert their effects from their fulfilment of some function for the individual observer, some need that satisfactory relationships serve and unsatisfactory ones — on the whole — do not. However, the theoretical step forward is an important one. The early, property-based approach was naturally difficult to translate into the explanation of decline or dissolution of relationships, as opposed to the explanation of dislike (initial dislike can be explained parsimoniously in such an approach by reference to the properties of the partners that pre-existed the relationship between them, since "dislike" does not necessarily imply the existence of any operative relationship between them). But since the very notion of deterioration of relationships itself contains the assumption of pre-existence of a working relationship that has now declined or is now declining in intimacy, explanations in terms purely of the pre-existing properties of individuals are inappropriate and unparsimonious: some explanation that uses the extra notions developed from work on "process" needs to be arrived at. This has become possible for two main reasons: first, a methodological growth has taken place in this area (McCarthy, 1981) and this enables the close study of social process, acquaintance and contemporary reporting of relationship experience — all of which are necessary to the study of relationship decline; secondly, theoretical growth is beginning (Hinde, 1981; Morton and Douglas, 1981). It is with the recent growth of theories of exchange in relationships (La Gaipa, 1977a; Burgess and Huston, 1979), equity (Walster *et al.* 1978; Hatfield and Traupmann, 1981), and information in acquaintance (Berger and Calabrese, 1975; Duck, 1976, 1977a) that a greater emphasis on such process in acquaintance has been established and may be brought to bear on the notions of breakdown, disaffection or dissolution of relationships.

In brief, several different process theories have developed to explain acquaintance growth and these, whilst often very different in detail (see Morton and Douglas, 1981; Huston, *et al.*, 1981), share certain central notions. Despite initial problems with the idea (e.g., Levinger *et al.*, 1970) it is now becoming more widely accepted that models of acquaintance growth will need to be stage models or filter models where the successive increases of intimacy in a relationship are contingent upon a partner's satisfaction of a sequence of separable criteria (Duck, 1977a; Hinde, 1979) or upon serial changes in expectation about the future reward probabilities in a relationship (La Gaipa, 1977a, b; Levinger and Huesmann, in press) or upon a succession of informational transformations in the participants (Berger, 1980). Certainly there is considerable debate about the relative merits of these different views (McCarthy, 1981; Morton and Douglas, 1981) but the essential similarity rests on the fact that each one supposes that acquaintance growth depends on different critical features at different points in the relationship's development.

Given these theoretical advances, can one best conceptualize the decline of intimacy in a relationship (itself a issue separable from the more general decline of "the relationship", see above) as consequent on acquaintance decline? Clearly not, for two reasons. Firstly, although knowledge of partner increases in acquaintance growth it probably does not decline significantly (except in amnesiacs) when acquaintance declines. It may nonetheless be re-interpreted or acted upon in different ways and it is these re-interpretations that researchers should be exploring. Secondly, the things that grow during relationship growth are more than merely knowledge (see above) and decline in intimacy may thus take a different form from intimacy growth. However, it may still reflect acquaintance growth by being subject to a similar series of criterial points, but in a reversed or different order. Alternatively, it may decline according to its own series of criteria that simply exemplify the same sequential process in a merely different form.

These are significant issues for research clarification but there is, unfortunately, little evidence that would presently help us answer such questions directly. (Braiker and Kelley, 1979, are concerned with a different but related question: how conflict actually helps to *develop* relationships.) Information-based approaches would presumably argue that, since relationship development is based in part on the development of a greater predictive accuracy about one's partner, the decline of intimacy could be explained parsimoniously in terms of an actual or perceived decline in such predictive accuracy (Miller and Parks, in preparation).

Such approaches are, perhaps, too strongly founded on cognitive assumptions and seem to place the responsibility for intimacy growth firmly and primarily upon cognitive operations in or between individuals (Crockett, 1980). The strong complementary effect of some of the *social* influences on individuals has already been alluded to and it remains to be seen whether such influences are translatable into cognitive language or can be added to the relationship equation in ways that give confidence that strongly cognitive approaches will prove to clarify the most important features of relationship breakdown, as they may do in the case of relationship growth (Stroebe and Stroebe, in preparation). It is nevertheless clear that there are important ways in which explanations of relationship decline, even if derived from explanations of relationship growth, cannot be cast in precisely the same terms.

One further point to note in this context is that vicarious exterior influences often cause decline rather than growth. Several researchers have noted that many sorts of relationships appear to have "make-or-break" points inherent in them, independently of the features of the participants involved. Thus Levinger (1976) has observed that a large number of couples report feeling a need to decide on the future of their courtship after it has lasted about 18 months; Hill *et al.*, (1976) noted the influence of time of year on the dissolution of affairs (e.g. student romances tended to reach a crisis at the end of an academic year or at that point of the year when people have to make arrangements about accommodation-sharing for the next session); and McCarthy (1976; McCarthy and Duck, 1976) identified a point in forming same-sex friendships (after 4–6 months) when individuals tested out their partner's suitability for future growth in intimacy. There is also the wider point that there are life-stages where such decisions are also important and promote re-evaluation of old relationships, as for example, after executives are promoted, when children leave home, or during family bereavement (Reisman, 1981; Chown, 1981). Apart from such dramatic crises, however, the nature of decline in intimacy is unclear, not only in theoretical terms but also from the point of view of the description of it as a subjective experience.

It is an open question for future research whether, and under what conditions, the decline of intimacy is merely a decline to a previous level of intimacy rather than a disruption of the whole possibility of a relationship at all, or a modification of the form of the relationship. Whilst one looks first to theories of intimacy growth for help in deciding such issues, it is clear that they must become conceptually more sophisticated. Once one recognizes that "acquaintance", "intimacy" and "relationship" are different entities or conceptual domains, it can also be seen that, to that extent, these theories are conceptually unprepared to be translated into explanations of relationship breakdown in any simple way. This, however, is not to suggest that the main part of any satisfactory explanation of relationship decline will not come from such theories: it is to say that, until further research has clarified the natures and connections of acquaintance, intimacy, and relationship, only an optimist would expect present theories to tell the whole story.

Components of Relationship Breakdown

In objecting to the contemporary work on relationships as he found it, McCall (1970) urged a sociological approach to relationships which eschewed the focus on abstractions propounded by role theory, or on the interpersonal theories of Freud and Sullivan, or on the narrow emphases of cognitive approaches like Heider's balance theory. McCall's approach stresses the view that social relationships are a form of social organization comparable to small groups, bureaucracies and communities, with rules and rituals governing entry and exit, and a host of little methods of controlling the form of a relationship. McCall's insight stood in stark contrast to the contemporary experimental social psychological approach which stressed the evaluative responses made by individuals attracted towards the formation of a relationship. However, it should not be distressing to find that relationships are so polymorphic and many-sided that investigators from different traditions find them full of interesting diversity even from their own discipline's viewpoint. Rather, it should encourage us to create a research perspective that draws on the contributions of many different disciplines.

One important contribution made by Hinde (1979; 1981) has therefore been to draw together work from several different disciplines (e.g., ethology, social psychology, developmental psychology) in order to indicate the large number of component activities, feelings, social processes and sorts of interaction that are implicit in the term "relationship". Thus important features are, for example, a series of interactions over an extended period of time, shared past experience, conjoint expectations of the future of the relationship, certain depths and types of feelings about the partner, socially defined norms and ideals for behaviour, and certain qualities of behaviour in interaction (Hinde, 1979; 1981). Also, one might add to that list the importance of activity *outside* the particular dyad, both in the sense of the other relational patterns which are available to each partner elsewhere (Kelley, 1979; Levinger, 1979c; La Gaipa, 1981a) and also in the sense of the planning, daydreaming, fantasizing, expecting and evaluating of the relationship that each person probably carries out (Duck, 1980). These aspects have been studied (or in some cases, have not been studied) by a range of different workers and we know varying amounts about each of them. We also know that each of them is an important component of a relationship and that, to an extent which is not yet known, each of them is independent of the others until critical points of a relationship's growth are reached. Indeed it is probable that the label "relationship" becomes justified as partners (and/or outsiders) start to recognize that several of the above features are no longer independent of one another. As Hinde (1979, 1981) makes clear, relationships have about them features which emerge and are not strictly present in either of the partners alone. In the present context we can note that what can emerge, can emerge badly or well.

It is thus of great significance to research on breakdown of relationships to note that they can break down in different ways, in a variety of forms, at a variety of levels, from a variety of causes. In much research this has been overlooked in the search for single, universal causes or in exploration of the most obvious influence: *decreased liking for, or reduced satisfaction with, the partner* (or disruption of any of the factors listed above, e.g. disturbance of conjoint expectations of the future). Relationship dissolution can also occur, among other reasons, because the *relationship has served its purpose* (e.g. relationships formed at points of life-crisis are likely to be dissolved once the crisis is passed). Furthermore, breakdown can result from faulty relational process and consequent *dissatisfaction with the relationship itself.* Such causes may include, for example, poor social skill in maintaining smooth interaction (cf. Trower, this volume); continual failure to provide appropriate types and levels of reward (Hatfield and Traupmann, 1981); unsatisfactory performance of implied role obligations (e.g. Murstein, 1977); inadequate sexual performance (Przybyla and Byrne, 1981); and so on. These should be added to the more traditional lists of "personal causes" (e.g. disaffection with partner's personality), "emergent causes" (e.g. the intimacy level of the relationship became inappropriately intense for one partner; or continuance of the relationship implied acceptance of an unrealistic view of oneself), or "circumstantial causes" (e.g. graduation and relocation of partners).

One additional component of "a relationship" — and hence one more thing that can be disrupted — consists in the formal or informal behavioural implications in many relationships. These cover such things as permitted sorts of physical contact (Jourard, 1966), expected sorts of intimate disclosure (Derlega, *et al.,* 1976), frequency of interaction expected with associates (Harré, 1977), and a whole range of semi-ritualistic behaviours that are expected to be performed in order to sustain and maintain a relationship at a particular level of intimacy (Berne, 1964; Harré, 1977). People in relationships — and outside observers, too, who can also institute a relationship dissolution by their observations or comments — have particular expectations about the performance of such behaviours if a relationship is to survive and, as Equity Theorists have observed (e.g. Hatfield and Traupmann, 1981), relationships can be disturbed if these expectations are not fulfilled. Indeed the discrepancy between expectations about a relationship and the actualities may itself accelerate or account for dissolution of the relationship. Not only may expectations about the nature or purpose of relationships be so disconfirmed but also expectations about correct or appropriate behaviours may be at odds with reality. Worthy of empirical investigation are the influence, in this context, of male or female sex role expectations, beliefs about appropriate relational activity at different ages in the life cycle, or norms for relational behaviour in different educational and socio-economic subgroups. A further source of such expectations (which may influence relationships and willingness to risk their dissolution) comes from cultural beliefs about the ages at which persons should be most active in their search for sexual partners.

Three important points for future research can thus be drawn from this discussion. One is the suggestion that "a relationship", being a *complex of independently developing features,* is something that can deteriorate at many possible levels and in many different ways, with consequent effects on different aspects of the future form of the relationship. The second point is that "a relationship" could end in some critical sense *before* the partners disengage from it. This suggests that, on the one hand, the usual research criterion for the end of a relationship (viz. partners leaving) is not necessarily a good criterion for establishing dissolution and it indicates that, since the relevant criterion may be an arbitrary one, incomparability between studies is likely to result. On the other hand, it may also be misleading or uninformative for researchers to compare experiences of partners immediately before leaving the relationship with those after leaving it if one is truly interested in relationship breakdown rather than, say, "the decision to leave" and its antecedents or its place in negotiated relationship dissolution. A third point to draw from the foregoing discussion is the probability that different sorts of relationships, having different social status, being formed for different reasons and from different antecedents (cf. friendship, courtship, cohabital relations, family relations) will not all grow or dissolve in the same sorts of ways, nor be associated with the same sorts of subjective experiences. Single-factor hypotheses have been shown *not* to explain the variety of relationship growth and cannot be expected to explain relationship breakdown. Nor should one expect them to explain both dissolution *and* the experiences associated with it: in the past, it has often seemed as if commentators are paying insufficient attention to the differences between relationship breakdown, the experiences of relationship breakdown, the experiences that precede (and maybe precipitate) it, and the experiential consequences of it. However, with such points made, I shall now go on to discuss past and possible future research into the nature, experiences, causes, course and consequences of relationship breakdown — all of which, though related, are psychologically distinct and must be so treated by research.

Researching Relationship Breakdown

The present section represents an attempt to distinguish features of declining relationships which will need separate sorts of investigation if anything approaching a complete picture of the process is to emerge. The consequent discussion of relationship dissolution is to be found elsewhere (Duck, in press, a). Because little existing research has yet tried to do so, I propose to distinguish several sorts of actual influence on relationship decline, to distinguish all of these from the experience of relationship decline and to try to place them relatively in terms of their psychological effects.

Types of cause

I have argued elsewhere that there are many possible ways in which a relationship can be dissolved (Duck, in press, a); here I am concerned that there are many possible courses for decline to take, many sorts of reasons that can be proposed, and many mixtures in which they can be combined, even if some high order principle may be common to many of them. It would be naive to expect that any simple model of causality will suffice to explain relationship decline or breakdown, or that any simple principles can be outlined to predict, in a given case, when decline will reach a point of dissolution (Duck, in press, b). It should also be remembered that actual mixtures of causes are perhaps best not assessed *only* in terms of one or both participants via causal attributions or narrative accounts, since such reports can be either a detached objective appraisal or an excuse that disguises what the reporter believes to have occurred, or even a reason for the decline itself. Witness the frequent ethical objection to research in this area: that having people analyse their relationships may itself cause their decline.

Since it is clear that "a relationship" is a compilation of many sorts of feelings, expectations, behaviours and social dynamics, it is extremely likely that these different features can be differently influenced or affected by different ranges of things and that each can decline, disintegrate or deteriorate in its own way (although this point has been overlooked by almost everybody). Breakdown of a relationship could occur because of a participant's view that one aspect was unsatisfactory just as much as because the participant felt disaffected with the partner in general or with the relationship as a whole. Although it makes sense to consider several of the features separately in this analysis, this should not mislead us into the belief that they are necessarily independent in any other way than in conceptual analysis. Furthermore, although both predisposing and precipitating factors may be identified separately, it is their interplay that is ultimately of importance.

Predisposing personal factors

Whilst constancy in friendship is a strong cultural imperative in most Western societies, there are nonetheless certain characteristics of individuals which seem to make them more prone to experience breakdown of relationships, whether through lack of competence, poor choice of partner, personal instability or some other cause. Given the interesting implications of the existence of such predispositions to disturbance in relationships and the social agonies that are often reported by those persons who suffer from them, a variety of research efforts has been directed towards the issues, in terms not only of the populations involved but also of the origins of the predispositions. It is important at the outset, however, to distinguish those chronically influential features that apparently afflict *all* of a person's relationships (e.g. neuroticism) from chronic but specific influence on certain types of relationships (e.g. females have been shown to be more likely to end 80% of courtships and to fall out of love more easily than males; Hill *et al.*, 1976; Rubin *et al.*, in press). Also it is commonly believed that at certain ages individuals are more likely to exhibit instabilities of choice (early childhood; early-mid-adolescence) but it is by no means clear how one should set about classifying such instabilities nor how one should best explain them (Duck *et al.*, 1980). An important additional disability in the present context would be an individual's perception that s/he is attractive for some forms of relationship but not others ("lots of people want me as a date but not as a spouse"). In such cases relationships may break down for the emergent reason that transition from one form of relationship to another is not desired or achieved yet continuance in the present form is not possible. Furthermore, work on social skill suggests (Trower, this volume) that some individuals are capable of setting up relationships in one form but not others, such that breakdown may be due to the progress of the relationship to a point beyond which they are not capable of taking it.

Evidence on the origin of more general forms of relational instability has been often disputed. Bowlby's (1951) controversial work on mother–infant separation has sometimes been interpreted as suggesting that maternally deprived infants grow into socially inadequate adults, rather as Harlow and Harlow (1965) have shown with monkeys. However the resemblance between infant humans and monkeys seems to wane somewhat during childhood, and follow-up studies of humans remain inconclusive and contradictory (Rutter, 1972). Whilst both the mechanisms and the degree of effect may be in dispute, however, there are many people who believe that early experience can influence both the social competence and the relational stability of individuals — although subsequent theoretical developments suggest that the most influential of such experiences occur in young childhood rather than in infancy as was first argued (see Foot *et al.*, 1980).

It is, nevertheless, possible to distinguish instability consequent on negative social experiences from the general instability of friendship choice in young childhood: children's choice patterns are quite labile at around the ages of 5–8 (Foot *et al.*, 1980). A recent explanation for this instability suggested that at these ages children's friendship choices are based on concretistic and particularistic features of interaction (e.g. sharing of sweets) such that someone who gives a child a sweet today will be a friend today but not tomorrow unless s/he also gives a sweet tomorrow (Duck *et al.*, 1980). Relationships of such children are thus likely to be inherently unstable, and the explanation for relationship problems in these cases can be found in the general features of children's propensities at these ages. A similar argument has been proposed for adolescents (Duck, 1975) and it has been claimed that adolescent friendship choices are based on similarity or consensual validation, particularly in those areas or layers of personality that are newly developing in the adolescent's system and hence are un-familiar and in greatest need of validational support from other people. Relationships in adolescence could, on this view, break down for three independent principal reasons: first, the adolescent is unable to find in the partner support for the parts of his developing personality system that need it most; second, the development of the system overtakes the requirement for similarity in the areas where it is present and so the partners disengage in order to seek other partners who support the newly developed aspects of their system; third, the relationship may break down because the partners lack the management or behavioural skills required to encode and reveal to their partners those similarities that are in fact present between them. These intriguing possibilities remain, however, for future investigators to explore. In essence the predisposing influence to relationship instability is tied closely to the function of consensual validation – in this case, personality validation and support.

Similar reasoning can be offered to explain other sorts of psychological predisposition to relationship instability. For example, Bloom *et al.* (1978) argue that neuroticism is a "premarital disability" that renders people liable to high rates of marital disruption and it is possible to contend that neuroticism raises the level of difficulty inherent in finding consensual validation for one's personality whilst simultaneously heightening its signifi-cance to the individual. In the first place, it seems to follow that neurotics would end up choosing other neurotics as partners (cf. Murstein, 1977) and that the conduct of relationships, rather than their psychological basis, would thus be strained and difficult. An alternative possibility is that neurotics become insecure in relationships (perhaps from some continual experience of failure to find validation in relationships) and have exaggerated expectations of instability in partners (Mehrabian and Ksionzky, 1974).

Whilst there is thus evidence to suggest the important influence of predisposing personal characteristics in the general aetiology of unstable relationships or relationship breakdown, the area of IPA (interpersonal attraction) research is full of examples of premature closure of efforts on a problem because workers unwisely supposed that identification of such predisposing characteristics was the end of the research enterprise. In the present case it clearly is not the end of the matter.

A further special danger here is that attention (and hence explanation) focusses on particular relationships in isolation from the other relationships in which the person is involved – an almost universal problem with the research until now (Andreyeva and Gozman, 1981; La Gaipa, 1981a). However any explanation of general characteristics predisposing a person to relational instability must be founded on the assumption that *all* their relationships are so afflicted (if not, why not?); whilst explanation for specific instances of breakdown against such a background is self-refuting unless one is prepared to argue that the particular relationship becomes dispensable because the functions that it serves are equally well satisfied within the nexus of other relationships available to the person — and hence that the effects of the general predisposing characteristics are in those instances therefore somehow neutralized.

Precipitating factors

Exterior influences on breakdown. Given the possible influence of a variety of potential predisposing factors, precipitating factors can themselves be divided conceptually in several ways. The first distinction here is between those that are exterior, (such as circumstantial events, the effects of other people on the relationship), and those that are interior (e.g. feelings about partner). The distinction is not an absolute one since even circumstantial events such as moving to new homes have to be *accepted* by the partners and "allowed" to upset a relationship: there is nothing *absolutely* wrecking about such separation, and many relationships survive over long distances. In one way of looking at the problem, then, the interior-exterior distinction is not a completely clear one. However, exterior influences are recognized in people's reports of broken relationships (Orvis *et al.*, 1976) and are often treated as neutral, unavoidable influences for which no blame can be attached to the partners themselves. As such, their influence on the experience of the termination of the relationship is likely to be significantly different from the influence of those causes which are not affectively neutral.

Amongst those causes for relationship breakdown which subjects have identified with such exculpatory resignation are "circumstances", as in Orvis *et al.* (1976), where subjects attributed some of the cause of their relationship dissolution to such things as relocation or change of employment. As has already been suggested, time of year is often another affectively neutral precipitator of breakdown although subjects rarely identify this as an influence and it is more likely to be seen as an influence by the researcher than by the participants themselves, who are far more likely to explain the breakdown in other terms.

Similar reasoning applies to another possible cause of breakdown: the appearance of a rival to one of the participants. Whilst the rival's appearance on the scene may appear to be the precipitator of breakdown, in the last analysis it is the *acceptance* of that rival by the other person and the expression of a preference for him/her that actually breaks up the partnership. Such reasons for breakdown of relationships are as likely to be markers or convenient excuses as they are to be causally precipitative, and this point needs to be borne in mind when one considers attributional studies of relationship dissolution. Such attributions may affect dissolution by their influence on other features of the relationship than simply liking — perhaps by influencing processual or management features of the relationship, such as exchange and equity.

Processual/behavioural/management features. A widely researched origin of relationship breakdown from this next cause is "social skill deficit" (Trower, this volume) where individuals lack the skills of timing, warmth and social rewardingness that are necessary to the smooth conduct of social interaction. Undoubtedly higher order deficits in social skill exist in the form of inability to comprehend higher order needs of intimate acquaintances, inadequacy of performance of the role of friend or acquaintance (La Gaipa, 1977b), mismanagement of relationships in public (Harré, 1977), and failure to establish complementary role relationships (Bloom *et al.*, 1978). Moreover, other theoretical notions seem to be applicable under this heading also; for example, the equitable conduct of relationships (Walster *et al.*, 1978) amounts to a management feature of it, and analyses exist for the breakdown of relationships through perception of inequity (Hatfield and Traupmann, 1981) assessed in terms of normative knowledge about relationships gained from sights of *other* relationships (one's own and other people's). The suggestion by Huesmann and Levinger (1976) that expectations of future reward contingencies in the relationship account in part for its growth in intimacy is also relevant under this heading. Presumably a partner who comes to expect lower rewards on the basis of his observations of present interaction processes, will feel an attraction to the prospect of withdrawal from the relationship. Also someone who is unable to conform to qualitative normative expectations about the shifting content of interactions as intimacy increases (cf. La Gaipa, 1977a) or who fails to conform to qualitative exchange expectations in interaction will also be likely to set the partner thinking of withdrawal or relationship breakdown.

Whilst disappointment with likely future exchanges may induce disaffection it seems that a further subtle related reason for decline may be found in quantitatively or qualitatively inappropriate exchange: thus, where one partner gives far too much of those resources that are appropriately exchanged only by more intimately related partners, disaffection is a predictable result. This finding had been observed many times in research on Self Disclosure (e.g. Miell *et al.*, 1979) where inappropriately intimate disclosure evokes not increased intimacy but hostility and withdrawal by the target of the disclosure. Furthermore there are societal expectations about sex roles in self disclosure and in resource investment in relationships which seem likely to affect satisfaction with relationships, desires to remain in them and intentions to leave. Thus, females are expected to be more disclosing in the early stages of relationships than are males and are expected to devote greater amounts of effort and attention to relationships than are men (Miell *et al.*, 1979). Disruption of such expectations may have unfavourable consequences for a relationship.

Another related point is the conclusion, from a range of literature, that many people (most of whom are clinically disturbed) are poor at appropriately indicating their feelings towards others (Trower *et al.*, 1978) and that their ability to conduct relationships is thereby restricted. A subtler version of this point is that some people may be normal when it comes to indicating certain levels of liking, but may act inappropriately or incompetently at deeper and more intimate levels. If this were the case, their relationships would be likely to falter or stagnate or breakdown not in the initial stages but at later ones. Unfortunately there is little evidence on this interesting possibility and "social skill" literature focusses, at present, mostly on the management of those superficial social encounters in which many normal people also feel most uncomfortable.

Emergent properties of relationships that cause decline. As two partners become better acquainted, so their relationship begins to develop properties that emerge from the interaction and are not strictly properties of the individuals themselves. One obvious example is that whilst the partners begin to develop a liking for each other, the relationship develops intimacy; also, the level of similarity between the partners, as it emerges in interaction, is not, in the true sense, a property of either partner separately. Such emergent properties as intimacy levels, similarity and "future of the relationship" can also become sources of decline or detachment. For example,

Orvis, *et al.* (1976), Harvey, *et al.* (1978) and Miell (in preparation) have all found that individuals sometimes explain withdrawal from the relationship in terms of relationship properties, such as: "The relationship was getting too intense", "It wasn't going anywhere", "It needed more commitment than I was prepared to give", "I felt stifled in it", "It was getting pretty obvious that we weren't as similar as we had thought (hoped?)". One cannot be sure here, however, that respondents were "really" focussing on the relationship rather than simply adopting a convenient social device for avoiding the open expression of dislike or negativity toward the partner — itself an interesting and researchable strategy! Nonetheless, in these instances the partners appear to regard the dissolution as caused by the relationship itself. Needless to say, this emergent influence of the functionally autonomous entity ("the relationship") has not been much researched until recently (Miell, in preparation).

Attributions and interpretations of causes of breakdown*. Attribution is, strictly, a judgement about the causality of a well-defined behaviour or event and I here use the word "interpretation" when I mean the looser notions that the term "attribution" has sometimes been used to convey.

Whilst several studies have explored the causal attributions that are made retrospectively about relationship breakdown, or have invited subjects to explain instances of conflict, it remains the case that analysis of and interpretation about a relationship can itself initiate a decline contemporaneously rather than retrospectively.

There are a variety of functions that attribution and interpretation may serve in relationship growth and decline, and it may be unfortunate that the research presently available for inspection focusses almost exclusively on one aspect: partners' retrospective analyses of the dissolution and of one another — *after* they know the fate of the relationship being described. Such work is likely to confuse the attribution of causality of the dissolution with the *function or meaning* that such an explanation has for the person. As Suttles (1970) notes, we do not know how the cultural and situational elements combine so that people can decipher the inception and course of their friendships. To that extent, therefore, we know neither whether there are certain *culturally*-defined/prescribed activities or omissions which are sufficient to set people thinking that their relationship must be declining, nor whether there are culturally standard sorts of "explanation" for relationship decline which are stated confidently but which do not actually obtain in a given case.

---

* I am very grateful to Charles Antaki for pointing out errors in a previous draft of this section and for his constructive suggestions about some of the arguments. For a detailed discussion of the differences between "attribution" and "explanation" the reader is referred to Antaki and Fielding (1981).

Such a point is also one with methodological consequences, given the recent growth of attributional data-gathering from couples involved in dissolved relationships. If a relationship is composed of both cognitive and social elements, and if it occurs in a social context and a network system by which the partners are influenced (Andreyeva and Gozman, 1981; La Gaipa, 1981a), then it will be ultimately unsatisfactory to explore merely the partners' attributions about one another's causal influence on the breakdown and dissolution of the relationship. Indeed, from anecdotal reports one might conclude that the imminent dissolution of a relationship is sometimes less obvious to its participants than it is to outsiders, such that, paradoxically, the members of a relationship *may* not *always* be the best or the only persons to ask about it. Furthermore, in some cases, observers may in fact be more informed than one of the participants about "the reasons" for breakdown, since they may have served as confidants or counsellors to one of the parties concerned.

Moreover, because dissolution of relationships is something that people usually try to avoid once they see the risk coming, it is often hard for psychologists to study it except retrospectively and the obvious risk here is that the participants' view of the decline may become re-interpreted as a consequence of definitions of success and failure that, in many societies, surround the conduct of relationships. As Perlman and Peplau (this volume) have observed, we usually talk of "failed" and "successful" relationships and in many people's minds their social standing or success is at least partly determined and indicated by the number of friends that they can reasonably claim to have at a given time. It is very likely therefore that views of one's own dissolved relationships will be clouded with a great deal of rationalization, self-serving bias and intra- or extra-punitiveness — expecially if, as some theorists contend, the decline is itself brought about by a felt loss of predictive accuracy about the partner. This observation does not, however, entail that attribution studies of dissolution should be abandoned; it merely counsels caution in their interpretation and points to a need for supplementary work that will clarify their application since "causal attribution" and "interpretation" need to be differentiated in such studies. Indeed, a whole area of research seems to be discoverable here: we simply do not know the systematic distortions of perception that occur in the process of accounting for and interpreting the course of a relationship's breakdown.

One further point here is that, for many of the reasons implied above, the threat to break up a relationship can be used not only as a source of power over a partner but as a means of re-establishing individuality as well: i.e. as a separation from *the relationship* rather than from the partner. So also, it should be noted, can the reasons for leaving a relationship be cast in such terms, even if they were not originally felt that way by the reporter. Indeed, in a formed relationship the memories are often shared or conjoint, whereas the nature and dynamics of breakdown itself sometimes mean that memories for the same events will often truly be divergent in content or in emphasis — or will be reported as such, itself perhaps an operational basis for study of relationship breakdown.

Finally, where decline is slow, a retrospective interpretation of the events must be viewed cautiously in view of the risks of participants imposing a specious coherence on a specious explanation. It is all too probable that interpretations or accounts of their decline are invested with considerable personal significance and this may be enough to distort or misestimate the significance of the various features of the breakdown.

None of this is to argue that such retrospective self-report data should not be collected or, worse, should be ignored: it is to argue that its interpretation is problematic unless and until it becomes possible to compare it with similar data gathered at the time of the decline. For all we know the *differences* between the two sets of data may be more interesting for psychologists than the similarities; and preliminary data suggest that this is indeed the case (Miell, in preparation; Duck and Miell, in preparation). It is clear that specific sorts of study are required to check out this possibility; not only longitudinal records of the progress of relationships by self report question-naires, via interviews and other varied time-sampling methods (cf. Wheeler and Nezlek's, 1977, study of social participation), but also observational data based on couples in conflict or in relationship growth so that researchers may compare the subjects' contemporary reports with their subsequent recollections and also with trained observers' own observations. Clearly, the progress of the research will be predicated on the solution to some advanced ethical dilemmas, but a major problem so far has been that insufficient data exist for us either to know the strengths and weaknesses of the ethical objection or to to be able to speak authoritatively on the nature of the problem of relationship decline.

Finally, it is the case that in this context different attributional possibilities are open to relationship partners from those that exist in other attributional contexts. Usual attribution theory language concerns questions like "Why did X do that?" and the emphasis is on the causal explanation of a unit of behaviour emitted by one person. In the context of relationships, however, (especially those where individuals know one another well) there are *additional* questions about the relationship unit, jointly created and jointly operated, like "What happened to *us*?" Also the person/environment or disposition/situation framework is inadequate to cope with the *directional* implications in two-way exchanges and interpersonal relations generally. Equally it underestimates the causal force of interpretation and beliefs about Self, Partner and Relationship in the development and decline of relationships. Attribution in relationships is a fundamental causal force through its creation of shared interpretation and conjoint experience of events.

One can, then, begin to distinguish five separate roles for such interpretation in the causation of relationship breakdown once one recognizes its probable functional significance:

(i)   Impressions and beliefs about the partner or about the relationship are themselves sometimes the basis of (desire for) dissolution (e.g. discovery that each person perceives the relationship differently and incompatibly, if, for instance, one appears to see it as "serious" and one does not);

(ii) attributions can identify the agreed cause of breakdown (e.g. both partners would agree that a given act of selfishness was the final straw);

(iii) attribution can be used to misidentify causes, and subsequent rationalizations may mask the decline or change the character of the relationship;

(iv) interpretations and beliefs can serve an essentially catalytic purpose in the process of decline;

(v)   attributions and their subsequent interpretation can serve to accentuate, accelerate the influence of, moderate or mediate the impact of any of the "causes" discussed earlier.

One problem with previous retrospective attributional work is that it tends to focus our attention on single causes, on an individual's behaviour as the origin of decline, on a dyadic frame of interpretation rather than a network one and on *when* the breakdown occurred. This is in sharp and intriguing contrast to explanations offered for development of acquaintance, with their stress on complex causation, on affect/cognition and on the "why and how" of development. We really need research to tell us whether and how far these differences in perspective actually matter.

At this point it should be re-iterated that although the present section has found it convenient to split up the causative mixture into separate constituent parts for separate discussion this is not to imply that there is an equally simple causative structure in the decline or breakdown of relationships. We should not be misled into underestimating the complexity of the processes, and the interweaving of those processes, that eventuate in the breakdown of relationships. Nor should we confuse problems of the causes of breakdown with the problems relating to the experience of breakdown — to which we now turn — even though the experience of decline may itself accelerate or cause the progress toward dissolution.

The experience of relationship breakdown

The experience of relationship breakdown as it occurs — the way it feels, the factors influencing the feelings, the consequences of the experience — have not been the explicit focus of much research but have nonetheless featured in much retrospective work unobtrusively. In the present author's view, such experiential features of the process are key elements in the overall understanding of the phenomenon and deserve fuller research — through contemporary self-reports, diaries, accounts, and so on — than has previously been provided. In the extension of such research, the following factors seem to provide fruitful questions for exploration.

If the causes for breakdown can be identified in categories similar to those outlined above, then the experience of relationship breakdown will presumably be moderated by the extent to which particular causes are perceived to contribute to the eventual breakdown, the type of relationship that is involved, and the psychological changes associated with the breakdown. An important influence on the experience of breakdown can be expected to be the source of the decision and the differences in "adjustment time" that it creates. In cases where the decision is a unilateral one, then the person who decides to break off has longer to adjust to the possible psychological consequences whilst the person at the receiving end is likely to experience a more sudden shock, anomie, loss of self esteem, anxiety and even temporary collapse of the value system or a sense of failure. Without data to constrain one, confident speculations can be made here: for example, that processes of re-assessment of the relationship are consequent upon (and presumably shaped by) the experience of the breakdown; or even that there are stages in re-adjusting to the breakup.

Furthermore that most thoroughly neglected area of research, the repair of relationships, would have relevance here if only there were work on it that could be consulted. Presumably there are mechanisms of repair which research has yet to describe and, presumably, the partners' experience of the effort involved in enacting them, the frequency of their attempted use and their perceived impact on the partners (or the relationship) will be relevant, with hindsight, to the experience of relationship decline. Indeed, this may produce a sense of "negotiated decline", which may itself produce a characteristic set of psychological phenomena, beliefs and feelings in the partners.

Indeed, even where partners do negotiate the termination (or reconciliation) this can involve stages of adjustment. As Fowles notes in *Daniel Martin* (p. 153)

> "changes . . . in the character of a relationship don't announce themselves dramatically; they steal slowly over months, masking themselves behind reconciliations, periods of happiness, new resolves. Like some form of lethal disease, they invite every myth of comforting explanation before they exact the truth."

The experience of breakdown is thus likely to be ambiguous and unclear in ways which simple retrospective analyses will fail to capture. However, one would expect future research to find that these experiences are reliably different from one another as a result of their placement on key dimensions, such as type and significance of the relationship to the partners, the degree to which the breakdown is a symptom of other psychological events (e.g. decline in stimulation derived from the relationship), a precipitator of psychological events (e.g. stress, anxiety, feelings of loneliness), or an agent of psychological change (e.g. in self esteem, self perception, or of beliefs about one's capacities in other, future relationships). Such questions, and many others raised here, are presently unanswerable given that the required styles and amounts of research are not yet being produced.

Signposts for Future Research

Although a number of general lines of research have been suggested during the course of this chapter, some of the major directions for future work seem to be the following. It is clear that such work must be predicated on a loud call for a shift of emphasis away from the study of the dyad in isolation from network systems and away from exclusive focus on particular sorts of relationships. The shift must go towards the distillation of *common* principles inherent in different types of relationship breakdown and the identification of *particular* features which are found in some instances of decline and not others. This will require not only a broader approach by social psychologists but also the assistance of workers in other fields. At present we have merely localized data that cannot be integrated against a general background or context, so we may be both generalizing unwisely and failing to descry points of considerable interest because we lack an adequate account of background patterns, a knowledge of cultural influences, and an adequate description of relationship growth and decline. This said, there are three broad and complementary but distinct targets for future research: the conceptual nature of relationship decline; the causes and course of decline; and the experience of decline.

The nature of relationship decline and breakdown. Much has been said in the course of this chapter on the present imbalance of current research towards the cognitive, and away from the social-processual. As with all such calls, the purpose is to redress the balance of the see-saw rather than to encourage intense study of social processes at the expense of further study of the cognitive elements. A view of the problems in ten or fifteen years will be able to tell us how social and cognitive processes interweave.

At present we are remarkably under-informed about the ways in which cultural and situational influences affect people's perceptions of the growth and deterioration of their relationships. Relationships are very largely taboo topics for analysis and research: indeed, part of the problem for the future will be to explore reasons for this. Goffman (1959), Suttles (1970) and McCall (1970) have shown several possible avenues for exploration during the course of their discussion of complementary issues in the nature of social relationships. Kurth (1970) has made several suggestions that would give us a means of exploring real differences between growth and deterioration of relationships (e.g. the "moves" and rituals of intimacy growth could be examined and compared with moves and rituals of decline). Denzin's (1970) work might suggest that we can unearth rituals and procedures of termination of relationships, but despite the existence of such useful starting points, the work remains to be done. Furthermore, Duck (1980) has suggested the likely importance of daydreaming and contemplation of relationships at a distance — both in their growth and in their decay. Such suggestions scarcely exhaust the stock of possibilities but they do highlight our present oversight of the investigation of the nature of relationship decline.

The causes and course of decline. Most previous studies give weight to such possible causes of relationship decay as decline in affect consequent on negative experiences like insults or faulty exchange, yet we know that relationships often survive such decline in affect even if we do not know how or why. (Indeed, a thoroughly under-researched area concerns repair of relationships in distress.) Little is known, too, of how or why people negotiate the decline of their relationships, how they test them or how they contract them or prevent their growth. Yet it will be theoretically instructive to learn about such features of relating. Also there exist some formulations of the course of decline (e.g. Levinger, 1979) but these are *predicated* on the fact that the relationship has gone sour, and we need to know how the souring occurs in the first place, what encourages or prevents it, and how it is different from simple conflict or other unpleasant effects on relationships that do *not* actually blight or destroy the relationship itself. Finally, practically nothing has yet been systematically discovered about the influence of outsiders on the preservation or destruction of relationships.

The experience of relationship decline. Whilst some research has been done on experiences of relationship decline these, as has been noted, are usually from a position of hindsight and this on its own is unhelpful as illustrated earlier. Diary accounts of relationships are one way around this problem (Duck and Miell, in preparation) although large amounts of data must be collected, given the ultimately serendipitous character of the occurrence of the *desired* observable data! Future research must, however, gather such data in order to create a clearer picture of the influences upon the experience of relationship decline and the ultimate place of that experience in our understanding of the phenomenon.

The value and application of such work are both self evident. However, to place ourselves in a position where such advantages can be gained, we must be prepared to encourage colleagues from other disciplines to assist us in elucidating the phenomena. It will not be adequate to apply simplistic general explanations for the wide varieties of relationship decline and breakdown that may be expected to be found once research into such phenomena becomes as extensive, as frequent and as sophisticated as it ought to be. Indeed, some of the most exciting and theoretically valuable possibilities arise out of the potential for cross-disciplinary fertilization — and it is this which provides a major source of optimism for the cartographer of relationship breakdown.

Acknowledgement

This chapter was prepared during tenure of Personal Research Grant HR5382/1 from the Social Science Research Council. I am grateful to Heather Gaebler, Robin Gilmour, Martin Lea and Dorothy Miell for their detailed, constructive and helpful reading of earlier drafts and to Charles Antaki for his generous expert comments on certain sections of the chapter.

CHAPTER 2

Toward a Social Psychology of Loneliness

Daniel Perlman and Letitia Anne Peplau

Loneliness is a common experience — probably few people avoid being lonely at some time in their life. It is also a distressing experience as many individual accounts bear out. For example, in interviews with journalist Suzanne Gordon (1976) one retired surgeon commented on the loneliness of old age, that, "You are alone, people have died and you look in the mirror and you look awful . . ."; while a middle-aged woman describing her unhappy marriage noted that "There was no one to talk to . . . To me, loneliness and depression were absolutely synonymous". Yet, despite the pervasiveness and importance of the phenomenon, it is only recently that social scientists have attempted a suitably empirical, theoretically-derived study of loneliness (e.g. see Hartog *et al.*, 1980; Peplau and Perlman, in press).

   The intention of the present chapter is to review the literature, drawing mainly on current empirical research, and to provide a conceptual perspective on loneliness. We start, therefore, by considering a more formal definition of the concept; in our view *loneliness* is the unpleasant experience that occurs when a person's network of social relations is deficient in some important way, either quantitatively or qualitatively; and although loneliness may at times reach pathological proportions, we are mostly concerned with "normal" ranges of loneliness among the general public. In this definition there are three general points to be noticed, which are also shared by other definitions that have been offered (see Peplau and Perlman, in press): first, loneliness results from deficiencies in the person's social relations; second, loneliness is a subjective phenomenon (it is not necessarily synonymous with objective isolation, so that people can be alone without being lonely); third, loneliness is unpleasant and distressing.

Conceptually, we draw upon an attributional approach (see Peplau *et al.*, 1979) and view loneliness as a discrepancy between one's desired and achieved levels of social relations. One advantage of this approach is that it draws attention to the levels of social contact that people need or desire as an important set of conditions producing loneliness, whereas, all too often, social scientists have ignored this aspect of the problem and focused solely on the low levels of social contact that people actually achieve. A discrepancy perspective thus gives a more comprehensive picture of the factors that contribute to loneliness and helps us to understand phenomena which might otherwise be anomalous.

A second major advantage of the discrepancy-attributional approach is that it takes account of cognitive factors mediating between interpersonal deficiency and emotional response. Cognitive processes such as causal attributions and perceived control are seen as affecting how we experience our situation subjectively. Most traditional views of loneliness (see Peplau and Perlman, in press), however, emphasize our human needs for intimacy, so that loneliness is seen as the inevitable direct consequence of failure to satisfy these needs and any intervening cognitive processes are almost entirely ignored.

In developing the approach indicated above the chapter will be divided into six parts: (1) the forms and measurement of loneliness, (2) manifestations of loneliness, (3) antecedents of loneliness, (4) cognitive processes that modulate the lonely experience, (5) how people react to loneliness in others, and (6) coping with loneliness.

Forms and Measurement of Loneliness

Forms

Various typologies have been used to distinguish different forms of loneliness (see de Jong-Gierveld and Raadschelders, in press) and three underlying factors have each been used in articulating types of loneliness.

The first factor used in classifying types of loneliness can be seen in the writing of Moustakas (1961). He distinguished between *loneliness anxiety* and *existential loneliness*. According to him, *loneliness anxiety* is aversive and results from "a basic alienation between man and man", whereas *existential loneliness* is an inevitable part of the human experience, involving periods of self-confrontation and providing an avenue for self-growth. While it can be painful, it can also lead to "triumphant creation". Thus, Moustakas, like others, sees a positive–negative dimension running through loneliness experiences. *Loneliness anxiety* is the negative form; *existential loneliness* is the positive form. In this chapter, we will primarily be concerned with what Moustakas calls *loneliness anxiety*.

Time has been used as a second basis of classification schemes. Loneliness can be seen as a temporary "state" perhaps linked to specific events such as moving to a new community; or, it can be seen as a more chronic "trait". The individual can have a short-term loneliness "experience", or s/he can be a "lonely person".

A third way of categorizing forms of loneliness has been on the basis of the social deficiency involved. Weiss (1973) distinguished emotional loneliness (based on the absence of a personal, intimate relationship) from social loneliness (based on the lack of social "connectedness" or sense of community). He believes emotional loneliness is a more acutely painful form of isolation; social loneliness is experienced as a mixture of feeling rejected or unacceptable, together with a sense of boredom.

In all these forms, loneliness is assumed to be an emotionally intense experience. Empirical work by de Jong-Gierveld and Raadschelders (in press) has identified yet one other type of loneliness. People in this group are passively resigned to their fate. Although they may lack both an intimate partner and friendships and they may see no end to their condition, they accept their social deprivations as unavoidable and are apathetic in their response.

Measuring loneliness

Researchers have used single items, uni-dimensional scales, and multi-dimensional approaches to measure loneliness (Russell, in press). In all cases, paper and pencil techniques (or verbal questioning) have been used, probably the most thoroughly developed and widely accepted of which is the University of California, Los Angeles (UCLA) Scale. This consists of twenty statements such as "I lack companionship" and "I am an outgoing person" and respondents taking the scale are instructed: "Indicate how often (never, rarely, sometimes or often) each of the following statements describes you". Scoring is done in an uni-dimensional manner.

The UCLA scale performs well on traditional psychometric criteria. It has a coefficient alpha of 0·94 and reasonably high test-retest reliability. An earlier form of the UCLA Scale correlated 0·74 and 0·72 with two other loneliness measures (Bradley's and Ellison and Paloutzian's). Several "at risk" groups of individuals (divorced adults, prison inmates, individuals seeking help with their social skills) have been administered the scale and, as expected, scored high on loneliness. The scale also has construct validity in that it correlates with activities (e.g. time alone per day) and feelings (e.g. sad) that theorists have linked with loneliness.

Finally, Russell and his colleagues have demonstrated the UCLA Scale's discriminant validity. It measures loneliness, *per se*, not related concepts such as depression, anxiety, or self-esteem. This is crucial not only for measuring loneliness but also for providing confidence in the importance of research findings in this area. If loneliness were inextricably confounded with another concept such as depression, one would always have lingering doubts that the presumed effects of loneliness were really only the result of the other factor. In real life it is probable that loneliness often occurs together with depression, anxiety and/or low self-esteem, but fortunately, the UCLA Scale in combination with careful research techniques permits the identification of loneliness *per se* and its unique consequences.

Manifestations of Loneliness

Several manifestations of loneliness can be identified. In the following section, manifestations of loneliness are divided into four categories: affective, motivational, behavioural and social problems associated with loneliness, of which the emotional or affective manifestations have been the most thoroughly studied.

Affective manifestations

Virtually by definition, loneliness is an unpleasant experience. Fromm-Reichmann (1959) described it as "painful and frightening" and other clinicians have commented on the frequent association of loneliness and depression. Further writers have associated loneliness with such feelings as dissatisfaction (Rubenstein *et al.*, 1979), anxiety (Moustakas, 1961), boredom (Weiss, 1973) and interpersonal hostility (Zilboorg, 1938).

Research provides empirical support for many of these postulated emotional correlates: for example, Sermat (1980) as well as Loucks (1974) reported data linking loneliness with hostility. In a study done at UCLA,

Russell *et al.*, (1978) found lonely students were apt to feel "angry", "self-enclosed", "empty", and "awkward". These students also described themselves as tense, restless and anxious. Similar results were obtained among a sample of senior citizens studied by Perlman, Gerson and Spinner (1978).

Another consistent finding has been that lonely individuals have a basically negative outlook: for instance, lonely respondents report being less happy, less satisfied, and more pessimistic (Russell *et al.*, 1978; Perlman *et al.*, 1978). When asked to list and then rate ten activities they did over the preceeding weekend, lonely respondents were less satisfied with how they spent their time (Perlman *et al.*, 1979).

Motivational and cognitive manifestations

Two seemingly contradictory viewpoints have been expressed concerning the motivational aspects of loneliness. On the one hand, some authors consider loneliness arousing: for instance, Sullivan (1953) believed loneliness was a "driving" force. He observed that loneliness motivates individuals to initiate social interaction despite the anxiety such interactions hold for lonely people. On the other hand, some authors believe that loneliness decreases motivation: for instance, Fromm-Reichmann (1959) contended that true loneliness creates a sense of "paralyzing hopelessness and unalterable futility". Similarly, Weiss (1973) claimed that for lonely people, tasks lose their meaning.

In one unpublished survey by Perlman, the answers of lonely respondents indicated apathy: for instance, lonely individuals endorsed such items as "At times I feel worn out for no special reason", and "My strength often seems to drain away from me", but rejected the statement "I have a lot of energy". In another study (Loucks, 1974), lonely students were found lacking in "vigor". Naturally, the despondency apparent in this evidence contrasts with the hyperactivity which can be engendered by anxiety.

Several factors may be helpful in resolving the apparently paradoxical motivational properties of loneliness. First, loneliness may arouse motivation for interpersonal contact but diminish motivation for other tasks. Secondly, loneliness may be arousing yet interfere with the effective channeling of one's energies to complete tasks. Thirdly, loneliness may have different motivational properties over time. Perhaps having perceived control over one's loneliness motivates people to seek ways of alleviating their experience. Last, but equally plausible, loneliness may influence the fluctuation in one's motivational state more than its "average" level. In other words, lonely individuals may alternate between periods of high and low motivational arousal.

Some of the motivational manifestations of loneliness emphasize cognitive processes. Perhaps the most salient of these is vigilance about interpersonal relationships. Weiss (1973, p. 21) commented on vigilance as follows:

> "The individual is forever appraising others for their potential as providers of the needed relationships, and forever appraising situations in terms of their potential for making the needed relationships available . . . (Loneliness) produces an oversensitivity to minimal cues and a tendency to misinterpret or to exaggerate the hostile or affectionate intent of others."

To date, very little systematic evidence has been presented to support these claims. What has, however, been established in several samples (see Jones *et al.*, in press) is that lonely respondents are high in self-consciousness: that is, they dwell on their actions, as well as the impression they think they are making on others.

Besides this vigilance, clinicians have observed that lonely individuals often have difficulty concentrating. The Manitoba data (i.e. Perlman's study) support this insight: lonely respondents were more apt to report being "easily distracted from a task", and, indeed, under distracting conditions, lonely subjects in a lab experiment made more errors in learning a list of paired associates than did non-lonely subjects (Perlman *et al.*, 1979). (There were no differences between the two groups in a non-distracting condition.)

Behavioural manifestations

In thinking about the behavioural manifestations of loneliness, it is at times difficult to distinguish behaviours that accompany loneliness, behaviours that lead to loneliness in the first place, and behavioural strategies for coping with loneliness. In this discussion, we consider social skill deficits in the context of antecedents of loneliness, and we consider affiliative behaviours such as attempting to meet new people, in a section on coping with loneliness.

Three possible behavioural manifestations of loneliness warrant attention. First, to the extent that loneliness creates anxiety or depression, lonely individuals may exhibit some of the characteristic behaviours which frequently accompany these states. Second, evidence shows that loneliness is correlated with a lack of assertiveness (Jones *et al.*, in press). The direction of causality here, is of course, open to debate: while being submissive may predispose people to loneliness, lonely people may also have difficulty mobilizing assertive behaviours. Third, it has been suggested (e.g. Fromm-Reichmann, 1959) that lonely people have difficulty talking about their loneliness with others.

Finally, while some research has been done on manifestations of loneliness, several crucial questions remain unanswered. For instance, do these manifestations inevitably accompany loneliness? Do the various manifestations occur together in one or more cohesive clusters of symptoms? If there is more than one cluster, what are these patterns or types of loneliness? While one tempting research strategy is to identify lonely people via their symptoms, such a technique appears premature. Possibly, such a technique will never be practical.

Social and medical problems

Popular writers have associated loneliness with a variety of social problems such as suicide, alcoholism and even illness: for instance, it has been noted that the death rate for surviving marital partners is atypically high in the period following their spouse's death; and some observers regard this as a consequence of loneliness. In his book, *The Broken Heart: The Medical Consequences of Loneliness,* James Lynch (1977) argued that loneliness also makes people susceptible to serious illness and promotes overuse of medical services. Lynch provided provocative evidence in behalf of his thesis, but it was mostly based on people who were socially isolated and, from our perspective, these individuals need not necessarily be lonely. Rubenstein and Shaver (1980) report a strong relationship between loneliness and a checklist of psychosomatic symptoms such as headaches, poor appetite and feeling tired. However, this checklist combines medical symptoms with cognitive problems (e.g., "worrying") and feelings of self worth.

Further evidence for the link between loneliness and social problems has been reported by Brennan and Auslander (1979). Their study was based on secondary analyses of several large scale surveys of American adolescents, and they found that loneliness was associated with poor grades, expulsion from school, running away from home, and engaging in delinquent acts such as theft, gambling and vandalism.

Antecedents of Loneliness

The possible antecedents of loneliness are numerous and it is useful to distinguish events that *precipitate* the onset of loneliness from factors that *predispose* individuals to become lonely or to persist in being lonely over time. Based on our definition of loneliness, precipitating events may be broadly categorized into changes in a person's achieved social relations and changes in a person's desired or expected social relations. Predisposing factors include the usual quantity and quality of one's social relationships, characteristics of the individual (e.g. personality, physical attributes) and more general characteristics of a given situation or culture. Predisposing variables are typically enduring aspects of the person's situation.

From a discrepancy viewpoint, most of these predisposing factors can be conceptualized as variables underlying the amount of social contact that the individual typically achieves and/or desires. Predisposing factors also shape and limit how people react to life changes that might alter the individual's desired or achieved levels of social contact. Thus, we see predisposing factors as putting people at risk of being lonely, but such factors are not necessarily the immediate cause of loneliness. However, independently of the way one conceptualizes the causal chain leading to loneliness, we would expect predisposing variables to be statistically associated with loneliness.

Changes in achieved social relations

Loneliness is frequently precipitated by changes in a person's social relationships that lead to a sub-optimal level of achieved social interaction. These changes may affect a single relationship, or may affect a person's total network of social relations.

Termination. The ending of a close emotional relationship is a common cause of loneliness so that, for example, widowhood has been associated with loneliness by several researchers (e.g. Weiss, 1973). Lopata (1969) reports that 48% of a random sample of urban widows viewed loneliness as the major problem in widowhood, while an additional 22% referred to loneliness in conjunction with other problems. Divorce is an increasingly common phenomenon which is also associated with loneliness (e.g. Weiss, 1973; Gordon, 1976); and at least one study (Hill *et al.,* 1976) finds that the breakup of dating relationships, too, is accompanied by feelings of loneliness and depression.

Physical separation. In a mobile society, separation from family and friends is a common occurrence. Separation reduces the frequency of interaction, makes the satisfactions provided by a relationship less available, and may raise fears that the relationship will be weakened by absence. Such events as moving to a new community, going away from home to summer camp or to university, or spending extended periods in institutions such as hospitals or prisons all affect social relationships, in addition the requirements of work often impinge on social relations outside of work in the form of business trips, extended hours spent working overtime, or the necessity of moving as part of career advancement. Evidence that physical separation puts people at risk for loneliness is readily available: for example Weiss (1973) has noted the difficulties experienced by wives forced to move by their husband's work. However, Rubenstein *et al.* (1979) maintain that the loneliness passes quickly for most people who move to a new community.

Status change. An individual's position within a group or organization has considerable impact on interaction with others both inside and outside the group. As a result, changes in status may lead to loneliness. For example, promotion in a business may weaken ties with former peers, and create loneliness until new peer relations are established. Persons who complete a term as president or chair of a group may also find that their contacts with others are reduced. Similarly, role loss through retirement or unemployment typically disrupts social ties with former co-workers and so may precipitate loneliness (see Rubenstein *et al.*, 1979). Bart (1972) documented the distress felt by mothers when their grown children leave home, and indicated that women who had invested the most in the maternal role suffered the most from having an "empty nest". The acquisition of new roles can also disrupt established social networks. For young adults, both marriage and parenthood may lead to major and often unanticipated changes in contact with friends and relatives (see Dickens and Perlman, 1981).

Changes in desired social relations

Loneliness may be precipitated when an increase in a person's desired social relations is not accompanied by an increase in achieved social relations.

Developmental changes. Age-related changes in a person's capacities and desire for social relations may precipitate loneliness. Sullivan (1953) posited a developmental sequence in which children of different ages have different needs and social skills. In his view, loneliness first becomes possible during the pre-adolescent era, in which a "need for intimacy" is added to earlier needs for tenderness, for peers and for acceptance. A rather different developmental approach is provided by cognitive psychologists who emphasize the growing child's changing intellectual capacities, such as role-taking ability (see Dickens and Perlman, 1981).

Developmental changes in desired social relations undoubtedly occur after adolescence as well. For example, Gail Sheehy (1976, p. 415) suggested that for many professionally successful people, "midlife may be a time to relax . . . and put more . . . into cultivating friendships, being a companion . . . , being more active in the community". Other experiences, such as psychotherapy or consciousness-raising groups, may also encourage individuals to re-assess the importance and the quality of their social relations.

Situational changes. A person's desire to be with others is not constant. Instead, it fluctuates frequently depending on the task, the physical setting, the person's mood and the like. Middlebrook (1974) found that nearly all students preferred being alone when tired or embarrassed, and being with companions when happy. Schachter's (1959) classic studies demonstrated that situations of stress or uncertainty can influence desire to be with others. Even holidays and seasonal changes can be important (Gilger, 1976).

Changes in expectations. A person's desired level of social relations is tempered, to some extent, by expectations about the sorts of relations that are possible or likely in a given situation. In some instances, expectations about future social contact help to prevent or minimize loneliness. For example, a woman entering hospital for surgery may correctly anticipate reduced social contacts, and so moderate her desired level of interaction in that situation. In other instances, however, expectations may increase the likelihood of loneliness. A young boy going away to camp may inappropriately expect to make friends quickly, and so raise his desires for social relationships to unrealistically high levels. By affecting the desired level of social contact, expectations may influence the extent of loneliness a person experiences.

The quantity and quality of social contacts

Quantity. Perhaps the most obvious determinant of loneliness is the level of a person's social relationships. Changes in social contacts have already been treated as a precipitating factor in loneliness. Here, we wish to discuss levels of contact, *per se,* as another causal ingredient in loneliness. Naturally, in cross-sectional surveys, reports of one's social relationships can reflect recent changes in one's situation: but, for the most part, we believe such reports reflect on-going levels of one's contacts. We therefore regard the quantitative aspects of one's social relationships as a predisposing factor in loneliness.

There are several indications that lonely people have fewer social contacts than do other people (see Jones, in press). For instance, lonely students have been found to date less, and report fewer social activities, and to spend more time alone; whilst lonely senior citizens have less frequent contacts with their friends (Perlman *et al.,* 1978).

Two interesting anomalies in the overall pattern of results are worth noting. First, in some surveys where global indices have been used, lonely and non-lonely respondents have reported a similar total number of friends. This may be because lonely respondents have a reasonable number of acquaintances but aren't actually very close to these "friends". Secondly, in a study where college students recorded their social interactions in a diary for two days, loneliness was not related to the total number of interactions the students had. The lonely diary-keepers did, however, report more interactions with strangers and casual acquaintances and fewer interactions with family and friends. Thus, even if lonely people have a number of brief superficial contacts, the overall pattern of data suggests their social contacts are deficient as one would suspect.

The quality of relationships. Loneliness is affected not only by the existence of social relationships and the frequency of social interaction, but also by the quality of relationships and the needs that they meet. For example, among senior citizens, marital dissatisfaction was associated with greater loneliness (Perlman *et al.,* 1978). Similarly, in Cutrona's (in press) study of UCLA students, dissatisfaction with one's friendships, dating life, and family relationships were all significant predictors of loneliness. Sermat (1980) suggested that loneliness is fostered by poor communication.

Our contact must also satisfy our needs. Weiss (1973) has delineated six "provisions" supplied by social relationships, which include feelings of personal attachment (as in intimate relations), social integration, the opportunity to receive nurturance, re-assurance of one's worth, and guidance. In Weiss' view, no one relationship is apt to satisfy all these needs and, instead, different kinds of relationships are apt to satisfy different needs. In the aforementioned UCLA study (Cutrona, in press), students rated how well their current relationships supplied them with each of Weiss' six provisions. As predicted, students whose needs were well met tended to be less lonely: in particular, having a set of relationships that provided social integration, a sense of worth, and guidance helped students avoid being lonely.

Thus, both the quantity and quality of social contacts do contribute to loneliness. However, it is worth re-iterating that according to our viewpoint, it is not achieved levels of contact *per se* that are crucial: rather, the relationship of achieved to desired (or needed) levels of contact should be taken into consideration. More will be said about this later in the chapter.

Personal factors contributing to loneliness

Individual characteristics that make it difficult for a person to establish or maintain satisfactory relationships increase the likelihood of loneliness. Such characteristics as shyness, self-esteem and physical attractiveness may affect loneliness in several related ways. First, characteristics that reduce a person's social desirability may limit the person's opportunities for social relations; secondly, personal characteristics influence a person's own behaviour in social situations; thirdly, personal qualities may determine how a person reacts to changes in his or her achieved social relations and so influence how effective the person is in avoiding, minimizing or alleviating loneliness. This section discusses characteristics that predispose individuals to loneliness.

Shyness. Shyness, defined as a "tendency to avoid social interactions and to fail to participate appropriately in social situations" (Pilkonis, 1977), may be an important contributor to loneliness. Significant correlations between self-reports of shyness and loneliness have been found by Zimbardo (1977) and Jones *et al.* (in press). Recent work by Pilkonis (1977) has begun to document ways in which shy people's verbal and nonverbal behaviours may hinder social interaction, for instance, by not taking the initiative in conversation. Work by Sermat (1980) has indicated that lonely men are lower in a measure of social risk-taking: while Cutrona's research (in press) has indicated that lonely students are introverted and lacking in assertiveness. Thus a cluster of related factors — shyness, low social risk-taking, lack of assertiveness, self-consciousness in social situations — may well contribute to loneliness.

Self-esteem. There is considerable evidence that low self-esteem goes hand in hand with greater loneliness (Loucks, 1974; Cutrona, in press). Jones *et al.* (in press) found a significant correlation between scores on the UCLA loneliness scale and on Coopersmith's self-esteem scale. Sermat (1980) reported that lonely individuals scored lower on the self-regard, self-actualization and inner-directedness subscales of the Shostrom Personal Orientation Inventory. Eddy (1961) found a significant correlation between loneliness and an indirect measure of self-esteem, the discrepancy between the person's actual and ideal self concepts.

The link between self-esteem and loneliness is reciprocal such that low self-esteem (and correlated factors such as shyness and unwillingness to take social risks) may foster loneliness but, at the same time, people with low self-esteem may blame themselves for social "failures" or for having low levels of social contact, and thus reinforce their own low self opinion.

Social skills. Weiss (1973) and others have suggested that a lack of social skills, perhaps stemming from childhood, may be associated with loneliness. In some instances, people with adequate social skills may be inhibited from performing effectively by anxiety or shyness. In other instances, individuals may not have learned essential social skills. Whatever the cause, lonely students (see Horowitz *et al.,* in press) report "inhibited sociability", that is, they report problems making friends, introducing themselves, participating in groups, enjoying parties, making phone calls to initiate social activities, and the like.

The argument here is that people with poor social skills have fewer or less satisfying social relationships, and so experience loneliness. A potential difficulty with the reasoning is evidence that loneliness is not invariably correlated with objective characteristics of a person's social life. For instance, young adults appear to have more contacts with friends than do senior citizens (see Dickens and Perlman, 1981) yet loneliness is more prevalent in young adulthood than in old age. Several factors may operate to produce these results. First, measures of "objective" social relationships, corresponding to the achieved level of social relations in our definition, do not consider the individual's desires for the number and kind of relationships to have. Perhaps seniors have fewer social needs than young adults. Our position suggests that objective indices of frequency of interaction are less appropriate predictors of loneliness than are indications of the discrepancy between achieved and desired levels of social interaction. In addition, it seems likely that over time, people with very low levels of social contact may adapt (see Weiss, 1973) and lower their desired level of social relations.

Regardless of the quantity of their social contacts, emerging evidence suggests that lonely people have a different style of interacting. Warren Jones (in press) videotaped conversations between strangers. Ratings of these tapes showed important differences between the social behaviours of lonely and non-lonely subjects. Lonely subjects made more self-statements, they asked fewer questions of their partners, and they changed the topic more frequently. Furthermore, lonely subjects responded more slowly to their partners' statements. Overall, Jones characterized the interaction style of lonely individuals as "self-focused and non-responsive", and concluded that this style had detrimental effects for the establishment and maintenance of relationships.

Similarity. A consistent finding in research on interpersonal attraction is that, other things being equal, similarity leads to liking (e.g. Dickens and Perlman, 1981). This suggests that the match between an individual and the social groups in which he or she participates will affect loneliness. In any given social situation, people who are "different" because of their racial or ethnic background, nationality, religion, age, or interests may be more likely to be lonely.

Demographic characteristics. Some data indicate that loneliness is correlated with gender, marital status, income and age. Although it may only reflect greater willingness to reveal their feelings, more women than men state that they are lonely (e.g. Weiss, 1973). For the UCLA loneliness scale, gender effects are small and usually nonsignificant. Loneliness is lower among married people than unmarried (Weiss, 1973). In one study, when the unmarried group was further subdivided, loneliness was higher among widowed and divorced people than among singles, who did not differ from marrieds (Gubrium, 1974). There is some indication that loneliness is higher among the poor (Weiss, 1973). Finally, while loneliness can occur at any age, it may be more common at particular points in the life cycle, especially late adolescence (Rubenstein *et al.*, 1979).

Childhood antecedents. Two findings from surveys (see Rubenstein *et al.*, 1979) regarding the childhood antecedents of loneliness are worth noting. First, people whose parents got divorced experience greater loneliness: the earlier the divorce occurred, the greater the sense of loneliness. Secondly, lonely respondents remembered their parents as being remote, less trustworthy, and disagreeable, whilst other respondents remembered their parents as warm, close, and helpful. Similar findings have been reported by Brennan and Auslander (1979, p. 200). They sum up their evidence by saying that lonely adolescents come from families manifesting "an absence of emotional nurturance, guidance or support. The climate is cold, violent, undisciplined, and irrational". Among other findings, their lonely adolescents reported higher levels of parental rejection, more parental use of rejection as a form of punishment and greater parental dissatisfaction with their choice of friends. Finally, lonely offspring felt their parents gave them very little encouragement to strive for popularity.

Cultural and situational factors contributing to loneliness

Both broad cultural values and characteristics of specific social situations may contribute to loneliness.

Cultural values. Sociologically oriented theorists have seen loneliness as resulting from cultural factors that prevent people from establishing satisfactory relationships. Bowman (1975) identified increased social mobility and decreased contacts with primary groups as key sources of loneliness. Riesman *et al.* (1961) characterized Americans as "other-directed", overconcerned about the evaluation of others to validate self worth: yet Riesman noted that "paradoxically (the other-directed person) remains a lonely member of the crowd because he never really comes close to others or to himself" (1961, p. 22). Slater (1970) emphasized a basic conflict between American values of competition, uninvolvement and independence on the one hand, and human needs for community, engagement and dependence on the other.

The conclusion reached by many sociologists is that pervasive cultural values emphasizing competition, rugged individualism and personal success increase the incidence of loneliness. These values affect the behaviour of individuals, and are reflected in the structuring of social institutions. Thus we might expect that in cultures such as China, where co-operation and group achievement are stressed, loneliness is less frequent (cf. Zimbardo's discussion of shyness, 1977).

Social norms. An individual's own expectations and desires for social relations are importantly affected by social norms. According to Gordon:

> "It is clear to the teenager that he or she should have a date after school, and it is clear to the average man or woman that he should have a mate, family, a circle of friends." (1976, p. 15)

Cultural expectations for social relationships change with age. For instance, while it is appropriate for young children to have their primary emotional attachment to their parents, young adults are expected to develop new attachments to dating partners and later to a spouse. When a person's social relationships do not keep pace with age-related changes in normative standards for relationships, he or she is likely to feel lonely.

One illustration of social norms can be seen in research by Larson *et al.* (in press). High school students were asked to wear electronic paging devices and, whenever they were paged, they indicated whether they were alone or with others and they indicated how lonely they were feeling. If students were alone on week nights, they reported only moderate feelings of loneliness, but students who were alone on Friday or Saturday nights reported intense feelings of loneliness. Here the expectation that weekends are for social activities appears to be changing students' reactions.

Situational constraints. In any social setting, factors that increase the frequency of interaction and foster group cohesiveness should affect the incidence of loneliness. This includes values (e.g. the extent to which a work group is competitive), but extends to other normative and structured factors in the situation as well. For example, a well-documented finding (e.g. Dickens and Perlman, 1981) is that physical proximity fosters liking. As a result, the architecture of housing units affects social interaction and friendship formation. The individual who lives or works in a physically isolated location may tend to be socially isolated as well.

Cognitive Processes that Modulate the Loneliness Experience

As indicated earlier, the discrepancy between desired and achieved social relations is typically perceived by the individual and labelled as loneliness. But, according to a cognitive perspective, this discrepancy does not lead directly and inevitably to loneliness. Several factors may affect the self-labelling process and the intensity of the person's reactions to their situation, and cognitive processes play a central role in modulating the loneliness experience. This section discusses how causal attributions, social comparison processes and perceptions of personal control affect loneliness. We will start however, with labelling.

Labelling

It is sometimes difficult to label subjective experiences accurately i.e. to decide if one is really lonely, or to distinguish loneliness from other psychological states such as anxiety or depression. Cultural beliefs about the nature of loneliness and when loneliness typically occurs may affect self-labelling. For instance, it is considered reasonable for a child to be homesick and lonely on a first trip to camp; and it is appropriate to feel lonely when a person has just moved to a new city. To some extent, people may match their own social situation with cultural definitions of loneliness, and so use social cues as guides to labelling their personal experience.

Cross-cultural studies suggest that language may also play a part in the self-labelling of loneliness. According to Robert Levy's (1973) ethnography of the Tahitians, there exist "no . . . terms for loneliness in the sense of being depressed or sad because of the lack of friends, companionship, and so on" (p. 306). Although Levy notes that the lack of specific vocabularly does not mean that this state is unexpressible, themes of loneliness were nonetheless rare in his interviews. In contrast, Jean Briggs' (1970) portrait of Eskimo life suggests that the Eskimo have several different words for loneliness. *Hujuujaq* is the most general term, meaning "to be unhappy because of the absence of other people". *Pai* refers more specifically to "being or feeling left behind; to miss a person who has gone". Finally *tumak* indicates being "silent and withdrawn in unhappiness, especially because of the absence of other people." It is interesting to note that the first term suggests a sort of angry loneliness including "hostility" whereas the latter suggests a more sad and depressed pattern of loneliness. The ways in which linguistic categories and folk understandings affect the experience of loneliness is an interesting area for further investigation.

Causal attributions

The search to understand the causes of loneliness is not limited to researchers and mental health professionals since lonely people are themselves also motivated to explain the reasons for their loneliness. For both groups, understanding the causes of loneliness is a first step toward predicting, controlling and ultimately alleviating loneliness. The growing body of psychological research on attribution theory indicates that people's own explanations for the causes of their behaviour can have important effects on their self esteem, expectancies for the future, affective reactions, and coping behaviour.

Of various attributional models, the work of Weiner and his colleagues (see Weiner *et al.*, 1978) is most relevant to our purposes. He has applied attribution theory to the achievement domain and this focus is useful for understanding loneliness because, in most western societies, one's social relationships are an indication of success; as Gordon (1976) observed about Americans, "To be lonely is to have failed". Weiner has demonstrated that causal attributions can be classified along two primary dimensions: locus of causality (internal or personal, versus external or situational) and stability (stable versus variable over time). For instance, saying "I'm lonely because I'm unattractive" would represent an internal, stable attribution whereas saying "I'm lonely because I've just moved" would represent an external, unstable attribution. More recently, Weiner has proposed the addition of a third dimension of *controllability*, which concerns whether or not people perceive themselves as having control over the factors that caused their behaviour.

Consequences of attributions

According to Weiner's model, the stability dimension is especially important for the person's future expectancies. Perceiving that loneliness is due to stable causes should lead a person to anticipate prolonged loneliness; unstable causes should lead to greater optimism about improving one's social life. The locus of attributions should have greater impact on the person's self-esteem, with self-blame and lowered self-worth accompanying internal attributions. Predictions linking attributions to affective states are somewhat more complicated (Weiner *et al.* 1978): internal attributions for loneliness should magnify feelings of shame and inadequacy but stable, internal attributions should heighten depression-related affects of feeling hopeless, helpless, aimless, or depressed. Finally, Weiner suggests that the dimension of controllability is most closely related to other people's evaluations of and liking for the lonely individual.

Several studies conducted at UCLA (Michela *et al.*, 1980; Peplau *et al.* 1979) have tested the applicability of Weiner's model to loneliness. One study (Michela *et al.*, 1980) examined students' perceptions of common causes of loneliness and found that dimensions of internality, stability and control were salient in lay conceptions of loneliness. Other studies of self-attributions for loneliness (summarized in Peplau *et al.*, 1979) have corroborated the proposed link between stable causes for loneliness and pessimism or low expectancies for the future. Evidence has also been found that feelings of depression are most likely to accompany loneliness when self-attributions are stable and internal. In the college samples, such relatively infrequent attributions for loneliness as low physical attractiveness and fear of rejection were associated with particularly high levels of depression.

Antecedents of attributions

Given the potential importance of attributions for the experience of loneliness, it is useful to consider how people make inferences about causality. Kelley (1967) and others have identified a number of principles concerning the attribution process. Their work suggests that lonely people should be most likely to make internal or personal attributions when they (1) feel lonely in many different situations (low distinctiveness), (2) know that most other people in similar situations are not lonely (low consensus), and (3) feel lonely over time (high consistency). In contrast, if loneliness is felt in only a few situations and is felt by others in those same situations, then external or situational attributions are more likely.

Two important implications of this analysis should be noted: first, prolonged loneliness should foster internal, stable attributions (results from studies of college students, Peplau et al. 1979, indicate that the duration of loneliness is related to internality of attributions); secondly, people may avoid talking about their loneliness, thereby creating a situation of pluralistic ignorance. If this is the case, lonely people may overestimate the uniqueness of their response, and assume that most other people have satisfactory social lives. This should also foster internal attributions.

Social comparison and perceived control

In the process of evaluating a social deficiency, several factors besides attributions may act to modulate one's experience of loneliness. In assessing one's social relations, social comparisons with others in similar situations may be important (Pettigrew, 1967). The lonely new college student may compare his or her success in making new friends to that of other students, and believing that others are doing better at making friends may increase feelings of loneliness. Evidence in support of this view comes from a longitudinal study of new students at college (Cutrona, in press). She found that loneliness was strongly related to satisfaction with one's social relationships, which in turn was related to comparisons with both one's peers and one's own previous relationships. It appears that social comparison processes may affect how large or important a social deficit is believed to be.

A final modulator of the loneliness experience is the extent to which an individual can exercise *personal control* over his or her relationships to achieve a desired level of contact. Existing evidence suggests that feelings of personal control may generally reduce stress (Averill, 1973) and enhance performance. More directly relevant evidence that personal control affects loneliness comes from a field study conducted in a nursing home for the aged, where the investigator, Schulz (1976), had undergraduates visit the elderly for a two-month period. The elderly residents who could choose or predict when their visitors would come reported less loneliness than residents whose visitor just dropped in, even though the total interaction time in both conditions was identical. Additional evidence bearing on this theme comes from a study of the break-up of college dating relationships where, although both members of a couple typically reported loneliness and depression as a result of the break-up, partners who wanted the relationship to end and initiated the break-up were less distressed (Hill *et al.*, 1976).

How People React to Loneliness in Others

Once people have become lonely, their friends and acquaintances may perceive and react to them in distinctive ways. On the one hand, these reactions can be considered the consequence of loneliness, so we have waited to discuss reactions to lonely people until after having considered the antecedents and moderators of their condition. However, on the other hand, reactions to lonely people can also become self-fulfilling prophecies that cause or perpetuate loneliness. Thus, these reactions could also have been discussed in the section of the chapter on the antecedents of loneliness.

How do others react to lonely individuals? While friends and acquaintances sometimes respond with warmth and compassion, this is not invariably the case, and the opposite tendency (for others to reject and avoid lonely people) has frequently been noted. Fromm-Reichmann (1959, p.6). suggested that "the lonely person may be displeasing if not frightening to his hearers, who may erect a psychological wall of ostracism and isolation around him as a means of protecting themselves". In her view, an attempt to defend against loneliness may also explain why so few researchers have investigated loneliness. Weiss has observed that "our image of the lonely often casts them as justifiably rejected" (1973, p. 12). An analysis of how people respond to lonely others must consider the interplay of several factors.

Stereotypes of lonely people. It has commonly been suggested that stereotypes of the lonely are harsh and negative, and Weiss (1973, p. 12) asserted that lonely people are seen as "unattractive, shy, intentionally reclusive, undignified in their complaints, self-absorbed and self-pitying". Gordon

(1976, p. 217) stated that even being "single" may be suspect: "to admit to being single would be to admit to having committed a cardinal sin in our culture — that of being unable to attract or hold a mate". Reactions may be especially harsh for single women. Lonely people are unsuccessful, inadequate people whom Riesman *et al.* (1961) characterized as "somehow pathetic without being tragic". If these postulated, stigmatizing stereotypes are widely held, they undoubtedly make it difficult for people to acknowledge their loneliness to others.

The available evidence suggests that Weiss, Gordon and Riesman were essentially correct. For instance Horowitz *et al.* (in press) had students describe a person they considered to be lonely, by writing down statements describing that person's thoughts, feelings and behaviour. Via cluster analysis, the predominant features of the lonely person were grouped into three main categories. According to the first set of descriptions, lonely people are stereotyped as isolated, different, separate from others, unloved and inferior; secondly, lonely people are perceived as bringing their condition upon themselves by avoiding social contacts and isolating themselves; thirdly, lonely people are seen as lacking trust in others as well as feeling angry and depressed.

Normative factors. Social norms help to define who should receive sympathy, and what situations merit support rather than rejection. For example, relatives and close friends should be accorded understanding and support in times of suffering. Similarly, norms prescribe that some situations, such as being recently widowed, are occasions for sympathy. Negative reactions should be more common when the lonely person is not known well, when the circumstances leading to loneliness are unknown or somehow suspect, and when the loneliness has continued for a long time.

Cost–reward considerations. Interaction with lonely people may often entail many costs and provide few rewards. To the extent that a lonely person lacks social skills, is highly anxious or depressed, or is unusually self-focused, interaction with him or her may not be very enjoyable. In interactions with a lonely person, others may feel constrained, for example, not to talk about their own successful social life or not to suggest activities that may make loneliness more salient. Lonely people may be perceived as making demands for emotional support, for advice, and ultimately for the establishment of a new relationship with the non-lonely other. While attention from a lonely person may be rewarding, there may be doubts about the lonely person's motives. Gordon (1976, p. 29) comments that "whomever is sought out of desperation will feel degraded by the sense that he or she is being used". It is more flattering to be sought out by a popular person than by one without friends.

Thus in general the rewards of interacting with a lonely person may be limited but two major exceptions to this generalization should be noted. First, people may react more positively if the lonely person is a high status or very attractive newcomer. In this instance, loneliness is attributable to situational factors, and the possibility of establishing an enduring relationship may have considerable appeal. Second, reactions to loneliness should be more positive if there is a pre-existing relationship with the lonely other. If the lonely person is a spouse, relative or friend, there may be a long history of shared helping and support, and the expectation of future reciprocity of nurturance. In this instance, being able to help an intimate may be perceived as rewarding.

Attributional factors. Reactions to a lonely person are affected by causal attributions about why the person became lonely or has continued to be lonely. Gordon (1976) suggested that, just as lonely people blame themselves for loneliness, so, too, observers may also blame the lonely, and hence react negatively. There are some data (Peplau *et al.*, 1979) to document the impact of perceived causal attributions on evaluations of lonely people. It appears that sympathy and liking are greatest for lonely people who are judged to have had little control over the initiation of their loneliness, and who have made an effort to overcome their loneliness.

Personality factors. Certain people may be more likely to sympathize with lonely individuals and this capacity to empathize with the lonely may be facilitated by personal experiences of loneliness, and by perceptions of being similar to the lonely individual. In a study of psychological androgyny, Bem *et al.* (1976) found that students whose self-conceptions were androgynous or feminine reacted more effectively in interactions with a confederate describing himself as a lonely transfer student than did those with masculine self-conceptions. Individual differences in beliefs about the extent to which people can control their outcomes as measured by scales of locus of control (e.g. Rotter, 1966) or belief in a just world (e.g. Rubin and Peplau, 1975) may also be relevant.

Regardless of whatever individual differences there may be in responses to lonely people, as we indicated earlier, we believe these responses may have implications for the persistence of loneliness since negative stereotypes and reactions may aggravate loneliness whilst sympathy and efforts to extend social support may help alleviate the problem of loneliness.

Of course, other people's reactions are not the only factor in how well people deal with loneliness: lonely people use a number of strategies to alleviate their condition, and helping professionals also have various therapeutic techniques for intervening (see Rook and Peplau, in press). In the last section of this chapter, we will review people's own efforts to

overcome loneliness and consider outcome research done to evaluate the
success of therapy for alleviating loneliness.

Coping with Loneliness

In line with our definition of loneliness, it is convenient to categorize coping
strategies into three broad groups. Coping strategies may alter (1) the
desired level of social contact, (2) the achieved level of social contact, and
(3) the importance and/or perceived magnitude of the gap between desired
and achieved levels of contact.

Changing one's desired level of social contact

One general approach to "loneliness management" is to reduce one's
desired level of contact, which may be accomplished in at least three
different ways.

Adaptation. Over time, people's expected and desired levels for social
relations tend to converge to their achieved level. For instance, Lowenthal
(1964) found that old people with a long history of social isolation, who had
been "loners" for some time, were less likely to report feeling lonely than
old people with higher levels of social participation. Weiss (1973, p. 228)
commented on the possibility that over time lonely individuals might
"change their standards for appraising their situations and feelings, and, in
particular, that standards might shrink to conform more closely to the shape
of bleak reality". Weiss does not, however, view this as an adequate solution
to loneliness.

Task choice. A second way people can alter their desired level of social
contact is to select tasks and situations that they enjoy alone. Consider a
person who enjoys reading alone, but only likes to go to movies with a
companion: this person might avoid arousing feelings of loneliness by
spending the evening reading rather than going to the movies alone. Interviews that Robert Brown (1979) has conducted with hermits and other
loners suggest that people who seek prolonged solitude have well-developed
repertoires of activities they find enjoyable doing alone. Some clinicians (see
Rook and Peplau, in press) have gone so far as to suggest greater involvement in solitary activities as a useful way of alleviating loneliness. People
who use this response to loneliness, report getting lonely less often
(Rubenstein and Shaver, 1980).

Changed standards. A third technique which people use to reduce their desired level of social contact is to change their standards for who is acceptable as a friend. As an example of this phenomenon, consider a professional who usually forms friendships with other high status professionals: if this person became lonely, he or she might be willing, even happy, to form friendships with a much wider set of people. In the UCLA study (Cutrona, in press), increased satisfaction with one's friendships was a strong predictor of recovering from loneliness.

Achieving higher levels of social contact

Perhaps the most obvious way of overcoming loneliness is to establish or improve social relationships, and in the UCLA study, "finding a boyfriend/ girlfriend" was perceived as being the best way to overcome loneliness. One can think of many ways of achieving higher social contact: making oneself more physically attractive, joining clubs, initiating conversations with other people, deepening existing relationships and the like.

In the UCLA study, Cutrona (in press) divided the initially lonely students into those who, during the year, did and did not overcome loneliness. In this study, neither a change in dating status nor the strategies used to form relationships had statistically significant effects on overcoming loneliness. However, as we would expect, a change in number of friendships was important: students increasing their friendship networks decreased their loneliness. Similarly, loneliness is less frequent and more transient for people who react to it by visiting or calling a friend (Rubenstein and Shaver, 1980).

Minimizing loneliness

A third major way to cope with loneliness is to alter the importance and/or perceived magnitude of the gap between desired and achieved levels of social interaction. At least four variations on this theme can be identified: first, lonely people may simply deny that there is a discrepancy between their desired and achieved levels of social relations; secondly, lonely people can devalue social contact and rationalize their plight by saying that other objectives are more important, or by contending that loneliness is a "positive growth experience", thirdly, people can try to reduce loneliness-induced deficits by gratifying their needs in alternative ways (for instance, if loneliness threatens a person's sense of self-esteem, he or she might engage in non-social means of bolstering self-regard); finally, people can engage in behaviours designed to alleviate the negative impact of loneliness. One example of this, consistent with speculation linking loneliness to alcoholism and drug use, would be drinking "to drown one's sorrows".

Therapeutic interventions

Given the diversity of factors that may precipitate and perpetuate loneliness, no single cure-all is likely to be found, but many strategies may be useful when appropriately employed (Rook and Peplau, in press). Our analysis of loneliness suggests a few guidelines for their use.

First, to be effective, interventions should be tailored to the specific problems of the lonely individual: a recent widow may need temporary social support whereas a college student who has never been on a date may need help with his/her social skills. The fairly extensive research on "heterosexual-social anxiety" (reviewed by Curran, 1977) suggests three specific approaches to aiding students who are fearful of dating. Depending on the individual, therapy might emphasize desensitization to overcome anxiety, the correction of faulty self-evaluations of performance in social settings, or social skills training to build a more adequate behavioural repertoire. A comprehensive analysis of the antecedents of loneliness and of the interactional styles of lonely people (Jones, in press) will undoubtedly facilitate the design of successful therapeutic interventions.

Second, interventions to help the lonely may need to consider the lonely individual's own explanations for the causes of his or her distress. Peplau *et al.* (1979) suggest that people may often *underestimate the importance of situational causes* of loneliness and overestimate the role of personal factors. On theoretical grounds, we would expect this tendency to be especially clear in cases where loneliness is severe and enduring. Consistent with this view in Cutrona's (in press) longitudinal study of UCIA students, attributing loneliness to internal, personal causes in the fall was associated with loneliness persisting over the academic year. Overestimating the importance of personal factors is encouraged by the emphasis in both folk wisdom and psychological thinking on a characterological theory of loneliness (Weiss, 1973). In fact, loneliness typically results from a poor match between the individual's interests, social skills or personal characteristics and his or her social environment. Careful consideration should be given to the interaction of both personal and situational causes for loneliness. Lonely people may also tend to *underestimate the potential changeability* of causes of loneliness. For example, they may focus on irrevocable precipitating events (e.g., the death of a spouse), rather than on factors that impede the development of a new, more satisfactory social life. These maintaining causes of loneliness, such as shyness or limited opportunities to meet people, may be more amenable to change. We would advise directing clients' attention to factors they can control.

Third, we believe lonely individuals should be encouraged to view their world more positively. Some degree of negativism may reflect the reality of their situations, but some of it is undoubtedly due to a negativity bias in their evaluations. For instance, after interacting with a randomly assigned stranger, lonely subjects rated their partners more negatively than did non-lonely subjects, an effect that appears to be in the eye of the beholder (Jones, in press). We believe that curbing such negative perceptions should help people overcome their loneliness.

Finally, efforts to reduce loneliness must go beyond the individual to consider social and cultural factors that foster loneliness. As Gordon (1976, p. 21) noted, "Mass loneliness is not just a problem that can be coped with by the particular individuals involved; it is an indication that things are dramatically amiss on a societal level". Social institutions might consider ways to assist such at-risk groups as new students, transferred business executives and their families, or nursing home residents. In addition, social programs for other groups such as the newly divorced or widowed who are not associated with a particular institution are useful. Indeed, it seems likely that interventions aimed at specific problems — such as retirement or moving to a new community — may be more effective than interventions directed more globally at "loneliness".

Outcome research on the success of therapy for alleviating loneliness

Although therapy outcome research on the treatment of loneliness is limited, it is encouraging. In our opinion, one of the most noteworthy studies was done by Jones (in press) and his colleagues. Jones' research group had identified three unique characteristics of the way lonely people interact in conversations: (a) they make fewer other-references and ask fewer questions of their partner; (b) they change the topic more often; and (c) they delay longer in filling gaps in the conversation. Jones therefore developed a short "social skills training program" to help students overcome these interpersonal deficits, incorporating explanation, modelling, practice with prompting, and feedback on the students' performance of target behaviours. Compared with a no treatment and a placebo treatment (conversation only) control group, the skills training produced desired changes in the participants' interactional styles and it reduced their loneliness. Indeed, the magnitude of the reduction in loneliness was appreciable compared to that reported in most psychological research.

Summary and Conclusions

We have now come full cycle in this review. We started with defining the concept and analyzing what leads up to it; then we indicated how cognitive factors moderate the intensity of affective reactions to deficits in sociability, and subsequently indicated how others react to lonely people; finally, we have indicated ways of reversing the process or alleviating loneliness.

At this time (circa 1981), loneliness is a topic ripe for research. Studies have documented that loneliness is an unpleasant and widespread experience. Loneliness is also associated with a variety of social problems, such as juvenile delinquency, alcohol abuse and suicide. The research literature on loneliness is relatively small (and thus easier to master) yet flourishing: and useful theoretical concepts and data collection instruments have been developed. Although the experimental manipulation of loneliness by researchers may be difficult and raises ethical issues, alternative research strategies have proved fruitful. Initial efforts to investigate loneliness empirically have been rewarded and available evidence suggests that psychologists are beginning to learn how to help people alleviate loneliness. Yet despite these advances in the field, many important questions remain unanswered.

All these factors make loneliness an attractive topic for research. Whatever else happened to the study of loneliness in the later 1970s, perhaps the most important development was that this research came "out of the closet". Loneliness is now justifiably a social science topic in good currency!

CHAPTER 3

Marital Breakdown

Michael D. Newcomb and P. M. Bentler

This chapter will evaluate the empirical evidence and available theoretical formulations bearing upon marital breakdown, as well as the research methods and strategies devised to study this phenomenon. To accomplish this task several major areas will be presented and discussed. The trends and contexts of marital breakdown, assessments of marital qualities, and methodological issues will be examined in terms of general research problems. Empirical research will then be presented regarding the antecedents, processes and consequences of marital breakdown. Finally a variety of theoretical perspectives will be discussed, followed by general conclusions and directions for future work.

The term and phenomenon of marital breakdown is familiar to most people either from first hand or vicarious experiences. It is usually a painful and disorienting event that touches the most personal and vulnerable aspects of a man and a woman, often piercing the very core of a person's identify and self-esteem. In addition, marital breakdown disrupts the family, one of the most valued institutions in society. What exactly is the phenomenon of marital breakdown that often carries with it such anguish and personal devastation? Most people think of it as the opposite of a well functioning and satisfying marriage; a marriage that is seen as in trouble or "on the rocks". However, beyond these simple definitions the term becomes ambiguous and difficult to define for both lay persons and researchers (Lively, 1969). Many terms are associated with marital breakdown, each somewhat different. Marital instability, unhappiness, dissatisfaction, maladjustment, disruption, failure, separation, and divorce are all related to marital breakdown, and vary in meaning from a subjective and at times difficult to assess feeling of unhappiness to an objective, legal and publicly recorded criterion of divorce. Although each of these terms and definitions has been used by researchers to indicate marital breakdown, many are not interchangeable. Even though divorce is the logical extreme of marital breakdown, not all married couples who separate get divorced nor do all marriages that are experienced as unhappy or dissatisfying reach separation (Landis, 1963). This issue of definitional inexactness will be discussed more fully later in this chapter. However, for clarity in this review marital breakdown will be used as a general term to indicate problems in a marriage that could be reflected in unhappiness, maladjustment or divorce. More specifically, we will follow the lead of Hicks and Platt (1970) who make a distinction between marital (in)stability and (un)happiness. Marital unhappiness will include maladjustment and dissatisfaction experienced by the partners. Marital instability, on the other hand, will include marital disruption and the likelihood or presence of separation or divorce.

Aside from this definitional confusion, marital breakdown is not a simple event resulting from a single cause. It is an immensely complicated phenomenon that researchers have not and may never come fully to grips with. Although admittedly artificial, it is heuristically useful to conceive of marital breakdown in three stages or processes: those influences or elements that contribute to marital unhappiness and instability; the process of marital dissolution, separation and divorce; and finally the eventual outcome of the marital dissolution for each person involved. Each of these events and processes occurs within a social and cultural context that has a powerful influence on each stage.

Researchers have been concerned with understanding the marital relationship and the problems that can occur within it for many decades. Most studies prior to 1960 were atheoretical in nature and typically tried to relate demographic, background, social and general personality variables to marital dissolution. There was no conceptual framework within which to understand and make sense of the various empirical findings. In the decade of the 1960s incipient theoretical formulations were attempted and occasionally tested, variables were more meticulously defined and validated, and concepts and constructs became better operationalized. The 1970s have seen an increase in behavioural measures, attempts to specify a typical family life cycle and an expansion of areas considered relevant to marital breakdown. For example, post-divorce adjustment of the ex-spouses and their children has received increasing attention. However, refining and honing of the various theoretical perspectives have proceeded rather slowly.

General Research Problems

Trends and contexts

This section will present trends in divorce rates and speculations regarding the causes of fluctuations in these rates. Although marital breakdown occurs at the dyadic level between a man and a woman, influences affecting the marital relationship can be observed at many levels simultaneously, and social and cultural norms and events have an important impact upon marital stability. They form the context, climate, and expectations within which personal relationships are formed and broken, such that it is useful to examine how marital breakdown has fluctuated over time in relation to social and cultural changes.

One indicator of severe marital breakdown or instability is divorce. A divorce is a public and legal declaration of marital dissolution that becomes a matter of public record in many countries. Because of this highly visible and accessible reflection of marital breakdown, it is possible to examine trends and social influences on marital dissolution by studying archives of divorce statistics. Norton and Glick (1979) studied United States census reports that covered a period of more than 55 years, ranging from 1920 to 1977. They examined rate trends of divorces, first marriages, and re-marriages in the light of social conditions and events. Only women were used in their tabulations since females are seen as a more consistent data base than men, who are more influenced by fluctuations in enlistments and discharges from the military service. Divorce, first marriage, and re-marriage rates all slumped immediately following the Depression of 1929, and then each rose sharply to a peak following World War II. After this peak and a general levelling down in the 1950s, each rate behaved rather differently. Beginning in the 1960s, the divorce rate started climbing and until recently has continued to accelerate to unprecedentedly high levels. Until recently the re-marriage trends have paralleled the divorce trends, which Norton and Glick (1979) interpret to mean that even when the divorce rate is high the institution of marriage has not been rejected, but rather only the first marriage partner. However, in the 1970s the re-marriage rate has diverged sharply from the divorce rate, indicating that large numbers of divorced people are not immediately re-marrying but are maintaining their singlehood. On the other hand, first marriage rates have steadily dropped following the post World

War II peak and since 1970 have dropped rapidly. In other words, more people are getting divorced while fewer are getting married or remarried. Concomitant with these changes in the past ten years has been an 8-fold increase in cohabitation, living together without marriage (see Newcomb, 1981 for a review). However, Newcomb and Bentler (1980a) conclude from an examination of their own data and a review of relevant literature, that cohabitation is not a rejection of or substitution for marriage *per se*, but rather will have the effect of delaying marriage to a later point in life.

Taking a longer historical perspective, based on a somewhat less defined data base, Scanzoni (1979) traced attitudes toward and incidence of divorce from the American Colonial days to the present. In the Colonial Period divorce was extremely rare and marriage was characterized by an "owner-property" arrangement, wherein the woman was totally subservient to the man. Since that time the marital power balance has gradually shifted to a currently more egalitarian position, where in many cases each partner has equal bargaining power within the relationship. Scanzoni implicates this increase in women's power in explaining the rise in divorce rate, although he is quick to stress that this is not a necessary outcome of marital equality except where there is little adaptation by males to egalitarian roles. This idea supports Norton and Glick's (1979) contention that roles have changed more rapidly than some people can adapt to them, and that once people more adequately adjust to the new patterns, the divorce rate will level off. In fact, their most recent figures support this prediction and it appears that the divorce rate may no longer be accelerating as previously.

Norton and Glick (1979) offer several explanations for the divorce rate changes they observed. They suggest that the uncertainties and pessimism created by the Depression made people resistant to making personal changes, such as divorce, marriage or re-marriage, and that the relief following World War II created an optimism in risking relationship changes, which led to high divorce, first marriage, and re-marriage rates. The recent upsurge in the divorce rate, during the past 15 to 20 years, they feel is the result of traditional value systems being thrown into question and into a state of rapid transition. People are accepting that divorce is a reasonable alternative to a failing marriage, while legal, economic and social constraints against divorce have become drastically minimized.

Other socio-cultural context factors influencing the likelihood of divorce have been presented by Bohmer and Lebow (1978). They consider the most important influence on changes in divorce patterns to be the degree of modernization, defined as an increase in urbanization, literacy, non-agrarian economy, and broad based taxation. Although modernization typically carries with it an increase in divorces, this is not universally the case and, according to other socio-cultural variables, modernization may make divorce more difficult. Bohmer and Lebow enumerate six important influences that interact to determine the ease or difficulty of divorcing in a particular situation: the type of kinship system prevalent in the society (whether it is matrilineal, patrilineal, or bilateral in nature); attitudes toward ownership and property; the status of women; religion and its political influence; the prevailing meaning of marriage; and the role of the state in regulating personal relationships (e.g. sexual behaviour). Variables such as these surely account for differences in divorce rates across societies, and this indicates how many factors outside the marital dyad significantly affect the way that relationship is negotiated and, if necessary, ended.

Assessment of marital (in)stability and (un)happiness

The conceptualization and operationalization of marital breakdown have varied widely from one researcher to another: many terms have been employed to reflect marital breakdown that do not all refer to the same concept. This raises many problems when trying to relate and compare various studies, since researchers have no common conceptualization and assessment of the phenomenon. A number of different ways of understanding the various forms of marital breakdown will be presented in this section, followed by the types of methods chosen to assess and measure these qualities.

Conceptualization

Early attempts to define marital breakdown conceived of a single continuum, from high to low levels of marital happiness and stability (e.g. Locke and Wallace, 1959). It was felt that although many factors related to and defined this omnibus concept — e.g. amount of conflict, ratings of happiness, perceived permanence of the relationship — all were interrelated and somehow reflective of an underlying general level of marital adjustment. Supporting this idea, Bentler and Newcomb (1978) found one large factor in their factor analysis of the Locke-Wallace Marital Adjustment Scale (Locke and Wallace, 1959), that accounted for 75% of the variance. However, other research using an expanded pool of items has thrown some doubt on the actual existence of only one underlying factor in marital happiness and adjustment. For instance, Hicks and Platt (1970) have suggested that there are at least two separate components of this general factor: marital happiness and marital stability. Marital happiness refers to the subjective level of satisfaction and adjustment in the marriage, while stability indicates the relative permanence of the relationship.

Although these two factors are related, such that levels of unhappiness predict high levels of instability and vice-versa (e.g. Bentler and Newcomb, 1978), they are not identical. Even though most couples who divorce — reflecting the extreme of instability — are unhappy, not all unhappy marriages eventuate in divorce (e.g. Landis, 1963). Conceptually, stability has remained undifferentiated, and although many variables have been implicated in determining the stability of a marriage, the concept itself has received little elaboration and attention. On the other hand, marital happiness, satisfaction, or adjustment have received extensive scrutiny, criticism, and modification. In fact, there have been so many confusing and different definitions and connotations applied to these terms that Lively (1969) feels there is justification for eliminating them from this field of study. Regarding the term "marital happiness", Lively points out that it is difficult to determine whether a spouse's (un)happiness is a result of the marriage or other life events, and that there is frequent disagreement between spouses about levels of marital happiness. Further, Burgess *et al.* (1963) have criticized the use of the term "marital satisfaction" since it ". . . is not by itself an adequate measure of success, for either husband or wife may be dissatisfied in marriage when there is no conflict or incompatibility, or they may be highly satisfied in a union that has unresolved problems of adjustment." In addition, these terms have at times been used as components of marital success and adjustment (e.g. Locke and Wallace, 1959) and a single criterion of marital happiness (e.g. Landis, 1963; Howard and Dawes 1976; Rollins and Feldman, 1970). A further complicating factor is that marital adjustment or happiness has the connotation of an ultimate and enduring condition, rather than a continuous state of adjustment, re-adjustment and negotiation (Hicks and Platt, 1970).

To clarify these many confusions, various researchers have attempted to specify different components of marital happiness or adjustment. Although many attempts have been made to determine the dimensions of marital happiness and adjustment, only a few will be presented for purposes of illustration. For example, Orden and Bradburn (1968) identified two independent factors that were significantly related to marital satisfaction. One factor was marital tension (number of perceived sources of friction), and the other factor was one of marital satisfactions (number of shared pleasurable activities). Gilford and Bengston (1979) also offered a two-dimensional model of marital happiness. They conceptualized marital happiness in terms of positive interaction (number of shared activities) and negative sentiment (frequency of negative affective interactions). Howard and Dawes (1976) combined two single-item dimensions into a composite index of marital happiness: they found that for a given period of time, the frequency of sexual intercourse, linearly combined with a measure of the number of arguments, predicted self-ratings of marital happiness.

Such two dimensional models of marital happiness have received criticism on the basis that they are too limited in scope and do not account for important aspects of the marital relationship. Marini (1976) examined the two dimensional model of Orden and Bradburn (1968) and found it lacking in important respects. In a secondary analysis of the Orden and Bradburn (1968) data, Marini found that marital companionship, defined as the amount of time spent together, is more important to marital happiness than marital satisfaction or tensions, even when the latter two factors are controlled for. Although these three dimensions (satisfactions, tensions, and companionship) were found to be the most essential ingredients of marital happiness, many other dimensions emerged with secondary importance. Spanier (1976) presented a four factor model of dyadic adjustment that purports to assess adjustment as a process rather than as a criterion state. The four factors he identified were marital satisfaction, consensus on matters of marital functioning, marital cohesion, and affective expression. The factor of marital cohesion seems most clearly related to marital stability, while the remaining three factors are most closely in line with marital happiness.

Many of these conceptualizations consider lack of conflict to be a major determinant of marital happiness, and it is clear that marital conflict is an important element (Barry, 1970). However, there has been a recent trend to acknowledge the prominence of conflict as an important and essential aspect of adjustment and, in fact, some popularized books advocate and teach ways to make disagreements and arguments a springboard to higher levels of marital happiness and adjustment (e.g. Bach and Wyden, 1971). It is the manner that conflict is dealt with rather than its occurrence *per se* that determines its beneficial or destructive influence on a marriage or its partners. However, no conceptualization of marital happiness or adjustment assesses the nature of the conflict, only the fact of it. It is apparent that a more diverse and multi-faceted concept of conflict is needed to assess marital happiness in a more adequate manner, reflecting the fact that conflict does not necessarily imply unhappiness, and could in fact, predict greater happiness in some instances. This is an example of how marital happiness needs to be assessed as a process rather than a criterion state.

Operationalizations

Aside from the difficulties in defining exactly what marital instability or unhappiness is composed of, a further degree of ambiguity is confronted when attempting to operationalize these inadequately defined concepts. Marital breakdown has been assessed in basically three ways: self-report, behavioural, and circumstantial, each of which will be briefly discussed.

Self-report. The most widely used technique of assessing marital happiness and stability is self-report, either through interviews or, most frequently, in self-administered questionnaires. In the simplest case, marital happiness is assessed by asking a couple or individual spouse to rate their marriage on a bipolar scale of happiness (e.g. Howard and Dawes, 1976), while stability is assessed most easily by asking the couple whether they are divorced or still married (e.g. Bentler and Newcomb, 1978). Most frequently, many items are presented that assess one or more dimensions of marital happiness or adjustment (e.g. Locke and Wallace, 1959; Spanier, 1976).

Shortcomings of these techniques include the fact that they are subjective, often influenced by social desirability, and frequently lack statistical reliability and validity.

Behavioural. Observational studies of marital happiness and stability have increased over the past ten years, although there is not yet a great deal of sophistication in these techniques. Monitoring the frequencies of sexual intercourse and arguments is a simple example of using behavioural information to assess marital happiness (Howard and Dawes, 1976). Wills *et al.* (1974) used daily records of spouses who tracked the frequencies of instrumental and affectional behaviours, which were found to be related to general levels of marital satisfaction. Birchler and Webb (1977) were able to discriminate happily from unhappily married couples in terms of the number of unresolved problems, choice of mutual involvement in elective free time activities, and shared sexuality. Haynes *et al.* (1979) found that observer ratings of specific behaviours in a marital interaction e.g. criticisms, positive physical contact, eye contact, could differentiate satisfied from dissatisfied couples.

Although these beginnings are encouraging, the designs are constructed and the results interpreted typically in relation to a reciprocity or exchange orientation which may be an overly narrow conceptualization. Future work needs to specify and behaviourally operationalize other important determinants of marital happiness, such as problem-solving abilities and coping behaviour.

Circumstantial. A final method used by researchers to assess marital breakdown is through the source of the sample. For example, couples seeking therapy would be presumed to have lower levels of marital happiness than intact couples not in therapy (e.g. Haynes *et al.* 1979). However, the only certainty that is assessed in making this distinction is that one group of couples is more willing than the other to seek therapy, assuming levels of marital happiness is much more confounded. On the other hand, the existence of marital instability has been assessed through public records of divorce (e.g. Bentler and Newcomb, 1978), population census statistics (e.g. Norton and Glick, 1979), or applicants for divorce (e.g. Levinger, 1979b). In each case, finding a couple in a particular manner implies a certain level of marital instability or unhappiness. Couples presumably high in marital happiness or stability are typically found in situations that do not cater to couples in trouble or with problems (e.g. church groups, clubs).

Methodological issues

Many problems have plagued the scientific study of marital breakdown. Some difficulties are specific to this field of study, while others are common to most investigations of psychological and interpersonal processes and behaviours. Specifically, this section will briefly examine issues related to samples, research designs, theorizing, instrumentation, and sexism bias.

Samples

There are three main criticisms leveled against the samples in many studies of marital breakdown: small size, unrepresentativeness, and the use of only one partner. Too often sample sizes are so small that the reliability of the results is thrown into question. In cases where large samples are employed, they are often atypical in some way and thus extremely unsound as a basis for generalization (Hicks and Platt, 1970). Often samples are located in a merely convenient manner, and the subjects are rarely drawn with a probability technique. Frequently when a probability sampling design is used, it is difficult to generalize beyond the group sampled (e.g. church groups, university organizations). In general, the subjects used are young (under 40 years old), white, middle-class and college educated. Clearly research on more diverse samples is needed, if a general understanding of the phenomenon is to be achieved.

One major exception to these difficulties might be provided by samples taken from national pollings, but rarely do these large samples provide the range of couple or individual variables needed to study the intricacies of a marital relationship or breakdown. A final fault related to sample selections is that many, but definitely not all, studies use only one partner of a marriage. Obviously a matter of convenience in most cases, this clearly presents an incomplete picture of people in relationship to each other, which is a defining feature of marriage. It is difficult and misleading to talk generally about a marital breakdown when only one person, and thus one viewpoint, of that relationship was assessed.

Designs

It is impossible to enumerate all of the research designs that have been used to study marital breakdown. In general, however, the most common is the cross-sectional, questionnaire study, and only very rarely have either cohort (e.g. Norton and Glick, 1979) or panel type (e.g. Bentler and Newcomb, 1978) longitudinal studies been used. In principle, panel designs permit much more certainty in understanding causal factors that lead to marital unhappiness and instability. Particularly when studying personality or attitudinal effects on marital breakdown, it is impossible to determine in a cross-sectional design whether an observed variable configuration is a cause or consequence of the marital breakdown. This is not so critical when studying demographic variables (e.g. age, previous divorce), since they do not change as a function of marriage.

Theorizing

One drawback of many studies of marital breakdown is that they are typically not based upon, nor do all the results fit comfortably into, the available theories that attempt to explain marital breakdown. To a significant extent the scientific method of deriving theory-based hypotheses, hypothesis testing, and theory modification based upon the empirical evidence, has not been widely practised in the field of marital breakdown. This is generally due to a pervasive lack of adequate theory development in this area of study. Over the past 50 or more years of data collection and empirical study only a handful of theories has emerged, and these few that have been put forward are often inadequate.

Instrumentation

However, despite the conceptual and operational problems noted above, on the independent variable side of the equation, there has been considerable advancement in the sophistication, reliability, and validity of the assessment tools used during the past 20–30 years. For example, early studies that attempted to link personality to marital breakdown tried to determine the influence of "personality" as a global, not clearly defined, influence (e.g. Terman and Oden, 1947). Recently, personality inventories have been used that assess "personality" to a much finer and more detailed degree, in a psychometrically reliable and valid manner (e.g. Bentler and Newcomb, 1978). Clearly, the assessment of independent variables as determinants of marital breakdown has improved immensely over the years, largely as a consequence of a general sophistication of psychological measurement tools.

Sexism

Taking a feminist perspective, Laws (1971) strongly questions and attacks the role ascribed to a woman in research on the marital relationship. She points out that the traditional role of a happily married woman is that of expressiveness (as opposed to the male instrumental role), child-bearing and rearing, and house-keeping. She claims that these qualities have become operationalized as partial definitions of positive marital adjustment. Times have changed, and this role is far too narrow to encompass the capabilities and desires of many women. However, the marriage institution has not adjusted as rapidly, nor have researchers changed their perspectives to account for and accept the fact that breaking up her marriage may be the only way for a woman to succeed fully in feeling and being a complete person. The traditional marriage has not adapted to the wider role of women in society, although this is fortunately changing, albeit slowly. Thus, a successful marriage has in the past been defined in part by those qualities that limit a woman's role and range of options. This is a bias that permeates much of the literature on marital adjustment or breakdown.

Empirical Research

Antecedents of marital breakdown

In this section, and the two following sections, the empirical evidence that bears upon marital breakdown will be examined. This section will be concerned with those factors that have been found to play a causal role in marital unhappiness or instability. Although the societal and cultural antecedents of marital breakdown could appropriately be included in this section, these have already been presented. For convenience, individual and dyadic antecedents will be discussed in four broad areas: individual, dyadic/relational, dyadic/structural, and adjustment cycles.

Typically, the research strategy used to study these types of variables has been to compare cross-sectionally couples or individuals high in marital happiness or stability with those low in marital happiness and stability. This strategy is generally not a problem when examining variables that are not influenced by the ravages of marriage — e.g. demographics, parental divorce. However, other types of variables can lead to interpretational difficulties when studied cross-sectionally. For example, if personality differences are found between married and divorced individuals in a cross-sectional design, it is impossible to determine whether the observed differences were the cause or consequence of the marital quality differences. These difficulties are far less troublesome in longitudinal designs, but studies incorporating such designs are very few in number.

Since the causes or antecedents of marital breakdown have received extensive attention from researchers, it will be possible, in this limited space, to enumerate only a sample of the more important and consistent findings.

Individual factors

Individual factors refer to those qualities that are brought to a marriage by each partner, which affect the quality and outcome of the marriage relatively independent of the other person. These are qualities that, in and of themselves, act against longevity and contentment in a marital relationship. Influences that will be examined include demographics (or background), personality, and previous sexual behaviour.

Demographic factors

Several demographic or background variables have a detrimental effect upon the quality and endurance of a marriage. One of the most consistently found determinants of marital breakdown has been age. In a large number of studies, it has been found that marrying at a young age predicts a lower degree of marital happiness and adjustment (e.g. Bentler and Newcomb, 1978) and a greater possibility of divorce (e.g. Mott and Moore, 1979) than is true for people who marry at a relatively older age. Traditionally, it has been noted that the more education one has obtained, the greater is the success probability of the marriage (e.g. Mott and Moore, 1979; Renne, 1970). However, there is some evidence suggesting that amount of education is curvilinearly related to divorce proneness, such that the stability is lowest for those with an elementary or high school education (Goode, *et al.*, 1971). Low occupational levels and low socioeconomic status have also been implicated as causes of high levels of marital unhappiness and instability (Bentler and Newcomb, 1978; Renne, 1970). It has been noted that there exists a higher rate of marital disruption in Black marriages, relative to White marriages (Renne, 1970). For males this ethnic difference all but disappears when socioeconomic variables are controlled for, but this is not the case for Black women (Renne, 1970). Black women remain significantly more dissatisfied in their marriages than White women, even when socioeconomic factors are controlled. Renne (1970) interprets this to mean that Black women are more susceptible to family disturbances and discontentment of living and being married in a White dominated society, than are Black men.

The experience of growing up in a home where one's parents are divorced or separated raises the probability of divorcing in one's own marriage as an adult. This pattern has been observed by many researchers (e.g. Pope and Mueller, 1979; Mott and Moore, 1979) but was not obtained in at least one study (Bentler and Newcomb, 1978). Attempts to explain this intergenerational transmission of marital instability have focused on the importance of the parental marriage as a role model for their children's later marriage.

Personality

Many psychological traits and personality factors have been implicated in marital breakdown. Even though background and demographic variables play an important role in marital disruption and maladjustment, Bentler and Newcomb (1978) have clearly shown that personality accounts for a much greater proportion of the variance in marital quality.

Individuals with gross psychiatric symptomology, as assessed on the MMPI, were found to have low marital adjustment and happiness (Murstein and Glaudin, 1968). In addition, people with a rigid defensive style and those with strong masculine interests also had low marital adjustment and happiness.

The amount of achievement motivation, competition, individualism, and ambition in a person are all positively related to high levels of marital unhappiness and instability (Bentler and Newcomb, 1978; Kirkpatrick, 1955). Presumably these qualities lower the priority, attention, and commitment an individual will devote to their marriage, and the marriage will suffer as a consequence (Blake, 1961; Newcomb and Bentler, 1980b). In a longitudinal study that compared divorced and married groups, and adjustment levels, in regard to personality traits that were assessed at the beginning of each marriage (Bentler and Newcomb, 1978), men and women displayed somewhat different predictive patterns. In general, variables that were assessed on women predicted marital unhappiness and instability more effectively than variables assessed on the men. This has also been found longitudinally by Hill et al. (1976) in regard to dating couples, and cross-sectionally by Murstein and Glaudin (1966) in regard to married couples. More specifically, Bentler and Newcomb (1978) found that men who perceived themselves as extraverted and invulnerable, and who had a high need for orderliness more often terminated their marriage by divorce, relative to men low on these personality traits. On the other hand, women who eventually divorced perceived themselves as more ambitious, intelligent, liberal, and unstable than women in intact marriages.

Premarital sexual experience

Sexual intercourse prior to marriage has shown a dramatic increase during the past decades (Athanasiou *et al.*, 1970), and there is some evidence demonstrating that this premarital sexual behaviour is a detrimental influence on a subsequent marriage (Reevy, 1963; Shope and Broderick, 1967). For example, the number of premarital sexual partners is negatively related to ratings of marital happiness and this negative relationship between amount of premarital sex and marital happiness persists even when intervening variables, such as romanticism and liberalism, are controlled (Athanasiou and Sarkin, 1974).

One of the many explanations of this relationship is that the amount and likelihood of premarital sexual experience is predictive of the occurrence of extra-marital sexual behaviour, which itself plays a prominent role in marital disruption in a large number of cases (Jaffe and Kanter, 1979; Gersick, 1979; Bukstel *et al.*, 1978). Finally, premarital pregnancy, obviously a possible consequence of premarital sexual behaviour, predicts low levels of marital happiness and stability (Furstenberg, 1979).

Dyadic/relational factors

These factors refer to the interactional qualities between a husband and wife in terms of behaviour, personality and expectations. Four areas will be examined: homogamy, complementarity, conflict, and marital roles.

Homogamy. One very consistent finding in the marital breakdown literature is that heterogamy, an unequal matching between marriage partners, or lack of homogamy, is conducive to marital unhappiness and instability. This has been found both longitudinally, on variables assessed prior to, or at the point of marriage (e.g. Bentler and Newcomb, 1978), and cross-sectionally, between married couples who report low and high levels of marital happiness (e.g. Cattell and Nesselroade, 1967). Heterogamy is disruptive to a marriage whether it is in terms of age (Bentler and Newcomb, 1978), race and/or religion (Burgess and Locke, 1953), personality (Cattell and Nesselroade, 1967), or marital expectations (Jaffe and Kanter, 1979). The typical explanation for this phenomenon is that dissimilarity (heterogamy) leads to conflict and dissatisfaction, which in turn create marital unhappiness and instability.

Complementarity. Some theorists have suggested that marital success is partially due to one partner compensating or complementing the other in terms of needs and personality (Winch, 1958). Conversely, marital break-down should occur when this balancing of spousal needs and personality is not successful. Although many attempts have been made to support this hypothesis, the majority of findings show no tendency for couples low in marital happiness or stability to be less complementary regarding needs (e.g. Meyer and Pepper, 1977) or personality (e.g. Bentler and Newcomb, 1978), relative to couples high in marital happiness or stability. In other words, there is little support for the idea that happy marriages, or unhappy or divorced marriages, are created by the presence or absence of one partner compensating or balancing the needs and/or personality of the other.

Conflict. Although conflict and disagreements occur in virtually all married couples, the manner, content, and style of the negotiations determines whether this conflict is a cause of marital disruption. In fact Scanzoni (1972) suggests that an over-avoidance of, or failure to engage in, conflict may exacerbate problems in a marriage, since conflict and negotiation are possible ways to ameliorate difficulties. However, he also points out that if the conflict is over very basic and fundamental issues in the relationship, the conflict will tend to be more dysfunctional and unresolvable. O'Brien (1972) noted that younger dissatisfied couples expressed their conflict in an "explosive", overt manner, while dissatisfied older couples were characterized by an "empty relationship", covert type of conflict.

The manner in which conflict is dealt with is critical in determining whether the conflict will be a precursor to marital dissolution. Effective (open) communication is associated with marital success and rewarding conflict negotiation (Hicks and Platt, 1970). Willingness to disclose feelings is also positively related to successful marriage (Levinger and Senn, 1967), and conversely, marital disruption is more likely when there is little mutual sharing of feelings. When one or both marriage partners are not willing to adjust, adapt and compromise, conflict becomes a pathway to marital disruption (Clements, 1967). Conflict negotiation where one partner consistently gives in to the other, rather than mutual compromise and give-and-take, is also an ingredient of marital breakdown (Bee, 1959).

Marital Roles. Marital disruption has been associated with an incongruity of attitudes and expectations of partners to their respective marital roles (Tharp, 1963). Where there is a great deal of specialization and differentiation of household duties and decisional roles in the dyad, marital happiness is generally low (Michel, 1971). High levels of marital adjustment have been noted in marriages with equalitarian roles (Pond *et al.*, 1963), while adjustment is relatively poor in marriage where one partner is overly dominant (Stryker, 1964).

Chadwick *et al.* (1976) found that the level of disagreement between spouses regarding expectations and performance of specific marital roles (e.g. providing, housekeeping, therapeutic) was highly correlated with willingness to marry their spouse again. Finally, Ericksen *et al.* (1979) found that a husband's income level was negatively related to shared marital roles, while the wife's educational level was positively related to shared marital roles.

Dyadic/structural factors

This factor concerns the structural placement of a marriage in a temporal and situational context. For example, a short acquaintanceship or engagement period, prior to marriage is associated with low marital happiness and stability (Goode, 1956). Although there are many possible structural placements a marriage might occupy, only two will be discussed, each of which has become more prominent in the past ten years: the temporal placement of cohabitation before marriage; and situational placement of the marital dyad in a communal living arrangement.

Premarital cohabitation. Nonmarital heterosexual cohabitation has increased markedly in acceptance and practice during the past ten years (see Newcomb, 1981 for a fuller review), and not surprisingly a growing number of marriages — almost half in one sample — are preceded by cohabitation (Newcomb and Bentler, 1980a). Although it has been the hope of some (e.g. Danziger, 1976) that cohabitation before marriage would reduce the divorce potential of the subsequent marriage, no differences have been found between marriages preceded and not preceded by cohabitation in regard to divorce rates (Bentler and Newcomb, 1978) nor happiness and adjustment (Newcomb and Bentler, 1980b). However, one interesting finding noted by Newcomb and Bentler (1980b) was that premarital cohabitors who eventually divorced did so while reporting significantly greater happiness and adjustment than non-premarital cohabitors who also divorced. Cole (1976) reported that cohabitors reported fewer barriers to terminating their relationship than married couples. Apparently this perception is maintained by cohabitors even when they marry, which could indicate that premarital cohabitors are less committed to their marriage and thus divorce when there are small signs of trouble. It is also possible that the premarital cohabitors may not base their happiness and adjustment solely on their marriage, and thus may divorce more amicably with less personal stress and deterioration, than non-premarital cohabitors who divorce. In any case, premarital cohabitation has no apparent direct influence on the disruption potential of a subsequent marriage.

Communal marriage. Jaffe and Kanter (1979) studied marital stress and separation within urban communal households. Based on interviews with 29 couples living in these communes, Jaffe and Kanter identified several influences that affected the marital bond and the proneness to marital disruption. One of the most striking features in this study was how the communal environment magnified and intensified intimate interactions and tensions. Although the environment was supportive in a variety of ways, there was clearly more support for the individual as opposed to the dyad and the couples felt deprived of intimate and personal space, both physically and psychologically. The environment enables a couple to be less inter-dependent to meet their needs, and consequently the emotional ties are weakened in the marital dyad. Other factors also lower the barriers to ending a relationship; for example, the negative aspects of singlehood are minimized (little isolation, broad range of emotional support, and close proximity of alternative sexual partners).

The general beliefs often held by commune members act against a lasting marriage in that environment. Jaffe and Kanter identified two aspects of this "ideological" encouragement to breakup: feminism and anti-familism. Feminist issues and the need to re-define sex-roles have allowed women to seek emotional support from additional sources than their husband (particu-larly other women), which are readily available in a communal environ-ment. On the other hand, communal household beliefs play down the importance of the nuclear family (sometimes actually rejecting it), exclusive relationships are negatively valued, and individual fulfilment is considered more important than couple maintenance.

Clearly, putting one's marriage in this context places severe stress and strain on the endurance of that union. In fact, in one study 70 percent of the married couples separated while living in communes (Zablocki, 1973). Obviously, there are powerful predisposing factors that would attract a couple to communal living that in themselves might make the dyad dissolu-tion prone, but even with these other contributing factors, the communal situation itself is stressful, and for many a deadly influence on the per-manence of a marriage.

These are only a few examples of how the temporal or situational context of a marriage affects the potential for marital breakdown. Other structural placements could include open marriage, wife-swapping, arranged marriages, and married couples living in their parents' household.

Adjustment cycles

Almost all physical and psychological events occur in some type of rhythmical patterns, cycles or stages. Levels of marital adjustment have been examined in regard to two cycles or stage processes: the developmental point in a marriage and the stage in one's life (age). The rationale behind this is that certain points in time or stages in cyles have unique configurations of needs, stresses, and vulnerabilities, and that these affect how a marriage is experi-enced and dealt with.

Family life-cycle. The life-cycle of a family has been defined in terms of the stages of raising children — e.g. pre-school, school age, adolescence, launching (Peterson *et al.,* 1979; Rollins and Feldman, 1970). However, such a conceptualization presupposes that all couples have children, and this is obviously not true. The presence of children in a marriage consistently lowers the amount of marital adjustment experienced by both men and women (Renne, 1970) even when confounding factors such as education, employment, and religion are controlled for (Houseknecht, 1979). In particular, marital cohesion and satisfaction were higher for childless couples, relative to couples with children (Houseknecht, 1979). However, a majority of people in unsatisfying marriages report that children are their sole satisfaction in the marriage (Luckey and Bain, 1970). In other words, the presence of children, in and of themselves, decreases marital satisfaction, through factors such as lowering husband–wife companionship time (Miller, 1976), yet these same children may be the only source of marital satisfaction and cohesion in a failing marriage.

There has typically been found a gradual decrease in marital happiness during the first ten years of marriage (Rollins and Feldman, 1970). This has been attributed to disenchantment, a negotiation of marital roles, and the transition of having children (Pineo, 1961). Burr (1970) assessed a variety of marital satisfaction indices over the family life-cycle and generally found a curvilinear relationship. Marital satisfaction was highest at the beginning of the marriage, with no children present, then satisfaction gradually decreased through the birth of the first child and reached a low when the oldest child was school aged (7–12 years old). Marital satisfaction then gradually increased until all children were out of the home and levelled off up to retirement. Clearly, low points in this cycle are particularly vulnerable times for marital disruption and breakdown.

Age. Although confounded by family life-cycle, age or personal life cycle is also related to marital happiness and satisfaction. Gilford and Bengston (1979) contrasted three age generations in regard to two dimensions of marital happiness and satisfaction. They found that their youngest married group (average age 22) had the highest levels of both positive interaction and negative sentiment and that there was a sharp decline in both of these marital quality indices for the middle married generation (average age 44). For the oldest married group (average age 67) negative sentiment continued to decline while positive interaction reversed its descending trend and made an upturn to a point much higher than the middle generation, but still lower than the youngest group. The youngest generation (with the highest levels of both positive interaction and negative sentiment) may be characterized by instability, role negotiation, conflict, and at the same time intimate and rewarding qualities: where partners are in the process of defining themselves in an intense and intimate personal relationship. The combination of forces operating in this younger group is also predictive of high divorce rates. The middle age group seems settled into their patterns, reporting the fewest good times together, but also few bad feelings; while the oldest group appears most content and peaceful, relative to the other generations, apparently enjoying, with little conflict, the post-parental and retirement years.

Process of Separation

All of the various influences and possible antecedents of marital breakdown discussed in the previous section are only potential and predisposing factors. For many, but not all couples, these adverse influences that undermine the marital relationship and structure also set the stage for marital dissolution and separation. They weaken the marital bond to a point where one or both partners would prefer to end the relationship rather than continue as a couple. In this section, we will discuss the triggering events or influences that catapult a married couple into separating, and the various phases or stages of separation.

Precipitating events

Precipitating events are those occurrences that end up being blamed for the marital breakdown. Renne (1970) found that spouses who reported high levels of isolation, depression, alcohol use, and physical illness or disability, were also very dissatisfied with their marriages. However, these may be only concomitants of marital trouble rather than causes or reasons to separate. On the other hand, Rasmussen and Ferraro (1979) found that problems such as adultery, alcohol abuse and financial difficulties were cited by divorced persons as major causes for their marital disruption. Other researchers have also found that extra-marital sexual involvement is a prominent cause and event that precipitates a marital separation or divorce (Bentler and Newcomb, 1978; Jaffe and Kanter, 1979). However, Jaffe and Kanter (1979) aptly point out that these events, admittedly extremely disruptive to a marriage, do not always lead to marital separation and divorce: but they may become precipitating causes for separation when the marriage has been previously weakened or undermined by more long standing problems and concerns. Rasmussen and Ferraro (1979) even suggest that these events are used to escalate the problems and tensions in an unsatisfying marriage in order to break the emotional ties and allow easier separation. In other words, the events may become the battle-ground or context within which to ventilate and express more long-standing dissatisfactions and disappointments with the marriage, and so provide the impetus for termination.

Sometimes the specific problems or precipitating events can illuminate the underlying conflicts. For example, Bentler and Newcomb (1978) found that divorced persons complained more about problems that were under some voluntary control for the individual (e.g. selfishness, bickering), rather than problems lacking voluntary control (e.g. ill health). One can infer that insufficient intent, ability, and motivation to change or help to ameliorate problem areas that are under voluntary control, contributes to marital instability and lack of cohesion. Johnson (1970) examined the correlates of extra-marital coitus and found that marital sexual satisfaction, adjustment, and involvement were negatively related to the occurrence of extra-marital sexual contact. In this case, problems in the relationship (unresolved conflict and dissatisfaction) allowed a major event to occur outside the dyad (adultery), which in turn could easily be considered grounds for separation and divorce. Physical abuse and violence have also been noted in divorce-prone couples (O'Brien, 1971), which could be construed in terms of a precipitating event that has roots in more long-standing hostility, dissatisfaction, and unresolved frustration patterns in the relationship.

There is some evidence suggesting that women are more dissatisfied and find greater fault with their relationships than men (e.g. Hill *et al.*, 1976; Levinger, 1966). Levinger (1966) found that, among applicants for divorce, women reported greater problems with physical and verbal abuse, finances, alcohol, neglect, mental cruelty, and lack of love significantly more often than men. Men, on the other hand, complained more about legal trouble and sexual incompatibility. Although not noting any sex differences, Newcomb (1976) found a significantly negative correlation between problem ratings of divorced husbands and wives, that is, one partner always felt more dissatisfied with the marriage than the other. There was no evidence for a mutual decision to separate; rather, the burden seems to have fallen on one member of the dyad to initiate the breakup.

A final concern involves what differentiates unhappy marriages that do and do not eventuate in separation and divorce. Marriages that are experienced as happy and fulfilling generally remain intact and are not divorce prone. Those marriages that are experienced as unhappy but which do not lead to divorce are characterized by the man marrying at an older age and having a low level of education, the woman having less education and being unemployed, and the couple having high religious commitment, relative to unhappy couples who divorce (Landis, 1963). Regarding the choice to separate when applying for a divorce, Levinger (1979b) found that husband's income, both partners' age, length of marriage, and number of children were positively related to staying together during the divorce process. With reference to the outcome of the divorce proceedings, Levinger found that the husband's income was positively related to reconciliation and dismissal of the court process, while the level of the wife's income was positively related to divorce as the outcome of the proceedings.

Phases and stress of separation

The decision to separate, the separation itself, and post-separation adjustment involve two different but essential processes in the role transition from a married identity to a divorced identity (Spanier and Casto, 1979). The first task involves the process of adjusting to the dissolution of the marriage, including emotional and physical loss. The second critical task is the process of developing a new life-style and creating an identity and life separate from the previous marriage. Six content issues have been identified that need to be redefined and renegotiated as a result of a divorce (Bohannon, 1970). There is the emotional divorce, focused on the task of uncoupling from the spouse; the legal divorce, played out in the court system; the coparental divorce, determining the future of any children involved; the economic divorce, settling property and financial issues; the community divorce, affecting social and friendship networks; and finally, the psychic divorce, the task of redefining oneself as an autonomous individual.

The loss of a marital companion through marital breakdown, and the resulting emotional response to divorce, have been likened to a grief or mourning reaction (Juhasz, 1979), and the loss of attachment to a loved one, as in a child's attachment to his/her parent (Bowlby, 1969; Weiss, 1979a). The stages of grieving the loss of a loved one — numbness, denial, bargaining, anger, depression, and acceptance — is a common pattern experienced by divorced individuals. Weiss (1979a) points out that while many of the components of love (e.g. trust, idealization, liking) decrease substantially, or even disappear, in a failing marriage, attachment to the spouse stubbornly persists and is less modifiable by the negative experiences of divorcing. This emotional attachment in the face of conflict, disruption and in some cases violence, often becomes the most difficult issue to deal with and adapt to in the divorce process. The process of uncoupling, of letting go of the emotional security and safety the other person provided makes many people feel anxious, fearful, or even terrified. It is often a period of depression, negative selfworth, and a very real sense of having lost an important, and at the time phenomenologically essential, segment of one's identity. At the same time, Weiss (1979a) has noted periods of euphoria interspersed with the separation distress. This is truly a transition point where the security and familiarity of the past is being forsaken, either voluntarily or not, for an uncertain future. That future can either be perceived as a terrifying and depressing void left by the former spouse or a vast potential for growth, development, and the creation of a new life. However, the former perception seems to be the dominant one to individuals in the throes of separation; though Chiriboga (1979) found that people in the process of divorcing reported significantly more negative *and* positive life experiences, than comparison groups experiencing other forms of life transition (e.g. first child, retirement, first marriage).

Berger and Kellner (1964) examined the interdependency of married couples, and found that a redefinition of self is necessary to form a marriage relationship, and Vaughan (1979) extrapolated from this notion to suggest that a radical redefinition of self is also necessary in terminating a marriage relationship. Vaughan clearly shows that the uncoupling process or sequence occurs much earlier in a marriage than the actual point of separation. Separation is only one stage in the uncoupling process that begins with one person's unresolved dissatisfactions and ends with divorce and a redefined identity. The dissatisfied person, when he/she cannot successfully negotiate change in the marriage, becomes the initiator of uncoupling by seeking self-validation outside the marital dyad. By obtaining self-gratification elsewhere, he/she has already begun to form an identity separate from the marriage and thus weakens the internal cohesion of the couple. Vaughan found that the initiator is less traumatized by the emotional separation than the non-initiator, since the one initiating has had an opportunity to progress further in uncoupling and self-redefinition. Yet, as other studies have pointed out, the initiator/non-initiator distinction only makes a minor difference in the amount of emotional distress experienced during separation (Goode, 1956; Weiss, 1979a). It is a major traumatizing event for both partners.

Different phases in the separation process have been shown to elicit differing levels of stress and disorientation. Holmes and Rahe (1967) found that, except for the death of one's spouse, divorce can create the most stressful demand for self-reorganization confronted in one's adult life. Goode (1956) identified the period of final separation as the greatest stress point in the divorce sequence. Chiriboga and Cutler (1977) examined a wider range of earlier stages, and while finding the final separation to be extremely stressful, they also found that the period prior to deciding to separate was equally distressing in many cases. However, in general they noted that the emotional stress and trauma was greater after separation than at any point in the marriage.

Some individual differences have been noted in responses to marital disruption as a stressful life event (Bloom et al., 1978). Blair (1970) found that post-divorce adjustment was more difficult for women who were older at the time of the divorce, had been married longer, had low self-esteem, did not initiate the divorce, and were financially unstable. Chiriboga *et al.* (1978) also found differing vulnerabilities to psychological distress and unhappiness during marital separation. They found that men were more unhappy than women, and that older people were more unhappy than younger people when coping with divorce. They also found that social context factors (e.g. education, religion, ethnic identity) when considered individually had little effect upon post-divorce adjustment, but when taken in concert have a moderate effect. They concluded that the qualities and character of the individual, in reference to the previous marriage, were much more predictive of adjustment than social context factors. Herman (1977) studied women's responses to divorce and found that it often leads to depression, feelings of hopelessness, and in some cases, suicide. She emphasized that inadequate role development, a pervasive characteristic of women prior to the feminist movement, makes this post-divorce adjustment more difficult and problematic since they do not have the experience or role expertise to integrate themselves effectively in the economic, legal, political and social aspects of society.

   Clearly, the process of uncoupling and adjusting to the emotional turmoil of loss is a major and frightening undertaking. Yet, Spanier and Casto (1979) found that the stress and uncertainty involved in developing a new life-style are equally, if not more, traumatic than the adjustment to loss. In fact, they consider the creation of a new independent life-style to be more crucial to successful adjustment, than coping with the marital dissolution. And further, feelings of attachment, regret and bitterness associated with uncoupling, may increase during the post-separation period if a new lifestyle is not launched successfully. For example, Spanier and Casto (1979) found that divorced individuals who developed new heterosexual relationships had fewer adjustment problems than those who did little dating or did not form a cohabital relationship with a new partner. Developing new romantic relationships seems to be extremely valuable in bolstering self-worth, self-esteem, self-confidence, and the reassurance that one has social, intimate and sexual value: areas that may have been devalued and minimized during the separation process. Old friendship networks, particularly mutual friends of the formerly married couple, tend to drift away following separation, emphasizing the necessity of creating a new or restructured social and friendship environment.

   In response to this traumatic upheaval in almost all areas of one's life following a divorce, various social groups have been formed to ease the transition from married to divorced (e.g. Weiss, 1975). There is evidence that contact and involvement with these programs and workshops aid in the adjustment process (Young, 1978a,b). In fact, Raschke (1977) found that those who had higher levels of social participation in these programs or support groups also had lower levels of stress. Apparently, the groups allow for the necessary sharing, support, and redefinition, as well as helping to mitigate the loneliness, confusion and depression, within this critical period. It is also a place to find new friends and romantic contacts.

Consequences of separation and divorce

An examination of marital breakdown would be incomplete without considering the pervasive consequences that result from it. The short term stresses and traumas associated with separation and divorce have just been discussed, so we will now focus on those adjustments that occur over a long period of time and involve more people than the ex-spouses. Such long term effects of marital dissolution will be discussed in regard to consequences for the ex-spouses, subsequent marriages, and the children involved.

Ex-spouses

Life stresses and traumas related to acquiring a divorced status do not occur solely in the circumscribed period of time surrounding the separation and divorce for the formerly married. Bloom *et al.* (1978) reviewed a wide variety of studies that consistently pointed to the fact that the divorced are at higher risk for many problems and crises that do not appear to be a direct outgrowth of the actual divorce. For example, they found that psychiatric hospital admissions were higher for divorced persons relative to married people, regardless of sex, age, or ethnicity. This greater use of mental health facilities by divorced individuals is also true for outpatient clinics. Other areas where divorced persons are at higher risk than married people include vehicle accidents, susceptibility to a variety of physical illnesses, and the likelihood of committing suicide or dying by homicide or disease. Clearly, a divorced status is far less healthy than being married.

Although the devastation resulting from the loss of a marriage partner through divorce is most acute at the point of separation, attachments can linger for a long period of time. Vaughan (1979) identified these persistent attachments as continuities, where some level of contact is often maintained between former marriage partners even if they have subsequently remarried. This effort to maintain some type of interaction with the ex-spouse may be actively constructed or unconscious, temporary or a permanent linkage. Vaughan (1979) provides several examples of these continuities, one of which is the following:

"The husband moves out, leaving his set of tools behind. Several years later, even after his remarriage, the tools are still there, and he comes to borrow them one at a time. The former wife is planning to move within the same city. The tools are boxed up, ready to be taken with her."

Although this need for continuing contact is not always present in the postdivorce period, it occurs frequently enough to emphasize the power and long term effects of deep, interpersonal attachment.

This desire for continued contact with the ex-spouse, as well as a growing realization that many divorces are not solely the fault of one partner, has led to a new style of negotiating post-divorce relationships between the ex-marital partners. For an increasing number of divorced couples, there are continued feelings of warmth and caring for each other, in spite of the fact that they cannot succeed at living together in a marriage relationship. There is an acceptance that each person has unique needs that cannot be met as a couple, or within the couple. Previously, the legal system has required an adversary and blaming process in order to confer a divorce (Spanier and Anderson, 1979), which helped eliminate any positive feelings left between the partners, and exaggerated the traumas already associated with separa-tion and divorce (Spanier and Anderson, 1979; Spanier and Casto, 1979). Fortunately, with the increase in no-fault divorce, this public humiliation and tearing down of the other person can be avoided in many cases (Blood and Blood, 1979).

For an increasing number of people, divorce is becoming more amicable with a concomitant increase in the likelihood of post-divorce contact and friendship (Blood and Blood, 1979). Juhasz (1979) suggests a possible redefinition of divorce for those couples who find they cannot live together as husband and wife, but also have a deep fondness, concern, and even love for each other. She contends that marriage is only one strand that helps link one person to another, rather than a bond that defines their entire relation-ship and if broken (divorce), terminates virtually all facets of that relation-ship. If we consider marriage as only one strand joining two people, then the act of divorce need not sever the many other factors that bind one person to the other and which can remain as sources of fulfilment and meaning even if the couple are no longer married. For some this may serve as a protracted uncoupling, spreading the detaching process over a more lengthy period of time. For others, it may become a permanent arrangement and source of gratification for a good part of their lives.

Turning next to financial issues faced by divorced persons, Espenshade (1979) reviewed the available data regarding the economic consequences of divorce. He found that divorced women suffered greater financial hardship during the post-divorce period than divorced males. In fact, in one study Espenshade cites (Hoffman, 1977), divorced women experienced a seven percent reduction in their standard of living over a six year period, while divorced men gained almost 17% in their living standard over the same period of time. Difficulty with finances was one of the three major problem areas reported by divorced women with children (Kohen *et al.*, 1979). The other two areas of concern were the control and conduct of family life, as well as the social stigma and discrimination involved in being a single, divorced woman heading a household. Weiss (1979b) estimated that about 10% of divorced men seek and receive sole custody of their children, and this group of single, divorced men raising their children report similar problems to their female counterparts. For example, Gersick (1979) found that divorced, single fathers experienced problems with finances, child care, and reduced social involvement.

The relative social status of women compared with men is related to high divorce levels (Pearson and Hendrix, 1979). Further, women returning to school for additional education has also been noted as a cause and consequence of divorce (Rice, 1978), clearly an example of the problem of self-image redefinition. Even though being "a divorced woman" carries with it many unappealing stigmas and problems, it can provide the opportunity for growth and development not possible in a traditional marriage. For example, aside from the negative aspects of being divorced, mentioned above, Kohen *et al.* (1979) also found that women experienced greater authority and control over finances and family matters, had a freer social life, felt more autonomous, and possessed a more positive self-concept than before the divorce. In fact, less than one quarter of this sample of women, divorced from one to five years, were seriously contemplating remarriage at the time of the study. Clearly, more rewards are associated with independence and autonomy, though many women also acknowledged the important and practical benefits of remarriage, such as security and financial improvement.

Remarriage

A real concern following divorce involves the possible fate of any subsequent marriage. Norton and Glick (1979) noted a decline in the remarriage rate during the 1970s. However, Carter and Glick (1976) point out that the lowest remarriage rate occurs in women over 35 and men over 50; in other words, by choice or, more likely, circumstance, women over 35 remarry proportionately less than men over 35. Glenn and Weaver (1977) suggest that this sex difference regarding remarriage rates is the result of two influences: first, the sex ratio of men to women during that age period is skewed toward the females, since the males have a higher mortality rate; and secondly, the "double standard of ageing" allows men to be more attractive on the marriage market as they get older, while women become less desirable the older they get. Yet, even with the decline in the remarriage rate and the sex difference noted, Carter and Glick (1976) estimate that 80% of all divorced persons will eventually remarry at some point in their lives.

What are the qualities of these second marriages? Glenn and Weaver (1977 pp. 15ff.) point out several positive and negative influences that could affect the stability and happiness of a remarriage. On the negative side, the tensions created by step-parent and step-child relationships, the male's financial burden of supporting two households, and the fact that there may be intrinsic qualities in a person that make them unsuccessful marriage material, could all have detrimental effects upon a second marriage. On the positive side, persons entering a second marriage may have greater maturity and experience, awareness of past mistakes, and a more realistic expectation of marriage, which may allow that second marriage to be more successful than the first.

Empirical data suggest that, typically, the stability of a second marriage is not as great as in a first marriage. In other words, there is a greater percentage of divorces in second marriages than in first marriages (e.g. Glick and Norton, 1971), although Glenn and Weaver (1977) point out that this difference in divorce rates between first and second marriages is far less pronounced than 20 or 30 years ago. In fact, one recent study found no significant differences in divorce rates between first and second marriages (Bentler and Newcomb, 1978). In terms of marital happiness, Glenn and Weaver (1977) found that men and women who had never been divorced were happier with their marriage than remarried persons, although only the female difference was significant. In other words, men are almost as happy in their second marriage as men in their first, while women are more dissatisfied in their second marriage, relative to women in their first marriage. An interesting confounding effect noted by Bentler and Newcomb (1978) was that women with children from a previous marriage were more stable (less likely to divorce) and better adjusted and happy, than women who did not have previous children.

A final area that has been studied regarding second marriages is the role of homogamy. Dean and Gurak (1978) compared levels of homogamy, based on age, education, and religious affiliation, of women in their first marriage with the first and second marriages of remarried women. They found that homogamy was significantly greater for women in their first marriage than either the first or second marriages of remarried women. They suggest that these differences are not primarily the result of marriage market constraints, but rather, because of some women's marriage concepts or mate selection criteria, they are more inclined to divorce and remarry than other women.

This tendency for low homogamy in both first and second marriages may partially explain the lower stability and happiness of second marriages relative to non-divorced first marriages. Perhaps the learning experience of divorcing and the awareness of previous mistakes is not as great as one would hope, or not great enough to permit individuals to counteract their individual "relational faults".

Children

The emotional impact of divorce upon children has received increasing attention during the past several years. Bane (1979) estimated that between 30 and 40 % of children born from the 1970s onwards will be directly affected by marital dissolution. Longfellow (1979) examined the emotional impact of parental divorce on children and concluded that the mere presence or absence of both parents is less critical to the child's development than other factors that affect the quality of parent/child interactions. For example, father absence and the economic hardships of being a single mother may most directly influence the mother, which can then indirectly have an impact on the child. Clearly, it is the quality of the mother/father and parent/child relationships that determines the development and adjustment of the child; so much so, that a child's well-being may best be served in an amicable, separated family, than in a conflict ridden and tumultuous intact family. Longfellow (1979) also points out that, all things being equal, divorce is more traumatic for younger children than it is for older children.

In a series of studies, Jacobson (1978a,b,c) examined a variety of variables and their impact on child adjustment following parental divorce. Children who received explicit and detailed explanation and discussion regarding the impending separation, before it actually occurred, were significantly better adjusted following the separation, relative to those children who did not receive such information and attention. Although this was the most predictive variable affecting child adjustment, amount of pre-separation parent hostility and the amount of time lost with the father both had a highly negative relationship to post-separation adjustment in the children.

Because of the type of findings noted above, Weiss (1979b) argued that a child's access to both parents is quite important to his/her development and adjustment following a divorce, so that a certain degree of joint custody is highly desirable for the child's welfare. Ahrons (1979) examined the familial effects of the increasing judicial decisions of joint custody, and found it to have generally positive effects. He reports that former spouses have been able to continue meaningful contact and work out equitable and satisfying arrangements in their coparental roles. Ahrons (1979) suggested the term "binuclear family" to refer to the phenomenon of ex-spouses developing their own separate households, remarriages, and lives, yet remain joined in their coparental function. In this case, children are the continuity that allows a certain level of attachment to remain between ex-spouses.

Theoretical Perspectives

Failure to develop a theoretical framework to understand marital breakdown has been a major stumbling block in this field of research. Few attempts have been made, and these are typically inadequate for a variety of reasons. A large body of empirical data has been accumulated but remains disparate and unorganized for lack of theoretical structures, while on the other hand the several attempts made to build a theoretical framework have met with varying degrees of success. In general, two approaches have been used to develop such a theory. A number of authors have taken an exchange theory perspective to help explain marital breakdown (e.g. Nye and Berardo, 1973), while a second method has been to develop an inductively derived theoretical model (e.g. Laner, 1978). Several of these theories will be presented and discussed below.

Structural models theory

Using the inductive method of grounded theory construction (Glaser and Strauss, 1967), Laner (1978) developed a theory of marital dissolution. She compiled over 1300 propositions that related a wide variety of variables to marital unhappiness and instability. These propositions were gleaned from source books and recent data based articles that addressed influences upon marital outcome. Conceptually, this profusion of data could be subsumed under and assigned by content to one of four general categories: cultural, societal, dyadic, and individual. The interaction of these four variables, and how they are negotiated through conflict, presumably determines the dissolution proneness of a marriage.

Within this theory, each of these categories of variables can independently have a positive or negative valence depending upon its helpful or hindering influence on the perpetuation of the relationship. Each of these categories needs to be briefly defined. The cultural context, which is taken as a given, includes extremely global factors that are related to high divorce rates, such as an increase in the use of subjective criteria for mate selection, bilateral kinship system, and a move from population homogeneity to heterogeneity. At the societal level, several influences are critical, including the social and economic independence of women, moving away from traditional male dominance, and high social mobility. These two factors also include those variables already presented and discussed in the section on Trends and Contexts. At the dyadic level, two sets of variables are prominent: structural and dynamic factors. The structural dyadic variables include heterogamy, short acquaintance prior to marriage, and income level. The dynamic factors at the dyadic level include communication effectiveness, role congruity, conflict compromise, and adjustment. The individual level also has two sets of variables: structural and reflexive, with structural components including age at marriage, previous divorce, parental divorce, and achievement motivation; while reflexive variables include degree of flexibility and adaptability, and the resultant satisfaction and happiness.

Taking the cultural context as a given and constant, there are eight combinations of the remaining three factors, when each can have a positive or negative valence. According to Laner (1978) the dyadic conflict emerging from these interactions will typically result in marital dissolution in three cases, non-dissolution in three cases, and ambiguous outcome in two cases. Dissolution will generally occur when all three factors are negative, where there is a high level of exacerbated conflict, low adjustment, low happiness, and non-supportive societal factors. Dissolution will also occur when both dyadic and individual factors are negative but societal is positive, since the positive societal influence cannot mitigate the difficulties within the relationship. Finally, dissolution will generally arise when societal and individual factors are negative and dyadic is positive, not because of unresolved conflict, but due to the low adaptability, low happiness, and the social situation's non-support. One configuration of these factors is dissolution prone (with occasional idiosyncratic non-dissolution), where there are negative societal and dyadic factors but a positive individual factor. Such a combination of exacerbated conflict, low adjustment, and societal pressure would generally result in dissolution, but in certain cases, the power of the individuals' flexibility and adaptability may prevent dissolution. The remaining configurations will typically result in non-dissolution or idiosyncratic dissolution.

There are many advantages of this theoretical perspective. It uses a systems approach combining several conceptually different levels of variables relating to the individuals, the relationship, and society, and it further allows diverse types of conflict and conflict negotiation to account for dissolution or non-dissolution. Although it is a simple and elegant theory, the simplicity is also a disadvantage since variations or gradations of the valences of the factors are not included, nor is any possible weighting of the factors presented. The theory will have problems when a particular factor has both positive and negative elements, which undoubtedly occurs in reality. It is possible that further refinement may allow for and actively deal with the subtleties and non-dichotomous nature of the variables and factors, but such refinements will necessitate more complex and sophisticated combinatorial mechanisms.

A social psychological perspective

Levinger (1979a) proposed a theory of marital breakdown that conceives of marital dissolution as a special case of social group or relationship dissolution, implying that similar processes are at work. He asserts that marital breakdown or cohesion is the result of three interacting factors: attractions within the relationship, barriers to terminating the relationship, and alternative attractions outside the relationship. These various factors are balanced or evaluated in terms of costs and rewards within an exchange theory perspective (Thibaut and Kelley, 1959), and the resultant equilibrium will determine whether a couple will remain together or separate. Conflict is not a prominent aspect of this approach and its range is limited to the dyadic level. Each of the factors and their composition will be discussed below.

Attraction to the marriage is determined by the rewards and costs incurred by being a member of that relationship. Rewards can take several forms including material, symbolic and affectional. Family income and home ownership are examples of material rewards, while symbolic rewards could include educational and occupational status, and social similarity. Sexual fulfilment and companionship are important types of affectional rewards possible within a marital relationship. Costs of membership within the marriage may involve time and energy investment, loyalty, exclusivity, and other commitments necessary to remaining in an intimate and enduring relationship.

In addition to attractions within the relationship, cohesion is also determined by the barrier forces that prevent the dissolution of the dyad. These restraining forces can be looked at in terms of material, symbolic, and affectional costs of terminating the marriage. Material costs would include financial expenses and possibly the loss of house, car, or other belongings. Obligations and commitment to the marital bond, religious prohibitions, as well as peer and community pressures, are symbolic costs to marital dissolution. Fear of loneliness, loss of a sexual partner, and feelings toward dependent children are affectional barriers to the termination of a marriage.

Finally, alternative attractions exterior to the marital relationship help determine the marital instability of a couple. The greater the number and/or strength of alternatives to the marriage, the more likely is it that dissolution will occur. Alternative attractions can also be material, symbolic, or affectional in form. Material rewards might include the woman's increase in economic and social independence. General independence and freedom for self-actualization are examples of symbolic attractions outside the marital dyad. Last, but certainly not least, are affective alternative attractions, that might include a wider range of preferable sex partners, in addition to greater companionship and friendship possibilities.

Dissolution will occur when internal attractions grow weak or too costly, barriers are few and with little power, and alternatives are attractive and salient. The basis for weighing these three factors is presumably logical and rational, but unfortunately (or fortunately) not all human decisions are made in this manner. Negotiation and conflict are not included in the theory, although they would seem to be important and essential ways to deal with imbalance and dissatisfaction with the reward/cost ratios. In addition, this theory presumes to address only the dyadic level of interaction, which leaves out the direct influence of social and individual factors. However, within these limitations, the theory seems to have broad appeal in terms of conceptual simplicity that can be applied to a variety of empirical data with a fair degree of explanatory power. Although the scope of this theory is far narrower than that offered by Laner (1978), Levinger's (1979a) perspective presents a much clearer and more meaningful representation of the dyadic level of interactional functioning and behaviour, with the apparent drawback that conflict is not overtly included in the theory.

The four-factor model

As an outgrowth of their study of married couples in urban communes, Jaffe and Kanter (1979) developed a four-factor model of marital breakdown. Although developed in the framework of communal living, with its particular stresses, the theory they offer has a broader application to break-ups and dissolution in other married dyads (Levinger and Moles, 1976). The four factors they presented are contextual conduciveness, systemic stresses, generalized beliefs, and precipitating events. Each will be discussed in turn below.

Contextual conduciveness refers to the social environment surrounding the marriage. Included within this factor are the presence of attractive alternatives within close proximity, and societal influences at a broader, more pervasive level. Alternative attractions could include another person, single-hood, or some other innovative lifestyle (e.g. cohabitation, mate swapping). Other influences within the contextual conduciveness factor include those previously discussed in the section on Contexts and Trends and the societal level factor of Laner (1978). Systemic stress includes those events or variables that create or cause tension within the dyad. Such stress could be the result of low intra-couple cohesion due to an incongruity of roles or values, weak internal attractions or barriers, or incompatible needs and expectations. This concept is similar to a combination of the dyadic and individual level factors in Laner's (1978) theory. Generalized beliefs involve those attitudes toward marriage, and the acceptance of divorce, by the marital partners and imposed by their peers, religious convictions, and social milieu. The symbolic barrier costs in Levinger's (1979a) theory fit nicely into this category (e.g. religious constraints). Finally, precipitating events are the motivators that propel a marriage in trouble, experiencing high systemic stress and low contextual conduciveness and support, into separating. Precipitating events can include a wide variety of disturbances within the couple, such as the discovery of an outside sexual affair.

This is a rather broad theory that can incorporate some of the important features of the other theories within it. However, without this filling in of the skeleton, the theory has little to offer in terms of detailed explanation of the process of marital breakdown or dissolution. In this sense it might serve best as a super-structure theory that can help organize and conceptualize other more limited range theoretical perspectives that have greater subtlety and detailed explanatory ability.

Exchange theory

Although many theories have an exchange orientation perspective as a component of them, a pure form of exchange theory has not been offered to explain marital breakdown. Even though Nye and Berardo (1973) have taken steps in this direction using a grounded theory approach, the general framework given by Thibaut and Kelley (1959), and more recently Kelley (1979), has remained largely in the broad area of close interpersonal relationships and has not been interpreted in the context of marital breakdown. In this section, a cursory translation of the relationship concepts offered by Kelley (1979) into a structure relevant to marital breakdown will be presented. It is beyond the scope of this chapter to elaborate and fully develop this direct application of exchange theory principles, although there is a clear need for such an effort.

There are three essential components or stages to the structure and processes given by Kelley (1979): outcome interdependence, transformation of motivation, and attribution of dispositions. Outcome interdependence refers to the fact that each person has an impact on the behaviour outcome of the other. Transformation of motivation refers to the capacity and quality of responding and transforming the interactional structure or pattern, as a function of the satisfaction, to the interdependence. Finally, based upon interactional shifts resulting from mutual

.ling to interdependency patterns, dispositional attributions are made
tners upon each other.

ıen applying this framework to marital breakdown, it is important to
rcı.. ember that marriage carries with it certain specific and probably
different expectations for each partner. Simplistically, this perspective can
be used to understand conflict negotiation, where problems can occur at any
of three stages. Marital breakdown can occur when one or both partners are
not satisfied (do not get what they want or need) from the interdependency
structure. This conflict will be further aggravated if there is a lack of or
inadequate response from the other to relieve the dissatisfaction. From this
type of interaction, a negative disposition can be attributed to the
inadequate responder (e.g. "He does not love me . . . care for me . . . want
me to be happy . . . care about the marriage" etc.). The more often these
unfulfilling transformations occur the more negative dispositions are
accumulated, eventually leading to marital breakdown and dissolution. Any
content issue could be involved from specific behaviours, to general
relationship concerns, to specific marital expectations, role performances,
or value incongruities.

It is apparent that this perspective can give a rather clear and precise
understanding of conflict negotiation and an explanatory device for a
microcosm of very important interactions within the marital dyad. It is
important to realize that marital breakdown is a special case of any close
interpersonal relationship breakdown (see Duck, this volume). Marital
breakdown does have differences, but not so much in structure as in content
and parameters. For example, a married couple has a legal, social and
personal contract to stay together, which might have an influence on their
commitment and motivation not to allow breakdown in the relationship.
This is an example of parameters that differentiate married relations from
other close interpersonal relationships. Similarly, there are traditional roles
and expectations for marriage partners that are imparted by parents, peers,
and society; these affect what one demands and wants from interdependency patterns. This is an example of content uniqueness in a marital
dyad. Further work is needed to elaborate this perspective more fully in
regard to marital breakdown, and to investigate its relevance to other
perspectives.

Reconciliation and synthesis

In all of these theories, perspective, or range, or amount of detail of
application is inadequate in the context of marital breakdown. Several of
them accurately convey an all-encompassing view of marital breakdown and
seem to enumerate the most important factors in a broad, general way (e.g.

Jaffe and Kanter, 1979; Laner, 1978). Unfortunately, these theories lack the ability to address and explain issues at a more detailed and finely tuned level of analysis. On the other hand, the remaining theories that attempt to explain smaller chunks of the marital breakdown process, do so rather effectively, albeit at the expense of leaving out other important factors identified in a more general perspective (e.g. Kelley, 1979; Levinger, 1979a; Nye and Berardo, 1973). A synthesis of these various theories would be extremely helpful to the extent that very broad, and at the same time quite detailed, understanding of marital breakdown could occur. This would also be useful in highlighting areas where there is totally inadequate or non-existent theory development (e.g. how societal and dyadic level influences interact). As previously noted, Jaffe and Kanter's (1979) four-factor model might serve well as a super-structure theoretical base within which to place the components of the other theories.

Future Directions

Even in the face of extremely high divorce rates — the most recent estimate is that 40 percent of all marriages will end in divorce — the institution of marriage does not seem to have lost its value as the most important relationship form in society. All but a few percent of all age groups have already married or plan to marry sometime in their lives. The personal meaning, importance, and commitment placed upon marriage has not waned to any appreciable degree, and almost all couples entering marriage consider the occasion to be anything but trivial. The potential rewards of a successful marriage seem to outweigh considerably the real counterforces that clearly disrupt a large minority of all marriages. However, people are probably entering marriage with less grandiose expectations and a more realistic perception of the difficulties and pitfalls of marriage in a changing society.

For many, traditional marriage may embody assumptions and roles that are at odds with emerging viewpoints in society, and marital breakdown might be a consequence. For example, there has been an increase in the value placed on independence, autonomy, and self-sufficiency during the past 20 years or so. Women are feeling stifled in their prescribed and limited role of wife. Unfortunately, the institution of marriage, and people's expectations from it, have not adapted enough to allow for individual as well as dyadic adjustment and growth. Traditionally, one has been sacrificed for the other. This has led some couples to seek relationship forms and structures that might have a greater possibility of permitting an individual to flourish and feel fulfilled as a person, while remaining in an intimate, close relationship with another person (e.g. cohabitation, communal marriage, open marriage).

Further research needs to be undertaken to determine what attitudes, expectations, and personality patterns can tolerate or even foster individual growth within a close, intimate relationship. Can people grow in different directions and still remain a couple that can meet each other's intimate needs? What are the essential ingredients and shared qualities that define a relationship and how do they relate to dyadic cohesion? Along these lines there is also the need to define a typology of marital relationships that could have research usefulness as descriptions of underlying dynamic or quality differences, and diagnostic usefulness in the treatment of relationship problems. Hicks and Platt (1970) suggest that there are at least two types of marriage relationships: institutional and companionate. The institutional marriage is characterized by traditional sex-typed roles, male oriented, and instrumental in nature, while companionship marriages are characterized by a greater emphasis placed on affective expression and needs, communication, egalitarian roles, and a focus on expressive factors. Hicks and Platt feel that the companionship marriage is a relatively new, emerging style, while the institutional type marriage has previously been predominant. Further refinement and detailed patterns of these and other marital types will help highlight the areas of greatest vulnerability to stress and divorce potential in a particular type of marriage.

The available theories on marital breakdown either effectively explain a small segment of the marital interaction, but lack the scope and range of the many factors involved, or else have the range and broad perspective, but lack detail and intricacy at the practical, dyadic level of analysis. Clearly, a theory is needed that can combine the broad perspective with the inclusion of many diverse levels of influential factors (e.g. cultural, dyadic), while also accurately accounting for the interaction of levels and the detailed analyses of the processes occurring in small segments of the relationship (e.g. conflict negotiation based on an exchange theory perspective). As pointed out earlier, a first step toward this goal might be to choose a theory that seems to portray accurately the broad scope of important influences at a macro level (e.g. Jaffe and Kanter, 1979; Laner, 1978), and then place the other theories that account for smaller, micro-level segments of the relationship, within the super-structure theory. Obviously, there will be many holes or voids where no existing theory has focused. For example, it is unclear how various levels of influences interact, such as the cultural level of analysis and the dyadic functioning level. Laner (1978) has offered some preliminary suggestions along these lines, but a great deal of theory development remains to be done.

An important ingredient that needs to be included in any theoretical perspective is the role of conflict. As mentioned earlier in this chapter, conflict, in and of itself, is not sufficient to predict marital breakdown. Rather, it is the style and content of the conflict that determines its beneficial or detrimental influences upon marriage. It is important that future research efforts focus on determining types of conflict, rather than simply noting the fact of it. Being able to specify types of conflict and processes of conflict management will be an immense help in understanding the nature of incongruities and disagreements and their impact on marital cohesion, or lack thereof.

Finally, theories of marital breakdown seem to consider divorce the limit of their domain. However, an adequate and inclusive theory of marital disruption should also predict how post-divorce adjustment will proceed and what specific factors in the relationship and individual prior to divorcing will determine post-divorce personal and life management. In other words, what features in the individual or relationship will hinder or help the post-divorce uncoupling or detachment process and the ability to create and develop a new life-style. For example, if a marriage is characterized by an over-dependence of one person upon the other, this may create problems in the relationship that could lead to divorce, and the post-divorce adjustment could be particularly painful for the dependent person who must relinquish his/her attachment to the former spouse and live a relatively terrifying life of independence. However, dependency is more than an individual factor since it takes at least two to be actualized, and thus there must be an interaction of individual and relationship quality factors that would influence post-divorce adjustment.

This chapter has examined a wide variety of influences and factors that help or hinder what life two people can make for themselves as a married couple. Marriage, its cultivation and nourishment, occupies a major portion of most people's lives and can be an invaluable source of satisfaction and confidence, or a place of pain and unhappiness. A clearer understanding of what can go wrong in that relationship may allow for even greater possi-bilities of growth and fulfillment within marriage. However, people's values and needs are in rapid transition, and people's marriages seem to be one of the fatalities of this changing world. Yet, oddly enough, the institution of marriage is not losing its importance to any great extent. People are rejecting their marriage partners in divorcing, but are not rejecting the institution itself. People are still seeking marriage as a vehicle or structure in forming close, intimate and rewarding relationship. Yet, many extra-marital needs and demands are putting a strain on marriage and the traditional role it has served. People's expectations for marriage need to expand and broaden in order to allow marriage to be a flexible and rewarding arrange-ment, rather than one that strangles. Many are disillusioned with its limita-tions and the fairy tale fantasy of "happily ever after". This is an age of the individual and marriage must change to accommodate the emphasis placed upon personal achievement and self-confidence. Hopefully, a balance can be reached where marriage can meet the intimate needs of the partners, but also allow for validation and meaning as individuals beyond its bounds. If not, marriage may very well join the dinosaurs, who also could not adapt to a changing world. It is doubtful that marriage will ever become extinct, but to survive it must change.

Acknowledgements

Preparation of this chapter was supported in part by USPHS grant DA01070. The first author would like to thank Leslie for showing him how problems arise in good relationships, and, hopefully Debbie, for teaching him how to work them through.

Section II

Disordered Relationships

CHAPTER 4

Social Skill Disorder

Peter Trower

Failure to meet the social demands of ordinary life, including the making of friends, is a common problem among psychiatric patients. Such failure is being increasingly interpreted in clinical psychology in terms of social skill deficiency, but this is an incomplete analysis that fails to account for many aspects of the problem. It can also be argued that social failure is a form of self-fulfilling prophecy in which negative expectations and other erroneous beliefs serve to channel information-processing and social interaction in such a way that outcomes are generated which verify the original beliefs. A circle is thus formed that is self-perpetuating and resistant to change.

In the first part of this chapter I will review studies which exemplify various aspects of this process. The second part traces, through experimental findings, the development of self-fulfilling prophecies; the long-term effects, namely behavioural consistency — a major feature of many patients, particularly chronic hospitalized schizophrenics; and the prevention or disruption of skill acquisition. It is concluded that social retraining programmes must include cognitive as well as behaviour modification components if they are to succeed, and intervention should occur earlier rather than later in the lives of individuals at risk.

Social Skill Disorder: Mechanisms of Failure

The commonplaceness of friendship belies its complexity as a social phenomenon, and its difficulty as a social task. Nearly everyone has friends yet it
appears that most people have difficulty in initiating friendships (Bryant and
Trower, 1974) and find encountering others a stressful experience (Givens,
1978). Psychiatric patients, perhaps to an even greater degree, seem also to
find problems in this area (cf. Bryant *et al.*, 1976).

Difficulty in making friends can be interpreted in terms of lack of social
skills; for instance in the Bryant *et al.* study it was found that ratings of
difficulty in starting up a friendship correlated most highly with independent
judgements of social inadequacy (unpublished data). In the case of psychiatric patients social skill deficiency is now recognized as a major feature
of a wide range of disorders, and the failure of many patients to relate to
others or cope with the social demands of ordinary life is increasingly being
seen in terms of such deficiencies with consequent need for correction
through skills training (e.g. Hersen, 1979). It would follow from this idea
that failure in friendship will often be due to maladaptive behavioural
responses which lead to rejection by others and withdrawal by the patient,
leading in turn to creation of, or worsening of, psychiatric symptoms.
However, while this is true in part, it is now clear that this is an incomplete
conceptualization of the problem, and an alternative model is needed to
account better for recent research findings.

Beginning with the simple notion that the eradication of maladaptive
behaviours and instigation of new, adaptive skills will "cure" the problem,
we have to ask why patients often do not learn in the ordinary course of
events to modify their own responses, and thus acquire skill. We should
expect from, for example, the social skills model (Argyle, 1969) that an
individual learns to modify his responses in the light of continuous, correc-
tive feedback from the social environment, from exposure to reinforcement
contingencies and learning models and so on, and indeed there is an abundance of support for such a learning process. Yet the evidence also shows
that many patients do not learn adaptive skills and their social inadequacy is
usually associated with "chronicity" of clinical symptoms. Indeed, Zigler
and his colleagues (Zigler and Phillips, 1961) have shown that level of
premorbid social competence is the best predictor of outcome, almost
irrespective of the diagnosis. Experience with social skills training shows too
that patients commonly fail to utilize skills in their own environments, even
though they appear to acquire them in training settings. The comparatively
low rates of generalization and maintenance of trained skills found in many
social skill studies also reflect this experience. What, then, is the blocking
mechanism?

One explanation is that the patients are suffering from a mental illness of which social impairment is a consequence, and that patients who show no change or get worse are simply showing outward signs of its course. However, a more parsimonious and testable account is the self-fulfilling prophecy theory. The essence of this account is that an individual brings about the very consequences of his own prediction simply by virtue of the effects of the prediction itself, thus forming a cycle that is self-perpetuating and for this reason resistant to change. This historically old theory has a wide range of explanatory applicability in sociology, politics and economics (Merton, 1948), and is a powerful explanatory tool within psychology (Rosenthal, 1973). Beck (1976) has made effective use of the theory in accounts of affective disorders. More recently Snyder (in press) and his colleagues have broken new ground theoretically and experimentally in the explanation of social psychological phenomena. The work of this group (Snyder, 1978, pp.1-2) has been to

> "chart the processes by which one individual's initially erroneous beliefs about another person can and do exert powerful channeling influences on subsequent information processing and social interaction such that: (a) the cognitive reality of these initially erroneous beliefs is bolstered and strengthened, and (b) actions of the individual based upon these impressions cause the actual behaviour of the target to confirm and validate the individual's initially erroneous impressions".

The first of these processes they name *cognitive bolstering*, the second they call *behavioural confirmation*. The perpetuating and central component of the cycle is a belief of some kind — variously described as prophecy, expectation, prediction, stereotype or schema. An example as applied to a clinical problem might be with an individual who has a belief that all people are against him, or that he is inherently unworthy or bad, and will always be rejected by others (Ellis, 1962; Beck, 1976). As a result of these beliefs he may (a) selectively attend to and interpret the behaviour of others in accordance with the beliefs (cognitive bolstering) and (b) behave in ways guided by the beliefs which tend to elicit responses from others which confirm the beliefs (behavioural confirmation). It will be argued in this chapter that in understanding the reasons for failure in friendship and other social tasks we need to look at both these processes in patients who exemplify social failure problems.

Cognitive bolstering

Individuals selectively filter information according to stereotypic beliefs which they hold about themselves and others. A number of investigators have shown the extraordinary degree to which strongly held stereotypes influence information processing such that new evidence that confirms these stereotypes is more easily noticed, remembered and brought to mind than is disconfirming evidence. When these beliefs take the form of negative evaluations about the self, they have a predictable effect on perception. A number of studies have shown that individuals low in measured "self-esteem" selectively attend to information that is self-defaming or otherwise punishing. For example, Young and Trower (in preparation) found that neurotic patients recalled more self-defaming words supposedly about themselves than did normal controls; Wener and Rehm (1975) found depressives attended to negative rather than positive feedback and Nelson and Craighead (1977) found that depressives tended to recall being reinforced on fewer trials and punished on more trials than nondepressed controls. Depressives also tended to self-reinforce less often.

Irrational beliefs. Beck (1976) and Ellis (1962) have independently developed the thesis that neurotics, particularly depressives and the socially anxious, hold central, evaluative, irrational self-beliefs or "schemas" such as "Unless I do everything perfectly I am a failure", which constitute the basis for screening out, differentiating and coding stimuli. Such schemas are seen as causal theories about reality. Empirical evidence has been found for the existence and operation of such schemas along these lines. Markus (1977) not only found that such "self-schemata" facilitated processing, retrieval and prediction of schema-relevant information, but also made individuals resistant to counter-schematic information. With such a biased information-base it is not difficult to see how individuals "cognitively bolster" a particular belief even when reality indicates a contrary conclusion.

The operation of such self-beliefs has been investigated in social problems. Clark and Arkowitz (1975) found that high-anxious men overestimated negative aspects of their performance in conversation with women volunteers, while low-anxious men did not. O'Banion and Arkowitz (1977) found that high-anxious women selectively remembered negative information about their performance in conversations with men.

Perception of others. Not only are such individuals more likely to differ from non-neurotics in the way they process self-related information, such as their performance, they are also likely to differ in their perceptions of others. Firstly, let us consider the degree and direction of awareness, or monitoring. There are complex, interacting mechanisms which may cause some patients to become external monitors (of others) and some patients to become internal monitors (of self) depending on type of belief ("Others are against me" versus "I am a failure"), and state of objective self-awareness

(Duval and Wicklund, 1972). It might be predicted, for example, that external monitors, such as paranoids, would actually be more aware of certain social cues, since they would be more vigilant monitors of those cues, believing them to be predictive of rejection. La Russo (1978) found that paranoid patients were indeed more sensitive — and accurate — in the perception of genuine as opposed to simulated negative nonverbal cues, compared with nonparanoid controls. Similarly, Cunningham (1977) found that neurotics were superior to controls in accuracy in decoding emotions and suggested that neurotics were motivated to be more vigilant given that they were psychologically more vulnerable. It is likely that externally oriented individuals caught in the self fulfilling prophecy cycle would become expert perceivers of cues to which they are continually exposed and which they continually monitor. The situation with internal monitors will take a different form (with poor external monitoring and increased self-monitoring), a problem to which we will return later.

Not only is level and direction of awareness of others affected by negative beliefs and other mechanisms, but the content of decoded information is likely to be distorted. Rothbart and Birrell (1977) showed that experi-mentally manipulated beliefs about the favourability or unfavourability of a confederate, affected recall by normal subjects, of actual physical expressive facial clues, such as whether the mouth was frowning or smiling, the eyes were cold or warm, hard or soft, or the expression cruel or kind. Dil (1972) found that emotionally disturbed children attributed more negative mean-ings to photographed facial emotional expressions. Forgus and DeWolfe (1974) found that delusional patients would selectively encode incoming information along dimensions relevant to their own delusional and halluc-inatory themes. Compared to controls, male patients perceived more negative interpersonal pressure (being persecuted), females more sexual pressure (e.g. terrified of sex) and both perceived more negative pressure coming from the environment.

The influence of strongly held beliefs on external monitoring is greatest in ambiguous situations where uncertainty is high yet firm inferences are drawn from sparse information. Young and Trower (in preparation) found, for example, that neurotics projected a negative interpretation upon ambi-guously defined social situations, whereas normals did not.

One situation where ambiguity is high is in first encounters, where it is well known that people perceive obvious physical and behavioural cues like attractiveness and smiling, and make inferences about the other's per-sonality, attitude and so on. The opportunity for negative interpretations and inferences is rife indeed, since in ordinary daily social encounters there is an abundance of aversive non-verbal signalling. Givens (1978) in an ethological study of unfocussed interaction (i.e. strangers passing each other in public places) found a characteristic pattern of contact avoidance cues as follows: lip compression, lip-bite, tongue show, tongue-in-cheek, downward, lateral and maximal-lateral gaze avoidance, hand-to-face, to hand, to body, hand-behind-head automanipulations, and postures involving flexion and adduction of the upper limbs. It is certain that some of these aversive cues would also be present in more focussed first encounters. However, as Givens (1978) notes, aversive signalling does not necessarily imply dislike or negative reactions, but simply responses to social anxiety. Approach and aversion signals often occur together, as in coyness where there is at once attraction and fear of approach. However, aversive cues are prime candidates for misinterpretation as cues of rejection and hostility, since such cues are ambiguous. Thus misinterpreted, they serve mistakenly to filter out the other as a potential friend and to further bolster negative beliefs about self and others.

Ambiguity of meaning applies not only to aversive cues but to most nonverbal communication. Several authors point out that non verbal communication is an implicit language of innuendo, its ambiguity serving an important social function. Labov and Fanshel (1977 p.46) write:

> "Speakers need a form of communication which is *deniable*. It is advantageous for them to express hostility, challenge the competence of others, or express friendliness and affection in a way that can be denied if they are explicitly held to account for it".

As we have seen, however, there are unfortunate consequences too.

Behavioural confirmation

Cognitive bolstering processes provide an evidence base that gives a compelling appearance of reality to beliefs about self or others. Snyder *et al.* (1977, pp. 657-658) point out that this reality is, of course, entirely cognitive.

> "It is in the eye and mind of the beholder. But stereotype-based attributions may serve as grounds for predictions about the target's future behaviour and may guide and influence the perceiver's interactions with the target. This process itself may generate behaviours on the part of the target that erroneously confirm the predictions and validate the attributions of the perceiver. How others treat us is, in large measure, a reflection of our treatment of them (cf. Bandura, 1977; Mischel, 1968; Raush, 1965). Thus when we use our social perceptions as guides for regulating our interactons with others, we may constrain their behavioral options (cf. Kelley and Stahelski, 1970)."

Of course self-fulfilling prophecy cycles may be virtuous or vicious. They are virtuous when they produce positive outcomes, such as when the other's attractiveness activates reciprocally reinforcing friendship responses (Snyder *et al.*, 1977). They are vicious when they produce negative outcomes such as when paranoid beliefs activate mutual rejection responses (Jones and Panitch, 1971). In the crucial opening stages of friendship formation the dangers are ever-present for a vicious cycle to begin its downward spiral, mainly because of the considerable tension and a sense of threat that is created by encounters between strangers, as mentioned earlier. However, there are also linguistic rituals and conventions such as greetings, partings and disclosure reciprocity which serve as cultural solutions to the problem of social tension in first encounters. In other words, a virtuous cycle of inter-action is bolstered by social rules of polite conduct and self-presentation (Goffman, 1955; 1972). Investigators have found, for example, that a rule of reciprocity of self-disclosure operates between strangers but not between friends (e.g. Derlega *et al.*, 1976). Conformity to such social rules seems essential in first encounters, and leads to impressions of increased attrac-tiveness and mental health (Berger, 1979).

On the other hand, it is not difficult to see the various ways that a vicious cycle would occur. The individual with strong negative expectations would be least likely to conform to affiliative conventions of etiquette, reciprocity or positive self-presentation, and most likely to exhibit defensive social responses. In a series of studies by the author and colleagues, patients who had been independently rated as socially inadequate were observed, in a standardized first encounter, to talk, smile and gesture less than controls, to avert gaze more and make posture shifts less often. They handed over the conversation less, showed little interest in the other, but too much interest in self, allowing personal problems and mood to intrude inappropriately into conversation. They were rated as less rewarding and colder (Trower, 1980; Bryant *et al.*, 1976).

Behaviour of this kind might be construed as breaking the rules of social etiquette in first encounters. Trower (1980) found evidence of a hierarchical structure of discourse rules, the most basic of which were being broken by unskilled patients. Evidence was found that the primary rule in first en-counters is the rule to talk, a theme echoed by a number of writers from Malinowski (1972) ("taciturnity means not only unfriendliness but indirectly a bad character") to Goffman (1955) ("undue lulls come to be potential signs of having nothing in common or of being insufficiently self-possessed to create something to say"). According to Malinowski and subsequent researchers, talk in these contexts serves the special function of "phatic communion" — the communion of words, which is the first act to establish links of fellowship.

Deviation from communication roles of the above kind leads to negative judgements such as "less attractive" and "less mentally healthy" (Berger *et al.*, 1976), and is likely to lead to rejections (usually no doubt in the form of a formalized polite routine). Patients are unlikely, however, to perceive the connection between their own actions and the other's reactions, given the common attribution tendencies between perceiving self and others (Jones and Nisbett, 1971).

Depression. Some depressives conform to the behavioural confirmation pattern; it seems they create, by the deployment of maladaptive skills, the environment they predict and dread. Such a pattern would be predicted for example by Beck's circular feedback model of depression (Beck, 1976). By expecting rejection and social failure the depressive may react in un-rewarding ways to others, and get less rewards in return. Libet and Lewinsohn (1973) found, among other things, that depressives used fewer initiating behaviours, less positive statements and longer response latencies than controls, and presumably as a consequence, elicited less social reinforcement. Learned helplessness (Seligman, 1975) may be construed in the same way — beliefs in the non-contingency of outcomes (i.e. that responses do not influence outcomes) lead to failure to attempt to influence outcomes, the final inactivity producing a predictable lack of social reward and possible rejection.

Coyne (1976b) takes the negative cycling effect further: while his results differ from those of Libet and Lewinsohn (1973), he finds nonetheless that depressives induced negative affect in those with whom they interacted and were rejected (an example of rejection was unwillingness to meet again). Both Coyne and others (e.g. Hammen and Peters, 1978) believe (with indirect evidence) that inappropriate (over-intimate) self-disclosure, e.g. about personal problems, and a dwelling upon pessimism, helplessness and negative self-image were the key factors leading to rejection.

A similar picture emerges from Dion and Dion (1978) who found that "defensive"women (those scoring high on the Marlowe-Crowne Social Desirability Scale) gave a less favourable self-presentation to men than nondefensive controls. They dwelt on their fears, self-consciousness, lone-liness and self-dissatisfaction. However, this study did not analyse others' reactions, nor the effect on self-beliefs.

Social phobia. Some types of social phobia seem also to conform to the behavioural confirmation cycle, as Beck and Emery (1979) point out. Situations which are perceived as a potential threat to self-esteem, also carry the potential for arousing anxiety. Once the fear is experienced, concomitant anxiety symptoms may disrupt performance to such an extent that the individual experiences failure and rejection again, thus confirming expec-tations and adding another twist to the vicious spiral. Evidence that overtly nervous individuals are indeed negatively evaluated in some situations

comes from Farina *et al.* (1978). They found that "job applicant" confederates, when apparently tense, were thought by their interviewers to get
along less well with other workers, have fewer assets and more liabilities, be
less reliable, less well-adjusted and valuable than "calm" confederates.

Lack of assertiveness. We have so far discussed negative self-beliefs or
other-beliefs which can produce aversive action – reaction cycles but this is
only one end of the spectrum. At the other end are positive action – reaction
cycles that have equally powerful *negative* belief-confirming outcomes. Such
individuals may equate assertiveness with hostility or aggression, and the
belief that any assertive act will lead to negative evaluation by others,
resulting in further self-deprecation as unlikeable. Alden and Safran (1978)
found, for example, that individuals who endorsed irrational beliefs (Ellis,
1962) were less assertive in behaviour and reported higher levels of discomfort than controls. Schwartz and Gottman (1976) found that a self-
critical cognitive set interfered with performance of assertive behaviour. It
seems probable that both assertive responses and submissive compliant
responses, will lead to behavioural confirmation of negative beliefs. Assertive responses, even appropriate ones, inevitably at times provoke aversive
reactions in others (Woolfolk and Dever, 1979) while submissive behaviour
will elicit dominance or disrespect — both reactions being readily interpreted as dislike or rejection. As with other forms of self-fulfilling prophecies, it is not enough just to analyse the behaviour of submissives and
apply behavioural assertive training.

Psychopathy. Another form of social skill deficiency that is prone to a
vicious cycle is found in psychopathy. Rime *et al.*, (1978) found psychopaths
used more gestures, leaned forward more, looked for longer periods, and
smiled less than nonpsychopathic subjects. The authors report a "spontaneous attitude of retreat" in the partner due to the psychopath's over-
intrusiveness. The psychopath thereby produces a situation that deprives
him of his greatest need — for stimulation — leading him to yet greater
intrusiveness. Hare (1970) suggested that the psychopath misses or ignores
many social cues that have important informational or emotional content.

Negative fit. The phenomenon of behavioural confirmation is common-
place in psychotherapy, though it is described more in terms of transference.
Patients' so-called unconscious or unmonitored attempts to elicit belief-
confirming responses from the therapist is the raw material for psychoanalysis and other orientations. However, it appears that psychotherapists
commonly fall into the transference trap. Luborsky and Singer (1974) noted
that in a statistically significant number of cases therapists responded to their
clients with "negative fit". Negative fit is defined as "the degree to which the
therapist actually responds in ways that fit the patient's preconceptions

about how people who have been important to him have responded". A number of conclusions emerged from the studies of these workers: first, the frequency of negative fit phenomena is much greater than commonly supposed. Secondly, two major types of "fit" were found: (a) the therapist's confirmation of the patient's fear of rejection by being critical, disapproving, condescending, cold and so on; and (b) the therapist's confirmation of the patient's expectations of being made weak and dependent by being too directive, domineering, and controlling. Both forms were considered by judges to be at least untherapeutic, if not anti-therapeutic.

Stigmatizing. The main thrust of the behavioural confirmation thesis is that individuals eventually bring about the reality that confirms their previously untrue beliefs. This gives a deeper insight and a new twist to the idea that psychiatric patients are to varying degrees out of touch with reality. Given that reality is remarkably tractable, how does this come about? An explanation is again provided by the self-fulfilling prophecy theory. Socially dysfunctioning individuals provide just the readily identifiable behavioural cues, or markers, that elicit stigmatizing beliefs and other negative stereotypes from others. For example, the labelling theory (Scheff, 1963) states that the cultural stereotype of mental illness (recently experimentally verified by Jones and Cochrane (1979)) acts as a self-fulfilling prophecy — others react to the potential patient in a uniform way that leads him to "play the expected role" and this tends to validate the original definition. It appears that the person labelled and the labeller act out stereotype roles that provide mutual support for the label.

Krause (1978) goes some way towards breaking down the stages by which "improper persons" are so labelled. The labeller first searches for a situational excuse to explain a behavioural "impropriety". If none is found the individual is labelled an "improper person" in the following way: if he meant to act that way and the impropriety is serious, he is bad, immoral, criminal or evil. If it was not intentional, but due to incapacity, then he is retarded, defective or incompetent. If neither intentional or due to incapacity, then it is behaviour "out of contact with reality" — or irrational, crazy, mad, insane.

The Development and Longer Term Effects of the Self-fulfilling Prophecy

A number of models and theories of social behaviour explain how people continually adapt to the social environment, yet these models do not so easily explain, as we have seen, how many people, such as psychiatric patients, appear not to learn, or at least use, adaptive skill. The self-fulfilling prophecy theory helps to explain how the normal learning process appears to be broken down by the effects of cognitive bolstering where perceptual input (on which learning depends) is distorted to fit negative beliefs: and also by the effects of behavioural confirmation in which the individual tends to generate, by means of his own performance, behavioural responses from the other that confirm his beliefs. The loop is thus closed and continually self-perpetuating. We will now briefly examine the development of the closed loop and the longer term effects on the patient's social interaction and social skills.

It seems certain that negative self-and other-schemas develop over time, with the accumulation of experience and the stabilization of particular theories (beliefs) which "fit" the facts. Evidence for this comes from Montemayor and Eisen (1977) who showed that in children self-references become less concrete and more abstract over time, and Rogers and Rogers (cited in Davis, 1979) apparently showed stronger recall for self-referring material in middle age as compared with younger subjects. Davis (1979 p.108) found evidence of self-schema development in depressives and he suggests that "when idiosyncratic cognitive distortions are employed over time their semantic inter-relatedness increases; this increase generates a self-schema".

Having established stable self-schemata, individuals are likely to be guided by their beliefs in the selection of behavioural strategies in dealing with others. Such behavioural strategies also become stable over time, and individuals, giving rise to cross-situational and cross-temporal consistency. For example, Bem and Allen (1974) found that individuals who identified themselves as consistent on a particular trait dimension exhibited substantial correspondence between self-description and behaviour and were also cross-situationally consistent in their behaviour.

Stable self-schemas also give rise, as we have seen, to perceptual distortion but also produce perceived similarity of various situations along dimensions congruent with self-schemata. It would be predicted that there would be congruence between situation perception and situation reaction, and indeed this is what Magnusson and Ekehammer (1978) found.

Individuals differ in the type and stability of their self-schemas, and in their awareness of them during social encounters. Snyder (1974) suggested that individuals differ in the extent to which social behaviour choices are guided from within, by dispositions and beliefs, or from outside, by situational specifications of appropriateness. Snyder (1974) and others have produced evidence for this difference between high and low "self-monitors" by showing that internally guided individuals are much more cross-situationally consistent. This difference is further profoundly affected by the individual's state of self-consciousness (Duval and Wicklund, 1972). Awareness of self not only produces greater consistency of behaviour (and congruence between behaviour and beliefs) but often generates poor and ineffective performance. This is again explainable in terms of the self-ful-filling prophecy since increased awareness of negative self-beliefs will simply speed up the negative cycle. A number of studies support this view: Brockner and Hulton (1978), for example, found that low self-esteem students performed significantly worse on a concept recognition task when made self-aware than did a group of high self-esteem students. It seems likely then that self-awareness is an additional component in the vicious cycle: poor performance produces self-awareness which fuels the predictive power of negative beliefs. This internal orientation then disrupts or reduces appropriate situation monitoring and reinforces internal guides to behaviour, producing both consistency and ineffectiveness in social behaviour. Consistency and ineffectiveness of social behaviour is a common feature of many psychiatric patients, and is the hallmark of the worst affected group: "chronic", hospitalized schizophrenics. Unfortunately, there have been only a few experimental investigations of this phenomenon, including those of Moos (1968), Snyder and Monson (1975) and Trower (1980). Trower, for example, found that patients who had been judged as unskilled on impressionistic ratings, not only were more consistent across variations in the situation than skilled patients (i.e. responded less to situa-tion cues) but performed at lower levels on all elements of behaviour measured (speech, gaze, smiling, gesture and posture).

The consistency of patients' behaviour is sure to produce consistency in others' responding, so that such patients are presented (indeed unwittingly present themselves) with an apparently homogeneous social environment, which provides certain "proof", by repeated verification, to the individual and his interacting partners that certain negative traits are indeed true.

All these processes interfere with, or prevent the learning of, social skills. Since they are internally focussed, some will fail to monitor important inter-personal and situation cues. If through behavioural confirmation processes others' behaviour will tend to become homogeneous, there will be little scope for discrimination, or trial and error learning. Some patients will distort feedback, ensuring that response alternatives they may try will be the wrong ones.

A final effect of self-fulfilling prophecies is that interaction will be invari-ably punishing, resulting in an insidious and relentless undermining of motivation to explore, innovate and experiment. Eventually the individual will isolate himself from social settings, thereby removing himself entirely from the social learning environment.

Summary and Practical Implications

Before considering the practical implications, it may help to review the argument put forward in this chapter. We began with the evidence that socially unskilled patients of various kinds seem to fail to learn appropriate tactics and strategies for coping with everyday social life. They appear to fail to benefit greatly either from the natural socialization processes or from special therapeutic programmes, even when these are designed to remedy their particular deficits. This led to the suggestion that one of the most important mechanisms that blocked learning was the formation of beliefs that served to channel cognitive processing and guide behaviour in such a way that the initial beliefs were repeatedly confirmed. Such beliefs therefore become self-fulfilling prophecies: i.e. the evidence seems to bolster the belief and subsequent behaviour produces effects that further confirm it. The first part of this process — cognitive bolstering — is well substantiated in the findings of a number of studies on psychiatric patients who seem prone to perceive evidence selectively or distortedly in accordance with — and probably because of — certain negative evaluations about their competence. The second part of the process, called behavioural confirmation, is also revealed, if less directly, in the way patients generate behavioural responses more as a result of internal beliefs than external situational cues, and in such a negative and unrewarding way, that others withdraw or react hostilely, fulfilling the patient's worst expectations. This happened, we noted, even in psychotherapy when the therapist should know better. The whole process, then, acts like a kind of psychological cancer, that grows on itself and gets ever more pernicious with every social encounter, often with no relief, even from those therapies and therapists who are supposed to be best fitted to help. It is not difficult to see why unskilled patients fail to learn — because they are not in *their* reality ever exposed to new learning situations and are not motivated to change because reality, forever confirms their pessimistic prophecies.

As the social psychological mechanisms of friendship-forming and other social tasks emerge from research investigations, therapeutic programmes to help those who fail in these tasks become increasingly practicable and important. However, if mechanisms such as self-fulfilling prophecy cycles do indeed occur, it would seem hazardous to embark on purely behavioural social skills training programmes as is now commonly practised, and to expect behaviour changes of a kind that patients themselves have failed to achieve in their natural environments and which they "validly" predict will not or cannot occur. If negative beliefs have powerful self-fulfilling effects, they will surely serve to work against such therapeutic attempts.

What is needed is a two-fold attack (Trower and O'Mahony, 1978). First, cognitive therapy is required to try to expose and modify the beliefs that block the normal process of skill acquisition, and secondly, social skills training programmes, allied with emotional control techniques, are needed to enable clients to efficiently and speedily acquire skills to reach desired objectives.

In addition, therapeutic interventions should be introduced earlier rather than later in the lives of individuals who are at risk, since beliefs become increasingly stable over time and ever more resistant to change. Since most of these programmes are based upon educative rather than medical models, they should fit quite naturally into school or college curricula alongside more traditional forms of learning. At least one traditional topic — language — is evolving away from being a purely academic subject separated from ordinary life, towards its study in the context of natural conversation or "discourse" (Coulthard, 1978), and such a shift in emphasis could be usefully linked with some form of personal development training, drawing upon ideas, findings and expertise from clinical and social psychology.

CHAPTER 5
Disordered Sexual Relationships

Maurice Yaffé

"Man survives earthquakes, epidemics, the horrors of illness, and all the tortures of the soul, but the most tormenting tragedy at all times has been, is and will be, the tragedy of the bedroom." (Leo Tolstoy: 1828 – 1910)

As Tolstoy so graphically notes, sexual relationships, and particularly the difficulties surrounding them, can assume major importance in individuals' lives. Thus sexual problems are a significant focus of concern to many, and no doubt have always been so even if local social and cultural conditions have often inhibited expression of that concern.

In the professional arena, sexual relationships and their disorders have interested clinicians and researchers from the beginning, even though it is only in the past 10 years or so that satisfactory short term directive treatment procedures have been available. This latter situation largely came about after the pioneering work of Masters and Johnson, and the publication in 1970 of their book "Human Sexual Inadequacy", as a result of which sex therapy has developed into a distinctive therapeutic speciality, although it is true to say that clinicians of many disciplines and theoretical orientations have been treating sexual problems for centuries.

When we discuss disordered sexual relationships we assume a concept of "disorder" which in turn implies some kind of understanding of what "ordered" sexual relationships might be like. An adequate treatment of that subject is certainly necessary but is impossible within the scope of the present chapter. Fortunately, it is dealt with elsewhere in this series of Personal Relationships volumes, for example by Przybyla and Byrne (1981) who discuss functioning within same and opposite sex relationships and also take account of age-related sexual changes.

To return to the area of dysfunction or disorder, Money (1980) provides a useful classification of the problems of human sexuality into dysfunctional or inadequate responses (the *hypophilias*); those which are excessive with respect to frequency or number of partners (the *hyperphilias*); and those involving inappropriate object choices (the *paraphilias*). These problems develop at specific stages of sexual or erotic pair-bonding which Money divides into three phases: *proceptive*, when attraction, solicitation and seduction occurs and which can include kissing, petting and foreplay; *acceptive*, which involves physical receptiveness and activity between partners; and *conceptive* — the sequel, in the ordinary course of events, to the previous phases which leads itself to parenthood. Hypophilias and paraphilias have been studied extensively but the hyperphilias have been neglected, probably because they are rarely presented as problems in Psychosexual Clinics. However, quite a number of husbands and some wives do make excessive sexual demands on their partners, and on the other hand there are many individuals who prefer to have an endless series of sexual relationships — for them the number of physical contacts with different people seems more important than the quality of each. Promiscuity is the pejorative term that has been used traditionally to describe these people, and it is likely that the term will continue to be applied to anyone who happens to be sexually active with rather more people than we are ourselves.

Classification of Problems

(1) Hypophilias

These occur at the acceptive phase of sexual pair-bonding, and can be divided usefully into *disorders of performance*, which prevent or significantly alter functioning during the sexual cycle; and *disorders of satisfaction*, which decrease enjoyment during the sexual cycle. In men, disorders of sexual performance can occur during any of the three phases of sexual response: excitement or arousal, penetration, or orgasm and ejaculation. Problems in men include those related to *erection* and *ejaculation* (which can be premature, retarded, or retrograde where semen is directed into the bladder); a further complaint is anapriapism where the erection is lost specifically at the point of penetration. These difficulties can be *primary*, where the dysfunction has always been present, or *secondary*, where the disturbed function was once intact; and, at the same time, they can also be *partial* or *complete*. In women disorders of performance include *dyspareunia* (pelvic or vaginal discomfort/pain associated with penetration and intercourse), and *vaginismus* (a spasm of the peri-vaginal musculature making penetration difficult if not impossible).

Disorders of satisfaction in males comprise: *split orgasms* (emission without forceful ejaculation, when semen leaks from the urethra) and *orgasm without pleasure* where there is emission and ejaculation but no concomitant pleasurable sensation. In females such disorders include: *general sexual dysfunction* which is identified by absence of vasocongestive genital response or subjective erotic feeling; *sexual anaesthesia* consisting of vaginal lubrication without the associated feeling of arousal or enjoyment; and *anorgasmia* (the inability to reach orgasm though sexual arousal is present).

Both performance and satisfaction disorders can occur during sexual activity with a partner, and usually present clinically when this is the case, but it is also possible that they occur during self-stimulation when the person is not in the company of others. Such a condition has diagnostic implications which will be dealt with later in this chapter.

In addition to the above, a third mixed but centrally related group of disorders has become apparent over the past few years as assessment procedures have gradually become more sophisticated and refined. These comprise: *diminished sexual desire* or interest; fears of *intimacy and romantic success*; specific *sexual phobias*; and *co-operation dysfunctions*.

Diminished sexual desire has been investigated fully by Kaplan (1979), and is claimed to be probably the most prevalent of all the sexual dysfunctions. The most extreme example is the sexual celibate who has had a life-long history of asexuality (sometimes as a result of personal choice), but the most usual is the person who reports a loss of sexual interest after previously experiencing a perfectly satisfactory level of sexual appetite. Fears of intimacy do not simply relate to sexual functioning; in Kaplan's terms they are associated with people who

> "tend to spectate rather than to participate together, watch television, play cards and video games rather than engage in intimate conversation. . . (they) are more afraid of intimacy than they are of sex. They find it easier to masturbate than to make love, to buy impersonal sex than to share love with a lover, to blot out the partner with drugs than to experience him/her fully."

Fears of romantic success and pleasure manifest themselves as avoidance responses when a person approaches his sexual and romantic goal, i.e. he experiences difficulty in having sex for himself. Until this time he has no conflict in his pursuit of sexual pleasure; but then, to quote Kaplan:

"when his goal is about to be reached, when the prize is in his hand, at the last inch, he will sabotage himself in any one of many possible ways — by provoking his partner, by conjuring up fears of failure or other negative thoughts during the sexual act, by merely getting anxious, by neglecting his appearance, by avoiding sex, etc."

Specific sexual phobias include: heterophobia/homophobia — phobic anxiety about the opposite/same sex, extreme dislike of sexual fluids (semen, vaginal secretions), concern about the adequacy of one's sexual performance, and phobic avoidance of sexual involvement with a partner.

Co-operation dysfunctions or interpersonal problems are somewhat different from the previous categories in that they usually involve both partners in a relationship and are exemplified by an inability to share, collaborate, act as a team, or agree on common goals, priorities or values. Couples compete with each other, and sex can be used by either partner as a weapon to deny the other any chance of pleasure.

(2) Paraphilias

According to Money (1980), who coined the term paraphilia, it is:

"an eroto-sexual condition of being recurrently responsive to, and obsessively dependent on, an unusual or unacceptable stimulus (e.g. animals, children, enemas), perceptual or in fantasy, in order to have a state of erotic arousal initiated or maintained, and in order to achieve or facilitate orgasm."

It is believed that the majority of paraphilias occur significantly more frequently in males than females. They range from the playful harmlessness of male fetishism for female undergarments to practices which are noxious and totally unacceptable to society, e.g. aggressive paedophilia and rape.

(3) Gender transpositions

Gender refers to a person's personal, social and legal status as male or female, or mixed, on the basis of physical and behavioural criteria which are more inclusive than the genital criterion alone. Two related concepts are *gender identity* and *gender role*: gender identity, according to Money (1980), is the private experience of gender role, and gender role is the public manifestation of gender identity. He points out that:

> "Gender identity is the sameness, unity and persistence of one's individuality as male, female, or ambivalent, in greater or lesser degree, especially as it is experienced in self-awareness and behaviour. Gender role is everything that a person says and does to indicate to others or to the self the degree that one is either male or female, or ambivalent; it includes but is not restricted to sexual arousal and response."

Gender transpositions can be *total, partial,* or *arbitrary* and they can be *chronic* or *episodic*. Examples of each of these categories are given below:

	Chronic	*Episodic*
Total	Transsexualism	Transvestism
Partial	Homosexuality	Bisexuality
Arbitrary	Androgyny of gender-coded education and work	Androgyny of gender-coded play and body-language

Gender transpositions occur at the proceptive phase of erotic pair-bonding, as do the paraphilias. Those with gender discordant behaviour who are suffering or causing concern to others may present clinically, but the presenting difficulty might well be dysfunctional in nature.

Incidence and Prevalence of Sexual Problems

The frequency of sexual problems presented in sex therapy clinics provides no information about how common these behaviours are in the community. It is likely that many people with hyperphilias and paraphilias do not seek help, and recent studies on the dysfunctions (Frank *et al.*, 1978; Nettelbladt and Uddenberg, 1979) confirm this view. Sexual difficulties rarely precipitate marital disruption (Dominian, 1979) and may even operate independently of one another (Hartman, 1980). In a study of 100 predominantly white, well-educated and "happily married" couples from Pittsburg (Frank *et al.*, 1978), 40% of the men reported erectile or ejaculatory dysfunction, and 63% of the women reported arousal or orgasmic dysfunction, though 50% of the men and 77% of the women were more concerned about other sexual difficulties, such as not being sexually attractive to partner, inability to relax or lack of interest. In the Swedish study of married men Nettelbladt and

Uddenberg (1979) found that 40% of their sample reported a tendency towards a sexual dysfunction. Both the American and the Swedish studies, then, suggest that some degree of sexual dysfunction is commonly to be found in the general population. This raises interesting questions about the conditions under which dysfunction becomes defined as a "problem" and one which requires treatment.

Causative Factors

For a thorough review of aetiological factors in sexual disorders the reader is referred to LoPiccolo and Hogan (1979); who list the major categories of factors as follows:

Anatomical and physiological. Physical illness can contribute indirectly to the onset of a sexual problem as a result of pain, fatigue or exhaustion. Specific neurological, endocrinological and vascular systems can be affected in disease and this can lead directly to sexual difficulties as can anatomical abnormalities, surgery and drugs (including alcohol) (Kaplan, 1974; 1979).

Psychological factors. Stress or concomitant anxiety is the most common psychological precipitant of sexual disorders, followed by depression, and anger/hostility towards the partner. Guilt and cognitive distortions, i.e. negative self-statements and irrational thoughts, also contribute to causation.

Psychiatric problems. In addition to depression and anxiety, psycho-pathology involving neuroses and psychoses and personality disorders may be relevant as antecedents of sexual disorders.

Marital relationship problems. Conflicts of power and control, expression of feelings, lack of commitment to partner, absence of caring or empathic feelings for partner and lack of trust may well have a central bearing on how the sexual problem was initiated and how it develops.

Environmental problems. Current and early background (pre-dyadic factors such as sexually repressive family mores, work and financial pressures) need to be taken into account here.

Poor skills, information, knowledge. Lack of sexual information, or mis-information and poor hetero-social skills are commonly found in those presenting with sexual disorders and contribute to the presenting problems.

Sexual orientation. In heterosexual dysfunctions one causative factor that has only recently received attention is whether the patient has homophilic interests (arousal responses and/or behaviour outlets) that interfere with the marital sexual relationships (Latham and White, 1978).

Assessment and Treatment

Given the wide variety of problems and the range of possible causative factors described above it is clear that careful assessment is crucial when disorders are presented for diagnosis and treatment. The nature of the appropriate therapy will depend on the outcome of assessment procedures whose more detailed results should suggest the content and the mode of specific interventions which will be focussed on constituent parts of the problem behaviour. A thorough and systematic assessment procedure is, therefore, essential and this should encompass both objective and subjective approaches in order to be adequately comprehensive and needs to focus on both individual and relationship aspects of the problem. Thus such procedures will include interviews, diary ratings and self-report devices; and they will also involve individual physiological measures of sexual arousal and response where appropriate (e.g. Barlow, 1976), as well as noting interpersonal indices such as the extent of behavioural excesses and deficits with respect to the communication patterns of the partners. It is only after working through an assessment schedule like the one indicated that a satisfactory treatment programme can be planned and executed. We go on now to consider the range of treatments currently available and these will be dealt with in relation to the hypophilias and the paraphilias, with a brief concluding section referring to special populations.

(1) Hypophilias

Masters and Johnson's (1970) account of the high level of therapeutic success attained using their package programme has made a great impression on those working in sex therapy over the past 10 years. However, most therapists have been unable to produce such impressive results: Zilbergeld and Evans (1980) in a detailed methodological analysis of that work explain why, pointing out that the duration of treatment was ofter longer than indicated; that criteria of failure, success and relapse are not clear; the issue of degree of change in patient situation with respect to their problems is ignored; there are deficiencies in sampling and follow-up; there is an absence of a category of deterioration as a result of therapy; there is no reporting of criteria for failure and relapse; inappropriate use is made of the Kinsey scale in the homosexual study, and in labelling homosexual dysfunctions; and replication of studies is impossible due to lack of the necessary detailed information. However, several techniques and approaches *have* proven their effectiveness in controlled-trial studies (Wright *et al.*, 1979), and comprehensive reviews of their appropriateness are available (e.g. Leiblum and Pervin, 1980; Jehu, 1979; Kaplan, 1979; Yaffé, 1980; Hawton, 1980; LoPiccolo and Hogan, 1979). These approaches include the following:

Sex education. When patients are lacking specific knowledge about sexual anatomy, physiology, behaviour or have misconceptions about specific issues or details, sex education aimed at correcting this is a valuable adjunct to therapy (e.g. see Barbach, 1974; Voss, 1980).

Anxiety reduction techniques. These cover a range of procedures, including desensitization, flooding, implosion and guided imagining. Desensitization involves exposing the patient to a hierarchy of sexual scenes (in imagination, on video, or in reality), which produce progessively higher levels of anxiety. During the presentation of the scenes relaxation is induced by systematic muscular exercises, hypnosis or with the aid of a chemical anxiolytic. *In vivo* desensitization is the treatment of choice for vaginismus (Ellison, 1972), and Masters and Johnson's (1970) therapy is a version of this. In flooding and implosion the intention is to proceed to the top of the anxiety-provoking hierarchy without delay in order to extinguish the anxiety response (e.g. Frankel, 1970). The guided imagining procedure involves the patient fantasizing about a continuous sexual scene that previously produced anxiety, and has met with some success (e.g. see Wolpin, 1969).

Skill training. Deficient sexual skills for example how to masturbate, how to apply the squeeze and pause techniques (for premature ejaculation), and how to massage a partner, can be conveyed accurately and quickly using audio-visual materials, especially videotapes, and this makes for useful feedback sessions with the therapist. Assertiveness training, on the other hand, helps patients to initiate sexual relationships; to decline a sexual invitation if they wish or to ask for one; or for specific kinds of activity and stimulation; or to convey disinclination for certain practices. Zilbergeld (1979) and Yulis (1976) have used this procedure effectively with single, sexually dysfunctional males.

Sensory awareness, cognitive therapy, and attitude change procedures. As a way of increasing sexual arousal and distracting patients' thoughts from producing interfering, intrusive themes, Kaplan (1974) recommends them to focus on the physical sensations experienced during sexual activities. Ellis

(1971) instructs his patients to substitute rational alternatives for irrational, anxiety-provoking thoughts about sexual performance, disappointment and failure. Other cognitive techniques such as re-labelling anxiety and tension as "sexual arousal" have also been found to be effective with patients who have been evaluating their sexual sensations inappropriately.

Behaviour change procedures. These are used to modify the frequency of specific target behaviours, the most straightforward involving instructions by therapists to engage in desirable activities like sensate focussing or oral-genital contact, or to refrain from others, such as trying to achieve orgasm or vaginal penetration. Operant techniques also have a positive contribution to make in this context and include positive reinforcement of the patient's behaviour by therapist and partner, and self-monitoring of sexual behaviour by the patient.

Marital therapy. Although the relationship between sexual dysfunction and marital conflict may be causal, a good sexual relationship is neither a necessary nor a sufficient component of a satisfactory marriage (Hartman, 1980). However it is often necessary to deal effectively with non-sexual aspects of a marital relationship before sexual ones can be resolved (Kaplan, 1974) especially with respect to erectile insufficiency and secondary orgasmic dysfunction. Where this is the case, some form of marital therapy is beneficial.

Medical intervention. These include drugs, surgery and other physical procedures. Anxiolytics and anti-depressant medication have general effects but more specifically, they can delay ejaculation and improve erectile functioning: and androgens, with counselling, may well have a useful role to play in the treatment of women with diminished sexual interest (Bancroft *et al.*, 1980). Surgical procedures for men with organogenic dysfunction are available and their use depends upon whether the problems are vascular or neurological in origin. In addition to such approaches prostheses have also been developed which make penetration possible in cases of erectile dysfunction. There do not, however, appear to be appropriate effective surgical interventions for female sexual dysfunction. The main physical procedure which has demonstrated its effectiveness in the treatment of female orgasmic dysfunction are Kegel's (1952) exercises directed at training the pelvic floor (pubo-coccygeal) musculature.

Therapy can be conducted on an individual, couple or group basis, depending on the availability and suitability of the partner participating in treatment sessions; and patients can be seen by the therapist, a co-therapy team or even sent instructions through the post, thus permitting minimum therapist contact and involvement. The main advantage of using two therapists rather than one seems to be didactic in that an experienced therapist can teach an inexperienced one appropriate strategies and tactics that are not readily apparent from simply reading about them (Mathews *et al.*, 1976).

(2) Paraphilias

Bancroft (1979) has reviewed the treatment options available for the paraphilias. He stresses, initially, the importance of determining the patient's motivation for change of sexual orientation, especially in cases where a patient is facing a charge for a sexual offence. Four principal objectives are then evaluated and this will subsequently determine the therapeutic strategy to be adopted. The objectives are:
  (a) The establishment of rewarding adult sexual relationships (hetero-
      sexual or homosexual);
  (b) The improvement of sexual function within an existing adult sexual
      relationship (heterosexual or homosexual);
  (c) Increase in self-control over sexual behaviour;
  (d) Adjustment to the deviant role.
Yaffé (1981) gives specific details of the techniques that can be considered in designing a therapy programme for paedophiles, and Barlow and Wincze (1980) present the treatment of 2 cases: one involving incest with a daughter, and the other involving multiple deviations, including a history of voyeurism, exhibitionism and incest. These accounts, along with that by Bancroft (1979), cover the range of therapeutic options available for the patient presenting with paraphiliac problems.

(3) Therapy with special populations

LoPiccolo and Hogan (1979) point out that until recently there has been a tendency to screen out those who were suffering from a chronic illness, were psychiatrically disturbed or advanced in years as patients for sex therapy. However, treatment programmes have now been especially devised for coronary, diabetic, renal failure and spinal-cord injured patients, as well as those who are pregnant and those in the post-partum period (see LoPiccolo and Hogan, 1979). In addition, Psychosexual Problems Clinics are starting to see patients from ethnic minority groups: here problems of verbal communication between therapist and patient will need to be resolved and the symbolic meaning of symptoms and normative standards of appropriate sexual conduct will need to be established before adequate therapeutic interventions can be made.

Factors Affecting Therapeutic Outcome

Hawton (1980) and Yaffé (1980) make a plea for continued research emphasis to be placed on evaluating which patients do well on which therapeutic regime. In general, positive outcome in sex therapy is directly related to high motivation for change, presence of a co-operative partner, higher socio-economic class, higher education, good non-sexual relationship and commitment to the relationship, perceived physical attractiveness of presenter to partner and good exercise (homework) practice at home. Negative outcome has been found to be significantly associated with poor living conditions (Storr, personal communication). Levay and Kagle (1977) studied treatment needs following sex therapy and identified three reasons for return to therapy: (1) treatment overload; (2) severity of symptoms; and, (3) presence of psychopathology relevant to the sexual dysfunction. Clearly future treatments will need to take account of these factors as well as a full working through of pleasure, intimacy and co-operation dysfunctions, if sex therapy is to have lasting effects.

Conclusions

As can be seen from the foregoing account, a considerable amount of work has been carried out in describing and classifying the various forms of disordered sexual relationships, which represent significant advances in our knowledge of the subject. Such advances have had distinct practical as well as theoretical outcomes; they have gone hand in hand with the development and improvement of therapeutic procedures designed to alleviate and correct the disorders. Clearly this is a great improvement over the situation that obtained in this area only a short while ago: yet it can be seen to be only a partial approach and partial solution to the general problem. In the long term a more adequate perspective would be one which includes positive as well as negative aspects of sexual relationships and concerns itself with the *avoidance* of disorders in these relationships rather than just the treatment of disorders when they arise. Thus Qualls *et al.* (1978) focus on the *prevention* of disorders in sexual relationships and bring forward the view that this is a more appropriate way to promote effective sexual functioning than present treatments, representing as they do a remedial effort at best. Sex education (starting in schools) would seem to be the obvious place to begin, though it does raise issues of invasion of individual privacy as well as an implication of the re-ordering of societal values which may make an effective educational programme impossible to implement. With regard to such a programme the essential point to note is that what is important is not so much factual information about sexual relationships, but the affect and the context associated with them: a value system positively rather than negatively oriented towards sexual relationships is crucial to the development of healthy sexual functioning.

Even if, as the preceding paragraph implies, we still have some way to go in eliminating disorder from sexual relationships much has already been accomplished. After all, it is only 25 years or so since sex in our society changed from being a devalued activity to being a required ability. Inevitably some people still manage aspects of their sexual relationships poorly but it is safe to say that now where "the tragedy of the bedroom" occurs it is very definitely resolvable. Tolstoy would be pleased.

CHAPTER 6

Disorders in the Family

Jim Orford and Paul O'Reilly

It has been notoriously difficult to define the family satisfactorily, although definitions usually focus on marriage, parenthood and common residence (Morgan, 1977). None of these is both necessary and sufficient, however, and each involves further problems of definition, whilst the institution itself both changes markedly over time and is related in a complicated manner to the cultural norms of a particular society (e.g. see Poster's historical analysis of 1978). In the present chapter we will be considering some of the issues which these problems pose for those who seek to understand and to help families in disorder. We will give some examples of the kinds of disorder that occur and then go on to analyse them in terms of the systems based approach implied by the above points about the relationship of the family to society at large.

Other writers have commented on recent changes: for instance Stueve and Gersons (1977) have pointed out that a prominent feature of modern marriage is "dyadic withdrawal" where the marital pair draw away from all but the most casual friendships outside. Furthermore, the greater mobility of our society makes it possible for family bonds to be weakened by distance and necessitates the parents themselves (rather than the extended family) taking more of the responsibility for their children's upbringing as the family grows. The new role of the parents in the family in modern society makes it a particularly demanding task to live up to, apart from the fact that the family, as an institution, is itself under attack from feminists and from the Left. The family is charged with maintaining the subordination and exploitation of women (and of children), and with reproducing the capitalist system from generation to generation (Gardiner, 1975; Oakley, 1974).

Analysis of disorder in the family thus needs to take account both of the internal pressures on the constituent members and of the exterior pressures that arise from the family's changing role in society. The themes that emerge in considering such families in detail are often to do with expectations for affection and intimacy; with the organization of family roles; with dependency versus independence; with the strains brought about by conflicting demands upon wives; with questions of sexual freedom and consciousness; with the problems of providing adequate parenting; with difficulties between generations; and with general malaise or depression — all problems shaped by the special predicament of the present-day family. Given such an analysis, we wish to argue strongly that disorders in the family should be seen as disorders of a *system* and that previous approaches focussing on *individuals* are inadequate. To make this case we shall consider different research approaches, giving some short illustrative examples, and then go on to outline a systems approach.

Research Approaches

The individual causal model

Family concepts of disordered or deviant behaviour are relatively new on the scene. Thinking of family matters within the health and social service disciplines and in related academic circles has continued to be dominated by notions of *individual* illness, pathology or social problems. *Individuals* have schizophrenia or alcoholism, have heart attacks or kidney failure, are physically or mentally handicapped, or perpetrate child abuse. The family is recognized to be important, but mainly these conditions have impact upon other family members, because the latter are consequently at risk themselves, and because they cope in response to this impact in a functional or not so functional fashion. Such a model of family functioning in the face of individual disorder has the apparent virtue of common sense and probably accords with the general public's understanding.

This disorder-impact-coping model of family disorder should not be dismissed out of hand. In certain instances it has the capacity to explain many of the known facts, and in some cases may be the model of choice. In many instances, however, it is found to be wanting in a number of respects. The case of excessive drinking by a family member illustrates the problems. The stress theory, the most influential during the last 20 years, supposes that alcoholism develops progressively, with little influence from the rest of the family but with increasing impact upon them. There is indeed evidence that the degree of hardship to which a wife has been exposed as a result of her partner's excessive drinking (loss of job, financial insecurity, infidelity, police involvement, rows and violence, social isolation, etc.) is correlated with the range of coping behaviour which she has used, and with likelihood of her complaining of psychological and psychosomatic distress, as well as with the short-term prognosis for the partner's excessive drinking (Orford 1975, 1980). There is also compelling evidence that where a parent drinks excessively, the children are exposed to certain hardships, particularly inter-ference with friendship formation and maintenance because of uncertainty and embarrassment over the parent's behaviour; and that the greater the degree of this hardship (particularly whether or not drinking is accompanied by violence) the greater the chances of children displaying problems them-selves, particularly in an anti-social form. Furthermore, the weight of evidence suggests that male children at least are themselves at considerably higher than normal risk of developing a problem with their own drinking later in life (Goodwin, 1971; Cotton, 1979).

Thus a model based on stress produced by individual disorder may explain much existing evidence, and may contribute to the humanitarian purpose of identifying groups who are at high risk of psychological distress or in need of greater psychological help than they may be currently receiving. Many clinicians would agree that spouses and children of problem drinkers have suffered, often in silence and isolation, and that their considerable needs have gone largely unrecognized. The same may be true for many conditions and problems. The stress of caring for a handicapped child has received more attention in recent years (e.g. Carr, 1975), and psychologists are beginning to notice the stress involved in living in a family with the con-sequences of major physical conditions such as renal failure (Nichols, 1980). Child abuse and neglect is perhaps one of the clearest examples of the apparent sense of a stress-impact view of family disorder. Whether the child abuser is viewed as intentionally delinquent or unintentionally affected by impaired emotional control, he or she is readily cast in the role of the villain, and the child is easily viewed as victim.

The stress-impact-and-coping view has its limitations, however. In the case of excessive drinking and the family, there are a number of findings which are difficult to incorporate within it. It is regularly found, for example, that a large proportion of problem drinkers who are married (around 50%) were drinking very heavily or excessively at the time of their marriage. Furthermore, some of the factors which might otherwise be attributed to the development of alcoholism during marriage — such as a relatively high level of anxiety in the spouse or an under-involvement of the drinking spouse in family tasks — were present in a large minority of such marriages from the beginning. A stress-impact theory would also predict the relief of symptoms and troubles upon removal of the stress. It has been found, however, that at least over a period of up to 12 months such factors as the spouse's anxiety level, her perception of her partner, as well as the arrangement of roles in marriage, remained remarkably constant (Orford, *et al.,* 1977).

Such research findings aside, many clinical practitioners have for a long time had difficulty working exclusively within a stress-impact model of excessive drinking in the family. Those who favoured a more dynamic approach were impressed by the apparent resistance to change of other family members, and they contributed anecdotal accounts which appeared to support the view that the non-drinking spouse had "chosen" a deviant partner, or had an "investment" in continued excessive drinking. An important part of this "psychopathology of the spouse" view was the so-called "decompensation" hypothesis which suggested the spouses were particularly likely to break down themselves when the identified patient gave up excessive drinking (Paolino and McCrady, 1977). The tables were turned: the spouse became the villain of the piece and one relatively straightforward account of the family gave way to another almost as simple.

Even in such an apparently open and shut case as that of child abuse, it is possible to identify a main strand in the literature on the subject which points to the child's own partial contribution to the problem (Allan, 1978; Belsky, 1978). There appears to be evidence that some children are more likely to be abused than others — those that are premature and of low birth weight, and perhaps those that are handicapped in some way, or those that cry a lot or otherwise have a temperament that makes them difficult and frustrating to care for.

The kind of serious, psychotic, disturbance which is often called schizophrenia and often results in hospitalization, has also been construed as a stress for family members (Clausen and Yarrow, 1955), but again research has borne out the clinical observation that matters are frequently more complicated. One line of research, recently reviewed by Kuipers (1979), has identified emotional expressiveness (EE) as a factor particularly likely to be present in families to which such patients return unsuccessfully after hospitalization. When a key family member (usually the patient's wife, husband or mother) reveals attitudes towards the patient which are either critical or over-involved, then the patient is significantly more likely to break down again or to be re-admitted to hospital within the following few months. But the matter is complicated: it is not possible to conclude that family EE *causes* relapse, let alone that it causes the psychotic disturbance in the first place. There is no simple formula here that enables us to attribute cause and effect in any straightforward fashion. In an early report of research in this area, Brown *et al.* (1962) attempted to bring some order by proposing three types of family: those in which EE is *consequent* upon a high level of disturbance in the patient; those in which high EE is due to unusual behaviour on the part of the relative; and the remaining cases for whom "it is possible that an interaction between the behaviour of the patient and that of the relative was responsible". However we choose to apportion causative influence, there is now some intriguing evidence concerning the psychophysiological concomitants of family emotion. In her review, Kuipers (1979) cites recent work suggesting that a patient habituates to a novel situation in the presence of a family member who shows low EE on interview, but does not habituate in the presence of a high EE relative.

Phobia is yet another topic which has provoked clinical comment suggesting that family members are influential as other than purely stress victims. Hafner (1977) studied 30 married women with agoraphobia, and included data from 26 of their husbands. For purposes of analysis, he divided the couples into two equal groups depending on the wives' scores on a questionnaire measure of hostility. Although the more hostile patients did quite well in treatment and for a few weeks after treatment, a number of them relapsed before the six months follow-up point. The husbands of women in this group showed an increase in self-dissatisfaction and in the number of psychoneurotic symptoms which they reported in the first three months following their wives' treatment. Also, within this group containing the more hostile wives, a positive association was found between symptomatic improvement in the wives and an *increase* in hostility in the husbands. None of these findings pertained in the group of less hostile wives and their husbands.

These findings accorded with clinical impressions. It was felt that many husbands in the former group found change in their wives difficult to accommodate because it aroused uncomfortable feelings in themselves. One husband who attempted suicide a few months after his wife's treatment said he felt useless and inadequate because his wife was no longer dependent on him. Two husbands became depressed when the focus of attention shifted from their wives' symptoms to their own sexual difficulties, and in three further cases the wives' improvement aroused abnormal jealousy leading to increased marital discord.

A very similar exercise in clinical sub-categorization is provided by the work of Rae and Drewery (1972) with male problem drinkers and their wives. When wives had high scores on the Pd (psychopathic deviate) scale of the MMPI, the pattern of interpersonal perception in the marriage was more abnormal (husbands describing their wives as more dominant and aggressive than the wives described themselves for example) and husbands were less likely to give up their excessive drinking (Rae, 1972). Their clinical impression was that wives in this group were hostile and uncooperative and lacked insight about the dynamic factors operating within their marriages. They tended to be caught in conflicts with their husbands over issues of dependence and independence, the relationships being competitive rather than complementary, and sexually threatening to the husbands. By contrast wives with low Pd scores gave the impression of reacting "normally" to the stress of their husbands' alcoholism.

The difficulty of ascribing causative influence to one particular member of the family is illustrated by further findings from Rae and Drewery's studies. High Pd wives tended to be married to husbands with job and previous relationship difficulties. Furthermore, dividing the marriages on the basis of the husbands' Pd scores produced rather similar results to those based upon wives' scores. The very fact that wives' hostility scores were used to divide couples into groups in Hafner's study also underlines the point: no simple one-way causal influence model for understanding families in disorder is complete.

We therefore wish to argue for an interactional, systems-based approach to the complexity of the family and we shall now illustrate by means of examples, some of the inadequacies of a one-way causal influence model in order to prepare the way for this argument. The case histories are intended to be illustrative rather than definitive. We do not have the space to detail the therapy programmes consequently undertaken, nor can we fully describe the circular patterns in family behaviour that present us with the best plank in our argument for an interactional approach. However, to illustrate the point is also to indicate the need for a different kind of theoretical model.

Four case histories

(1) *The B. Family.* Mr. B. had a lengthy history of excessive drinking and had recently come home after several months in an alcoholism treatment unit. He was unemployed and lived in a small house with Mrs B. and their five children (three daughters and two sons). A difficulty about communication had grown between Mr. and Mrs. B. over the years. She described "a wall" between them. Mrs. B. was ambivalent about their relationship and future prospects. She tended to avoid Mr. B. when he was drunk and refused to enter into unproductive arguments. Discussions between them were observed to escalate rapidly into rows. When Mr. B. was sober, Mrs. B. avoided antagonizing him in order to preserve the temporary peace. Mr.

B.'s relationship with his eldest daughter was crucial. She, like the other older children, was resentful of the effects of Mr. B.'s drinking on her relationships with her friends. She had been ashamed and embarrassed by him in public and felt unable to invite friends home. Other members of the family were especially sensitive to the tension in this relationship, particularly because this daughter had a large role in caring for the youngest child, in a strong alliance with Mrs. B. The eldest daughter was more punishing than Mrs. B. about her father's drinking, having attempted, on a number of occasions, to persuade Mrs. B. to leave. If the relationship between Mr. B. and his eldest daughter became tense, the whole family became tense also.

(2) *The F. Family*. Mrs. F., now in her early thirties, had Mark (11) after a casual affair. Six years ago she married a divorced man, Mr. F., now in his early forties, and who had adopted Mark. The couple have a two-year-old son of their own, Matthew. Mark was the identified patient (IP); rebellious, stealing money from his parents' business (a public house), playing truant, and fighting with the other village children. Mr. F. and Mark related only as rivals, and Mrs. F. usually supported Mark in disagreements, making statements understanding of him. Matthew was a happy, adventurous boy who related easily with Mark, more easily with his father and somewhat uneasily with his mother.

Mrs. F. had been a successful businesswoman before her marriage and she knew that she had coped very well with, and about, Mark. She wished to carry on "being her own woman" with enough personal space and an equal say in the running of the pub (for which she had provided most of the initial capital). Mr. F. was a man who found it difficult to show emotion, who thought he alone should be the provider in the family and certainly considered that he should make all the decisions. He found it difficult to be affectionate to anyone, other than Matthew. When the couple argued about this matter (frequently!), Mark distracted all three. Mark was most useful, practically, in the family because he looked after Matthew in the evenings when his parents worked in the pub (Mrs. F. cooking the pub meals; Mr. F. serving in the bar).

(3) *The P. Family*. Alan P. (22 years) had been in an adolescent in-patient unit for one year when aged 16. He had then worked for four years, with difficulty, and he had recently been at home for a year, living as a recluse, before being formally admitted to the local psychiatric hospital. Mr. P., in his early sixties, drank a lot of alcohol, though nobody in the family complained about this. Mrs P. (early fifties) worked part-time, but only for a few hours per week. Diane P. (20 years old) worked locally with a fairly responsible job, drove her own car (the only car in the family) and was infrequently

at home in the evenings.

Mr. P. thought that perhaps Alan should leave home but *knew* that Alan could not. Mrs. P. thought Alan should leave home and considered that, with help, he could learn to be independent, but was unsure. Diane thought he should and could. Alan wanted to leave home sometimes, but felt that he had some responsibility for "taking care of his unhappy parents". He continually inserted himself between them and, at home, interrupted them when they attempted to be alone together. He stopped them arguing with each other by becoming delinquent in his behaviour.

Mr. and Mrs. P. and Alan found it difficult to look at one another. No-one could find anything positive to say about anyone else without a good deal of accompanying non-verbal disqualifying behaviour such as eye-rolling, interrupting, sudden movements, ignoring of directed statements, and looking bored. The exception was Diane: the others had no complaints about her, insisted she was very well and attempted not to have her present in therapy sessions.

(4) *The W. Family.* This family consists of Mr. and Mrs. W. (who married eleven years previously), Rachel (12 years old), Samantha (10), David (7), and Debbie (6). Rachel was the IP, still enuretic at night-time. Rachel was conceived by Mrs. W. while she was relating to Mr. W. but he was not the father (Mrs. W. insisted). This was a secret in the family though Rachel was able to say that she "felt she was different in some way". When Rachel was dry at night, David wetted the bed. David was very reluctant to attend school and it needed a good deal of attention by the others to get him up and out to school in the morning. Debbie was epileptic, but this was another secret and her fits (every two/three weeks) were described to the others as "fainting spells, nothing more".

Both parents work for the same Government organization, but on shift-work so that they see each other relatively infrequently. Mr. W.'s mother looks after the children at weekends and before and after school. Mrs. W.'s mother also helps and is often present in the evenings. Mrs. W. has a close friend who lives locally and who is generally in the W. home when Mrs. W. is home, whether or not Mr. W. is home. Thus the children hardly ever see their parents together alone. On the occasions Mr. and Mrs. W. are together they tend to argue. Mrs. W. becomes "depressed" quite often and if not depressed she is usually feeling angry, but unable to specify why. Mr. W. feels incompetent when Mrs. W. is depressed and when she is angry he feels he must not disagree with her about anything.

All these families are different each from the others and yet common themes emerge. They illustrate the complexity of family functioning and highlight how "blinkered" might be an approach concerning itself with only an individual. They begin to illustrate also how symptoms, or symptomatic individuals are useful in families; how they protect, or prevent examination of, strained relationships. The themes present are those of dependency and independency, (the lack of) affection, role conflicts, parenting difficulties, problems created by desire for autonomy, the coalitions and alliances formed, the way individuals are "triangled" and problems of cohesion.

Though these are very brief descriptions, it is possible to see that single individually centred cause-effect explanations may be impossible. A systems based approach looks a more fruitful way of dealing with, for example, the circularity of behaviour patterns that can be observed, and doing justice to the interactive nature of family disorders. In the next section we will go on to consider some interactional approaches which attempt to adopt such a perspective.

Interactional approaches

From clinical observation many concepts have arisen which appear to do greater justice to the complexity of family process by treating the family, or at least a relationship within it, as the unit of observation. For example, Moos and his colleague (e.g. Moos and Moos, 1976) have employed the concept of family climate or atmosphere, using his own 90-item family environment scale (FES) to elicit family members' perceptions. The scale assesses 10 perceptual dimensions, particularly important amongst which would appear to be *cohesion*; "the extent to which family members are concerned and committed to the family and the degree to which they are helpful and supportive to each other".

The importance of cohesion as a variable which is both descriptive of important differences between families and predictive of movement towards greater or reduced family integration, has been argued elsewhere (Orford, 1980). Briefly the argument is that families, like small groups studied by social psychologists, are relatively more or less cohesive, and that in the context of family life, with its high expectations for affection and commitment, this is of vital significance. Families in disorder are quite often thought to be highly conflictual or disharmonious and the outcome for the disorder may depend very much upon the existence or revival of cohesion. There is by no means full agreement in the literature on the correctness of this simple view however. Olson *et al.* (1979), for example, whilst agreeing that cohesion is one of the most significant dimensions for describing family systems, believe that the relationship between cohesion and disorder is curvilinear. They argue that a balance between cohesion and lack of it is ideal and that too much cohesion is as harmful as too little. In support of their view they cite concepts described by other clinical authorities — "enmeshment", "dependence", and "pseudomutuality", for example — each of which captures the observation that high cohesion may limit personal fulfilment and growth.

There have now been a large number of family interaction simulation studies. The methods employed for simulating normal family interaction have been varied and ingenious but all suffer from lack of convincing evidence of their validity as methods which truly simulate everyday family interaction. These methods include the revealed differences technique (RDT) (e.g. Farina and Holzberg, 1968), SIMFAM (e.g. Russell, 1979), "improvisational scenes" (e.g. Billings, 1979), and many others (see Riskin and Faunce, 1972, for a dictionary of procedures and terms employed in this literature). Work in this area up until the mid-1970s was comprehensively reviewed by Jacob (1975). He divided such studies in two ways. Firstly studies where the identified individual problem in the family was one of schizophrenia, versus all other studies. The latter was a large and very mixed group including families where the identified individual problem was one of non-psychotic mental disorder, in others the problem was delinquency, in others non-specific maladjustment. Secondly he divided interactional indices employed into four groups: conflict, dominance, affect, and communication clarity. All studies compared clinic or problem families with control groups consisting of families with no such identified problem. Findings were on the whole mixed and inconsistent, with one notable exception. The clearest results involved measures of affect in non-schizophrenia problem or clinic families versus controls. Of 33 such comparisons, five indicated significantly more positive affect (supportive, affectionate, warm, involving laughter, etc.) in control than in problem or clinic families, and ten indicated significantly more negative affect (defensive, hostile, anxious involvement, rejection, etc.) in problem or clinic families than in controls. However Jacob warns that all affect measures were based upon observer ratings and that such results could conceivably be the result of rating bias or demand characteristics of the research setting.

These results support a straightforward descriptive view of families in disorder: such families are relatively low on expressions of positive emotion, and relatively high on negative expressions between family members. This is consistent with self-reports by psychiatric patients in at least one recent study (Henderson et al., 1978). Research on family EE, outlined above, as well as work showing the favourable outcome of drinking problems when family cohesion is high (Orford et al., 1976), suggest that this major dimension contrasting favourable or pleasant family interaction with interaction which is unfavourable or unpleasant may have predictive significance also.

Nevertheless, Jacob's (1975) general conclusion was that "family interaction studies, though based on potentially sound methodological strategy, have not yet isolated family patterns that reliably differentiate disturbed from normal families". It is likely that current research methods are insufficiently sensitive to detect some of the more subtle aspects of disordered family interaction. One such aspect may be that captured by the influential concept of the "double-bind" (Bateson *et al.*, 1956). This concept is highly complex and easily misunderstood. As Sluzki and Ransom (1976) make clear, it refers both to the quality of *ongoing family interaction* and to the nature of particular *incidents* which occur within the context of that relationship. Not surprisingly, therefore, attempts at operational definition and systematic research of double-bind phenomena have so far been inconclusive.

The family process literature in fact abounds with concepts of similar sophistication and complexity with which research has made little progress. Two further examples are "role reversal" and "pseudomutuality". The first, suggested to be important in the etiology of child abuse (Morris and Gould, 1963), postulates that normal parenting of young children requires the maintenance of a certain level of parental nurturance in the face of limited or uncertain rewards in return. Sometimes, it is argued, roles may be partially reversed and the parent may have higher expectations of the child than the latter can fulfil. There are *cognitive* elements in this idea (e.g. faulty knowledge of developmental norms leading to unrealistic expectations of what a young child can do), as well as *emotional* (e.g. low tolerance to the frustration of a young child crying), and *personality* elements (to do with the parent's feelings of security, self-worth and self-esteem). The concept of pseudomutuality (Wynne *et al.*, 1958) is similarly complex combining ideas of high apparent family cohesion, isolation from inputs from outside the family, restrictions on the autonomy of individual family members particularly the children, and myths about the degree of affection and support in the family.

Many of the concepts with which family process researchers have been struggling are static in nature, complicated though they may be. As examples of more dynamic conceptions of families in disorder, mention will be made of three separate research programmes. The first, conducted by Ferreira (e.g. Ferreira and Winter, 1968) was of the simulated family interaction type and therefore provides a link between attempts at quantitative family research of that type and the less quantitative work of most writers who have favoured a more transactional or systems theory approach. Ferreira and Winter's work suggested that families containing a member with an identified psychological problem tended to differ from control families by displaying less "spontaneous agreement"; showing longer "decision time" when asked to reach family consensus; their final decisions producing less "choice fulfilment" for individual family members; spending a greater proportion of time in silence; and displaying relatively little clear "information exchange". On this basis they postulated a positive feedback "family pathology cycle" of events leading into greater levels of disturbance of communication. This is one of the few research approaches which concerns itself with the circular patterns of behaviour so evident clinically.

The second programme of research, conducted by Steinglass on family dyads, at least one of whom had a drinking problem, is also in the observed family interaction tradition, although procedures were less formal and his research largely non-quantitative and based upon detailed analysis of individual couples. In the course of his research (Steinglass *et al.*, 1977; Steinglass, 1981) marital couples as well as father-and-son and brother-brother pairs were observed during both sobriety and intoxication. In general, couples were found to have difficulty reporting accurately about their interactional behaviour during intoxication, and observation of such interaction produced many surprises. Some couples, for example, displayed more warmth and closeness when the "problem drinker" was intoxicated. Others showed a change in dominance patterns, with a formerly unassertive member taking on a different role. On the basis of this research, Steinglass (1981) has speculated that excessive drinking serves to stabilize some families temporarily in the face of threats to the family's stability which are most clearly felt when the family system is in a "sober" phase.

Finally, recently reported work by Billings (1979) demonstrates how research may begin to do justice to both the dynamic aspects of disordered family interaction and the more static, structural aspects. He compared the interactions of 12 maritally satisfied couples and 12 relatively dissatisfied couples engaged in the "wife-distant" and "husband-distant" family improvisational role playing scenes devised by Raush *et al.* (1974) where one spouse was asked to recall and act out an occasion when they felt distant or aloof from their partner. Firstly he demonstrated a clear difference in the *structure* of interactional behaviour using the Interpersonal Behaviour Rating System developed by Leary (1957). Consistent with the findings of Jacob's review (1975), dissatisfied couples displayed significantly more hostile behaviour, both of a dominant and submissive nature, and relatively little friendly behaviour. Billings was more interested, however, in *contingencies* displayed in interaction and he examined this by comparing each "act" (the antecedent) with the following "act" (consequent). Satisfied couples showed a particularly high frequency of friendly–dominant consequents following hostile–submissive antecedents, and vice versa.

Dissatisfied couples, on the other hand, showed a particularly high frequency of reciprocated hostile–dominance sequences. Finally Billings showed group differences in the *temporal sequence* of interaction during the course of a scene. When playing the "distant" role, some subjects with satisfied marriages showed a marked reduction in hostility from beginning to end of the scene. This was rare in maritally dissatisfied subjects. In contrast, many maritally dissatisfied subjects displayed a marked increase in hostile acts from beginning to end of the scene when their partners were playing the "distant" role, and this was rare for satisfied subjects.

Although it has been argued elsewhere (Orford, 1980) that models of interaction based upon ideas of contingency, such as those proposed by Leary (1957) and Benjamin (1977), can usefully form the basis for a theory of disordered families which does justice to both structural and dynamic aspects, no clear theoretical position has yet emerged which unites the extant conceptions and research findings in this field. Many writers on disordered family process now look to general and social systems theory for an overall perspective and in the following section we will examine this approach in some detail.

General Systems Theory and Family Disorder

It is not possible within the scope of the present chapter to discuss the background of General Systems Theory (G.S.T.) in any great detail, and in this section we will limit ourselves to some of the approaches to family theorizing and family therapy that "nest" within G.S.T. thinking. (For a broader consideration of a systems approach and its specific reference to personal relationships, see La Gaipa, 1981a). Generally, though, we are using G.S.T. as a perspective, a way of thinking, rather than as a simple articulated "theory" in the traditional sense. In particular, it is a perspective which emphasises the dynamic inter-relatedness of parts of a system, and the necessity for molar rather than molecular or atomic approaches, and as such it is especially suitable as a framework for examining the family and family disorders. We shall take a number of concepts from G.S.T. and show how they help us to understand the origins and continuation of disorders within the family.

(1) *There is a strong interaction between parts.* Even though the strength may sometimes not be obvious, there is usually a strong interaction between the members of family systems. Actions and statements by one affect all other members; emotions, especially strong emotions, experienced by one

affect all; in the extreme case, death of one member affects the others, often severely, and occasionally that effect lasts a long time. Strong interactions in families have an obvious historical context, by which we mean that they are based in past history, affect the present and have implications, or create expectations, for the future. Frequently they are inescapable. Such inter-actions are more properly termed transactions — emphasizing the important temporal aspect. For example, in the F. family, Mrs. F's desire to be relatively independent, "to be her own person", caused stress for Mr. F., whose reactions further reinforced Mrs. F.'s views about the necessity for her to be independent.

(2) *The whole is greater than the sum of the parts.* It is proposed here that a system is not understandable solely in terms of the additive effects of its parts. In families the names, ages, occupations and schools, hopes, desires, needs and personal psychodynamics may be known for each individual (though not likely in a large family) but these will not predict how the family system operates when all the members are present. A family system has its own particular rules, peculiar history and unique rituals and circularities of behaviour that have meaning only in terms of the family system as a whole.

If the couple alone had been seen in the F. family (as they were eventually) the role of Mark in their disagreements — as a distractor — would not have been seen so clearly. Mark's other role, as a caretaker for his little half-brother, could not have been observed, and Matthew's role — to introduce laughter — could hardly have been predicted.

This concept of the whole being greater than the sum of the parts is the most revolutionary in GST. It compels observers/scientists to discard a simple causal model. Instead the circularities present in the system, the interaction of all the parts, must be observed and described. Such obser-vation and description is powerful in its potential for effecting change in the system. In the case of the family there is a natural but arbitrary decision taken by most workers to observe only the family, which might be regarded as a sub-system of the wider community of which it is a part.

(3) *Morphogenesis and morphostasis (dynamic equilibrium).* These two terms, morphogenesis and morphostasis, are terms used by Wertheim (1973), replacing the concepts of homeostasis and heterostasis used by von Bertalanffy (1968). They refer to similar phenomena, but those used by Wertheim are more relevant with respect to living organisms and systems. In any living system there is constant energy for change, arising partly from biological aspects (children growing, parents aging) and also from external influences on the system such as legal, financial and political factors. Morphogenesis describes this energy, this tendency for change. But continual change without order or regularity is chaotic and a family system

attempts to impose order so that living is tolerable. Morphostasis is the state of rest, of no change, that families tend towards. These two phenomena, existing together, lead to a state of dynamic equilibrium — there being energy for change and a striving for growth and adaptation, along with a desire for continuity, certainty and a steady state.

Disorder can occur then in family systems which are too near either end of the morphogenesis–morphostasis continuum. Too much change, too quickly, produces uneasiness. Attempting to remain in a fixed state e.g. a family system which maintains children in a dependent role, no matter what age, causes discomfort also. This uneasiness may then be experienced by one individual primarily, so that the others can carry on. In the P. family Alan expressed the discomfort of the system. The parents were unhappy about, and with, each other. They needed children around, no matter how old, in order to be "parents" only, so as not to have to be adult partners, alone together.

(4) *Hierarchic order.* Systems are organized in an orderly and hierarchic manner. Family systems consist of a series of sub-systems — there is the sub-system "parents", composed of two further sub-systems, usually "man" and "woman" (but sometimes "man" *or* "woman"). There is the sub-system "siblings", which consists yet again of a number of sub-systems. In turn the family is a sub-system of its neighbourhood. Hierarchic order is an intrinsic property of systems. No ideal or necessary state is implied in this concept. In the family the children are not a sub-system of the parents, they are a sub-system of the family system. However power may be vested in one of the sub-systems only. The alliance between Mrs. B. and her eldest daughter produced a particularly powerful sub-system (alliance) in that family which overrode all the others and diminished the marital sub-system.

(5) *Open and closed systems.* Closed systems are systems which do not interact with the environment: in the biological world they are possible in theory only. Living systems are open — there is exchange of energy with the environment. The family is such an open system. However, open systems can tend towards a more or less closed state. The degree of interaction with the environment is partly dependent on the boundaries around the system. In the W. family the boundaries around the parents and children are diffuse, so that other possible care-givers may move into and out of the system freely, perhaps too freely.

An ideal boundary for a family system is one which permits interaction with the environment and therefore allows movement in the system, at the same time as serving to satisfactorily define the family for all the members. Minuchin (1974) suggests that families vary along a continuum, from those with loose indeterminate boundaries to those with fixed, very rigid boundaries. Most families lie between these two, perhaps oscillating about a fixed point. Boundaries can exist around family sub-systems too, and within systems the degree of permeability of internal boundaries may vary. In some families, children, no matter their age, may belong only to the sibling sub-system, not being permitted to move between adult and childlike states.

Family Therapy and its Outcome

Much current theorizing about the family arises from the practice of family therapy and this partly accounts for the major difficulty that theorists and clinicians have about families — that we do not have a useful, operationalizable theory of family change. Not surprisingly, then, there has been, until recently, a dearth of outcome studies of family therapy. More importantly, many of the studies carried out are deficient in measurement or design so that results are obscure, even when allowance is made for those special difficulties such as how to assess the impact of family therapy on the whole family system, and how to describe that therapy in a public manner (Gale, 1979). Indeed, Wells *et al.*, (1972) reviewed the previous twenty years of family therapy outcome research and there was *no* study which they felt to be adequate in terms of design. Equally, Olson (1970) and Haley (1972) come to depressing conclusions about marital/family therapy — that there is no substantive evidence that family therapy is effective in enabling maladaptive family systems to move to a more adaptive level of functioning. Gurman (1973) is somewhat more optimistic when reviewing the previous twenty-two years' work on marital therapy, concluding that there was improvement in 66% of the cases in all the studies he reviewed. He had many reservations, however, about the quality of much of the work carried out.

More recently, Gurman and Kniskern (1978) carried out a very extensive and wide-ranging review of outcome research in marital and family therapy. Again many studies are defective in terms of design and measurement. They consider non-behavioural marital and family therapy first. In the former, therapy produced beneficial effects in 61% of cases and in the latter 73% of cases improved overall. When the Identified Patient (IP) was a child 71% of families improved and when the IP was an adult there was a 65% improvement. Results vary also within treatment settings. Family therapy with outpatients yielded 76% improvement, with day-patients 59% and with inpatients 74%. A very important finding, and a disturbing one, is that between five and ten per cent of cases show a deterioration in the marital/family system.

When marital/family therapy is compared with other treatment methods

Gurman and Kniskern (1978) find that the former is superior in terms of rates of improvement. But Wells and Dezen (1978) in their survey of the literature in this area found that there were only eight comparative studies with acceptable design. Of these, family therapy was superior at follow-up in four, and in one of these the results were equivocal. They conclude that family therapy has not been able to demonstrate more than equivalence with non-formal treatment.

Gurman and Kniskern (1978) also examined studies of behavioural marital/family therapy, where the word "behavioural" is used to refer to therapy based on a social learning theory approach and which is primarily concerned with the number and type of rewarding interactions that occur in families. Marital therapy is beneficial in 64% of cases using this approach. Figures for family therapy are not presented (nor presentable) as a percentage figure at the moment. The authors conclude that "Family therapy appears to be at least as effective as, and possibly more effective than, individual therapy for a wide variety of problems, both 'apparent' individual difficulties and more obvious family conflicts". Wells and Dezen (1978) reach similarly optimistic conclusions:— "At the very broad level it is apparent that (family therapy) has been legitimized". They add, more cautiously, "But data are still scanty and do not support the more specific (and sometimes extravagant) claims of family therapy proponents".

We have major reservations about these conclusions. Throughout, the term "improvement" is unclear. Gurman and Kniskern (1978) use it to refer to gross improvement on a three-point scale — improved, no change, worse. "Improved" ranges from "very much" to "somewhat" improved according to ratings *made by the original authors*. Therapy is often not specific and may be short, medium or long term. Assessment of outcome may occur at termination, at three or six months follow-up or, occasionally, longer than this. All of these raise serious doubts. Studies are included which the authors find inadequate in design criteria and in many cases the outcome figures are based on therapist ratings alone. A further difficulty is in the use of the term "behavioural family therapy". It appears that behaviourally based intervention in families may often be very effective, although as yet such intervention is not based on a systems view of the family. Rather, parents are trained in ways of managing children, there being little acknowledgement of the circularities that are observable from a systems theory perspective.

We must conclude then, that the evidence for the usefulness of systems-based family therapy is, at best, equivocal. Despite the enormous amount of work done, the figures for improvement rates are often highly questionable in themselves and do not differ significantly from figures for remission in no-treatment groups in well designed studies. This failure to demonstrate the usefulness of the family therapy approach is partly due to the lack of an adequate theory of family change, partly due to the inability of researchers to measure change in system terms and partly due, we feel, to the over-ambitious nature of much of the research. We suggest that a more fruitful way of assessing family therapy intervention with disordered families would be in making detailed hypotheses about the system, and interventions that might be effective, that can be tested in individual family therapy sessions, in a rigorous manner. (This is what clinicians probably do anyway, though not rigorously and hardly publicly) We could then move on to the second stage — that of assessing whether or not change effected in a therapy session endures over time and after termination.

Conclusions

Although there is little evidence to date that it has led to practices which are demonstrably efficacious in reducing disorders in families, we believe a general systems theory offers an approach within which family theorists and practitioners of varying persuasions can feel comfortable. This is important because it augurs well for the development of theory which will command widespread respect and may advance our knowledge in this field. As it stands, systems theory has too high a level of abstraction to provide this way forward in itself. It is a perspective rather than a theory (La Gaipa, 1981a). On the other hand, research approaches, some of which have been des-cribed in this chapter, have represented only partial approaches which fail to do justice to the wholeness and complexity of the disordered family, let alone to the array of family types to be found across time and culture.

Hence our plea, a familiar one, is for a "middle level" theory about families and family disorder. Such a theory should be capable of doing the things we expect of all theories: it should serve to organize findings to date, guide future research, and be amenable to change depending upon research findings. At the same time it must offer an adequate account of the main processes which we think we see at work in families such as those described briefly earlier in this chapter.

Section III

Relationships in Disordered People

CHAPTER 7

The Relationships of Problem Children in Nursery Schools

M. Manning and J. Herrmann

In this chapter we are concerned particularly with *relationships* of problem children, perhaps the most important and fundamental characteristic to be investigated. Not only is it apparent that relationships are almost always abnormal in difficult children but it is likely that a study of the nature of these abnormalities will tell us a great deal about the factors underlying the children's difficulties. The establishment of interpersonal relationships is one of the most important activities of the human infant and child and much of his motivation is bound up in this. It is therefore probable that disturbed behaviour will be reflected in and possibly originate from disturbed relationships. This is apparent when we consider the question "What is a problem child in a nursery?" Many consider that, rather than talking about a disturbed child in the clinical sense, we are dealing with one who cannot adapt himself well to nursery life. Indeed, there are those who would argue that there is nothing necessarily wrong with a so-called problem child and that one should not expect everyone to conform to the nursery-school world: perhaps such a child is simply better adapted to a different type of environment.

This attitude is supported by some aspects of the behaviour of problem children. While the difficulties they present are mainly those of management, the children are also seen by the teachers as failing to use and enjoy the facilities offered by the nursery. Most British nurseries today present a free unstructured environment where a child can do many different kinds of things; physical things, constructive things, fantasy games and so on. The children regarded as difficult tend either to concentrate on wild, noisy, fighting games or to flit from activity to activity, pursuing none with any real interest and often hovering on the edge of groups, looking on or sometimes interfering. (Real "loners" who scarcely interact at all, may also be included, but they are relatively rare.) Such evidence might well suggest that nurseries are not in some way fulfilling the needs of these children and their uncooperative, contrary behaviour could be viewed as simply an expression of their dissatisfaction.

However, questioned further, teachers also express concern about the relationships of difficult children, both with their peers and with adults. Many problem children appear to avoid contact with teachers and few, on their own initiative, will start up a friendly conversation with them. Among peers, they are described as having few friends, as often quarrelling and fighting, as failing to cope with difficulties or with opposition, as failing to persuade or invite but instead making mainly physical or demanding approaches. They are also described as often unhappy or at least as changeable in their moods. These views were expressed in a questionnaire presented by Manning and Sluckin (1979) to teachers in four nursery schools in Edinburgh, regarding children whom the teachers themselves had named as difficult — and the findings suggest that something more serious might underlie the troublesome behaviour described, given that experienced teachers are likely to be sensitive to those aspects of a child's behaviour which are important for social development.

Moreover, the described behaviour accords clearly with that observed in clinically disturbed children. Wolff (1967) looked at behaviour characteristics which distinguished children referred to a psychiatric clinic from normal ones among the 5–12 age group. Most of the significant characteristics fell into three groups, those concerned with conduct disorders, those concerned with relationships and those concerned with discontent or anxiety. A similar cluster of characteristics was described in a survey of problem three-year-olds in nursery schools, by Richman et al. (1975) who concluded that about 7% of these children had moderate to severe behaviour problems, a proportion very close to that of the difficult children selected by teachers in the Edinburgh nurseries in the study by Manning and Sluckin (1979). It is likely, then, that Edinburgh's "difficult" children correspond to Richman's "problem" children and that a number of them may show incipient disturbance or else be set upon a deviant course which could lead to that end.

The Significance of Relationships at Nursery School

For the three to five-year-old, nursery school usually represents his first step into the social world outside his family. The relationships that he develops are likely to affect his whole future life. They are part of the process of being and becoming "social"; of communicating with others, doing things with others, adjusting to and co-operating with others. All interactions aid this process; relationships, which are uniquely personal, mutual and continuous, enable it to go much further.

Yet it is apparent that some children form good relationships with their peers, naturally and without difficulty, whilst others do not. Theories about the reasons for this are influenced by further theories regarding the factors which underlie this process and its meaning to the child. Many writers concentrate on the nature of the learning processes concerned, on progressive adaptation, on negotiation, on the elaboration of rule structures and ceremonials (Harré, 1979; Goffman 1961, 1967; 1972). But often they do not consider why the child should in himself want to pursue these aims, nor do they address themselves to the deeper structure of relationships. As Shotter (1974) has pointed out: "Personal relationships and other human groupings do not exist and function as matters of fact, but are maintained by *the intention* of their members to maintain them; without such intention they collapse". Many of the negotiations, rule structures and so on serve to control and elaborate interactions, allowing adjustment to the needs of each partner. Yet their development does not explain why the child should strive to interact in the first place. Some workers refer to Piaget's ideas of the "power of mastery" (Piaget, 1971), others suggest that relationships are stimulated by the exchange of rewards such as love, status, information, goods, services, money (Foa and Foa, 1974).

On the other hand, Trevarthen (1979) has suggested that human infants have innate *motivation* and *capacity* for the development of intimate relationships and co-operative understanding with people. The *motivation* is to strive towards, and engage actively in, all communicative processes, while the *capacity* (which Trevarthen has called intersubjectivity) is for an awareness of affective states and intentions in others, an ability to communicate this awareness, to express similar personal states and to explore the potentialities of mutual understanding and shared experience. From this viewpoint, an infant, even a very young baby, has always an "intention" to interact and form relationships. There is no need to postulate extrinsic rewards, the rewards are intrinsic and part of the mechanism, as in all instinctive behaviour. A baby actively enjoys interacting with people, no other rewards are required. It is by no means far-fetched to suggest that humans possess an instinct for social behaviour. We are essentially communicative and co-operative creatures and owe much of our success to this fact. Hence natural selection is likely to have operated to evolve mechanisms which pre-adapt an infant for co-operative life and which make a child "need" relationships in the same way as he needs food, sleep and protection.

Harré (1974) has argued that mother–child relationships are essentially different from later peer relationships. The first he regards as concerned with emotional bonds, the need for love and comfort and protection (as envisaged by Bowlby, 1969; 1979) and these (he argues) have no place in the genesis of social order, which he sees as the essence of peer interactions. In doing so he would seem to be underestimating (indeed ignoring) the interacting, communicating side of the mother–child relationship. Such interactions support and strengthen the bond; recent work on attachment suggests that mothers who form the best bonds are sensitive and responsive, talk to their babies, and are able to anticipate and adjust to their babies' needs (Ainsworth, 1967; Ainsworth *et al.,* 1974; Dunn, 1977; Schaffer, 1977). But the two processes (i.e. comfort and communication) are separate and probably have separate functions: Harlow's baby rhesus monkeys were able to obtain comfort and assurance from surrogate cloth mothers (and so were able to explore the inanimate world) but they could not interact or communicate with them, and so were inadequate socially (Harlow 1961; 1963).

It is possible, then, that peer interactions are a continuation of mother–child interpersonal communication but not of the caring bond. Young children who are well-cared for by their mothers, do not normally seek comfort, help and protection from each other; but they do seek interactions and there is little doubt that they bring strong emotions to bear upon this. Observations suggest that good relationships in nursery school children are still primarily concerned with and motivated by the enjoyment of communicating and sharing. Children enjoy doing things together; they like to dance, dress up, run, climb, play fantasy games, but especially they like to do these things together. In addition they like to tell of their own enjoyable experiences and show objects they possess or models or paintings they have made. When they achieve some degree of sharing in this way their enjoyment and enthusiasm is unmistakable. It seems similar in essence to that described by Trevarthen and Hubley (1978) for a 40-week old girl with her mother "in playing with objects they shared the effects almost equally, Tracy looking up and smiling when an entertaining effect was produced".

If this interpretation is correct then one may conclude that children with peers, as with mothers, strive to interact because they have an inborn tendency to do so. Recent work by Murray in Trevarthen's laboratory (Trevarthen *et al.,* 1981) shows that when mothers fail to respond to their infants, or when they do not respond in synchrony with the child's social behaviour, then the latter shows clear signs of distress and withdrawal. It is as if the child has an expectation of and a striving for a good reciprocal relationship with its mother and is distressed if this does not occur. In the same way, nursery school children become angry, distressed, sulky or withdrawn if their attempts to develop a co-operative game break down or are disrupted. It would seem that the same motivations, the same rewards, the same emotions are involved in both mother–child and peer–peer relationships. Obviously there will be many differences of content and form in the two cases (e.g. less nurturance and controlling between peers) and there will be different negotiations and different rules which reflect this: although details of style often remain the same. Manning *et al.* (1978) showed that many aspects of the relationships of eight-year-old, well-adjusted children with their mothers, with much conversation and joking, resembled those established by the same children with their peers. This strongly suggests continuity.

A Comparison of Difficult and Well-adjusted Children

Before considering what these theories imply in terms of what can go wrong, it is useful to look more closely at the nature of the relationships of difficult children. The behaviour of a problem child often seems strangely unadaptive; he seems to be acting against his own interests as well as those of others. Yet it is likely that his behaviour makes some sense in its own terms. Even behaviour which may be considered pathological, destructive and defeating its own ends, is likely to have its roots in forces and goals which are, in other circumstances, adaptive. To assess this, it is necessary to observe all the behaviour of a child and consider its implications in terms of goals and needs. Both Montagner (1978) and Manning *et al.* (1978) have considered different styles of behaviour in nursery school children; Roper and Hinde (1978) have analysed different types of social interaction; and Wolkind and Everett (1974) have considered clusters of behavioural characteristics and picked out two which suggest disturbance. The following account will refer to all these works as well as to recent unpublished observations directly comparing disturbed (Herrmann, 1978) or difficult (Manning and Sluckin, 1979; 1980) children with those well-adjusted to the nursery.

It is not to be expected that all difficult children will be the same and the assortment of characteristics discussed above does not necessarily apply to each individual child. A number of different styles of behaviour have been described both by Montagner and by Manning, and among these descriptions there seems to be agreement upon three distinct styles.

The first is the *well-adjusted style*. Montagner calls children showing this profile "leaders" or "dominated but resembling leaders" according to their degree of self-assertion. Montagner stresses the non-verbal appeasement, soliciting, bonding acts shown by these children; offering, inclining the head, kissing, taking by the hand. Manning stresses their friendliness, their love of conversation and their limited employment of aggression mainly in disputes over specific problems (i.e. with evident purpose). Teachers also stress their co-operativeness, their willingness to talk, and their happiness in the nursery.

The second style may be called the *aggressive style*. Here there are few bonding acts (Montagner), much less friendly talk (Manning), and a tendency for spontaneous and unexpected aggression which may appear to be unrelated to the situation. Montagner distinguishes two types of child employing this style, the dominant aggressive and the dominated aggressive. Manning also separates two groups of teasers according to their relative assertiveness. The dominant aggressives are the children most commonly picked as problem children in nursery schools. They present management problems, frequently play rough games, seek to dominate others and use aggression to do so. They also tend to be defiant and may avoid teachers. Wolkind's cluster of "management problems, temper tantrums, poor peer relationships, fears, worrying, bedwetting" would seem to fit here too.

The third style may be called the *dependent style*. Montagner calls it the timid dominated style and he describes such a child as dependent, often soliciting teachers, normally friendly, with some bonding acts but prone to unexpected outbreaks of violence. The behaviour is similar to that of Manning's "games specialist" — timid and "anxious to please", but prone to wild, uncontrolled behaviour in the more permissive atmosphere of a game. Wolkind's cluster of "dependency, separation anxiety, fears, habits, worrying, bedwetting" may also be related. Teachers often complain that such children are demanding and want everything done for them.

Thus there appear to be two fairly distinct ways of being difficult in a nursery school and they will be considered separately here because these different styles affect relationships in different ways. It is likely that the constraints of the nursery situation make members of each group appear more similar than they are. However, Montagner (1978) stresses that many of the behavioural characteristics which he describes are recognizable from a very early age and he claims that he can distinguish potential leaders and potential dominant aggressives at 18–20 months. Hence they may not be styles of behaviour acquired at nursery school, but originate perhaps from very early relationships. However it may not be the styles themselves which are so persistent, but the needs or distortions which create them.

Friends, games and interactions

It has already been stated that, in the view of teachers, difficult children fail to make many friends and do not adequately sample the resources of the nursery whereas, among well-adjusted children, type of play and friendship groupings tend to be linked. Vivienne Atkinson (1981) has shown that, at least in one nursery, those children who spend a great deal of time in fantasy play, and who develop elaborate fantasy games, tend to form tight, rather exclusive, groups of friends which may be quite large. Here the relationships are often complex but continuing and quite stable, the children tending to stay together even outside the fantasy situations, sitting together for snacks and so on. The children who like to spend more time doing quieter, more personal, constructive activities (e.g. puzzles, paintings, etc.) form looser groups and are more prepared to be friends with anyone. They like to talk about their activites and share their interests.

Difficult children, where games are concerned, tend to fall into two categories. Either they play wild, rough games most of the time, or they tend mainly to flit around, or to look on and sometimes to play wild games. In general, the aggressive type of child belongs to the first category and the dependent child to the second. The noisy rough games developed by both types are usually fantasy games of adventure, excitement and power although dependent children sometimes enjoy quieter fantasies too (in role-games as doctors, postmen or families in the Wendy House). In aggressive fantasies the children are Tarzans or Batmen or Daleks or witches with magic powers and they attack almost everyone, even bystanders or children engaged in other pursuits who have no part in their game. Usually aggressive children lead and dominate such games but dependent children, when they take part, are sometimes unexpectedly violent. Unlike similar games of well-adjusted children, these games are loosely organized and the relationships between the participants are unstable. Quarrels and temporary rejections are common. The aggressive children sometimes seem quite popular, for often they are inventive and their games are exciting even if they do not develop. Most children enjoy chasing, play fighting and monsters and they are attracted to them; indeed these emotionally-charged fantasies seem to play an important part in normal development. However, when difficult children are involved, the games may become too frightening or too violent.

The dependent children appear often to be *trying* to play with other children but are not prepared to take the initiative themselves. They hover on the edge of a group, waiting to be invited, they come and stand silently at a sand-tray gazing, or more often glaring at the children playing together there. Sometimes they harass such groups, snatching their toys or challenging them, for example, by bringing up an opposing car or boat. One boy would submit to almost anything to get himself into a game with others: he would allow himself to be dragged along the floor, tied up or generally knocked around. These children are in general unpopular; usually they have little of interest to contribute to a game, for it seems enough for them simply to have got into one. Occasionally, however, they develop rather possessive relationships, usually with one other child. In such cases the difficult child may dominate the fantasies once they have started and it is typical that he or she will be reluctant to let the friend either go away or change the direction of the game. You may see such a child literally tugging another back into the Wendy House or hospital which the latter is trying to leave; or you may see her pursuing another pleading, "You said we were friends, you said we'd be princesses and dress up together and get married". If finally rejected such a child is likely to perform malicious acts of revenge. However, the pair "make up" eventually. Clearly, there is some attraction between them although, again, the relationship is unstable. It is usually apparent that the difficult child is pursuing and seeking out the other, who occasionally tolerates, occasionally rejects.

One important similarity between these two types of child (and a difference perhaps of fundamental importance between them and well-adjusted children) lies in the apparent self-centredness of the way in which they play fantasy games, for often there are no roles for others. A well-adjusted child clearly wants to include others in his game. He will say "I'll be the driver and you can be the guard" or he will indicate sharing by saying "We'll make this our space ship, shall we?" A difficult child is more likely to say "I'll be Tarzan" with no concern about his friends. Even when he develops quite elaborate fantasies, this tendency remains. One girl said, "Let's pretend I am Father Christmas and I come up on a sleigh with lots of parcels and climb down the chimney". In addition he or she is likely to make unacceptable rules concerning the activities of others. Simon perpetually cried, as others approached him, "You can't come here. You're dead. I shot you" — although he himself had been repeatedly "shot". Colin, in a football game, organized others into specified places and then proceeded to kick the ball to and fro with his special friend. When others ran forward to intercept, he declared "No, no you mustn't come up and try to get the ball. Go back to your place".

Neil, a more well-adjusted child, by contrast, although doing a lot of ordering in an adventure game with carts was nevertheless assigning roles and jobs to others so that they felt part of the game. Thus Neil: "No you run. You come in Stuart, give me your coat. Craig, we're the ones to keep the coats". Because there are more roles in them, a well-adjusted child's games tend to develop because each participant contributes ideas. A train may have a driver, a guard, a ticket collector as well as passengers and each may suggest some happening on the journey. A difficult child will often oppose innovations, except those suggested by himself.

These self-centred tendencies in difficult children are of some interest since Chandler (1972, 1973) has demonstrated a link between poor role-taking skills and antisocial and delinquent behaviour in older children. However, it cannot be assumed that difficult nursery school children are necessarily "egocentric" in Piagetian terms, i.e. that they are incapable of taking another's point of view. On occasions they show that they can do this perfectly well, as they also show they want and need to co-operate and be friendly with others. It seems that, for much of the time, other needs override these tendencies.

Observations regarding the tendency to interact at all and motivations underlying this, seem to support the idea of "other needs". Most workers investigating social participation have viewed it on a single scale: self play, parallel play through to varying degrees of social participation in more elaborate games. There is a clear tendency, as would be expected, for social participation to increase with age, both in amount and complexity (Parten, 1932; Smith, 1973). However Roper and Hinde (1978) find that other dimensions are involved and that some children who play freely in groups, also play a lot alone. They also show that playing alone is not always associated with looking-on or being unoccupied. They suggest that to be playing alone does not necessarily imply that a child is lacking in sociability and they predict perhaps a more confident quality about the self-play of those who can also play in groups.

These conclusions are supported by other observational work which suggests that some of the other relevant dimensions concern the social adjustment of the child and his confidence in his ability to establish satisfactory relationships. The child who is equally happy at almost any "stage" of social participation, seems to be the well-adjusted child who has no apparent problems about establishing easy and friendly relationships. Such children will sometimes be seen to be completely absorbed in a model or a painting, not to be distracted even by a fight proceeding close by. Alternatively they may be seen to be playing in parallel, at the sand or water, usually then making interesting comments about their own or others' activity. Yet on other occasions they will show themselves well able to participate in quite complex games.

On the other hand, difficult children come, in general, rather lower on the social participation scale (they rarely achieve complex integrated relationships) although their total amount of self-play may be variable. Most aggressive children play rather little alone, although they may occasionally be deserted by all their companions. Herrmann (1978), comparing two disturbed children with five normal ones, found that her disturbed boys were distinguished from other children in that they spent more of their time in a group and played very little alone. The figures are:

% time in	Disturbed children		Others
Group play	68	41	41,29,28,21,17
Alone	20	21	22,30,36,43,68

Dependent children may play quite often alone but, with them, this tendency is highly associated with hovering and looking on. This is not the case for most well-adjusted children.

Moreover the self-play of difficult children both aggressive and dependent tends to be different from that of well-adjusted children in that long periods of interested, concentrated self-play are rarely seen. Aggressive children may concentrate for a short time on a painting, or perhaps on a sword or on a frightening mask for later display. More often, when alone, they will be seen to be displaying; perhaps hammering very loudly at the woodwork bench, painting with exaggerated flourishes of the paintbrush, dropping objects with a great splash into the water, shouting across the room to a friend or running across to tease (as described below). Dependent children will sometimes watch rather than try to attract attention, but they too will not be attending very closely to their own activities. One boy was often to be seen at the sand, letting sand trickle through his fingers (rather than do anything else with it) meanwhile looking longingly at an interacting group nearby. Herrmann (1978) found that her two disturbed children interacted more than normal children in most situations but especially in those where interactions are not so appropriate or expected (they came first and second in rank orders for time spent interacting in painting, manipulative play and transitional periods). In quiet activities, looking at books, playing with puzzles, making models or simply moving from one activity to another, normal children do not always seek to communicate but difficult children do. It is as if they are never really content not to be interacting. Normal children seem already to have developed a balance between self-sufficient and social play before nursery-school age. Difficult children have not and their constant striving for social interaction suggests needs and anxieties which can only be satisfied therein.

Quality of interactions and relationships with peers

It is revealing also to look at the quality of interactions and types of relationship achieved by difficult children. Herrmann (1978) found that her two disturbed children ranked 5th and 7th (out of 7) for the number of different peers with whom they were involved in friendly interactions although they came first and second as regards those interacted with in total. The figures are:

No. of different peers interacted with per unit of observation time (x 100)

	Disturbed children	Others
All peers per total time	57,44	32,29,6,5,5
Friendly peers per friendly interaction time	9,19	12,20,22,25,30
Dispute peers per dispute interaction time	32,27	7,18,26,29,36

In other words, as described earlier, they are extremely interested in interacting but they can develop friendly relationships with only a few of their peers, although they dispute with many more. These relationships are sometimes intense but usually unstable. With others, and often with their friends too, their interactions are different in nature from those of well-adjusted children. Manning and Sluckin are investigating these differences further.

From what has already been said it is apparent that while the interactions of well-adjusted children seem to be concerned mainly with communicating, sharing and co-operating, those of difficult children only sometimes appear to have this goal; more often they are concerned with quite different, self-centred interests. This is not easily revealed by consideration of the form or even the function of speech and acts in isolation. It is necessary to assess their meaning in the context in which they occur.

Manning and Sluckin (1979, 1980) have developed categories which attempt to do this although in some cases they have to be defined in terms of the manner in which the relevant acts are normally received. Five main categories distinguish acts which are *friendly* (communicating, sharing, helping); *organizing* (attempting to make a child modify his immediate behaviour); *contrary* (in opposition to what is being done or is proposed); *annoying* (hurtful or against the interests of another child); or *submissive* (giving way against one's own interests).

Some of these categories are subdivided, especially *friendly*, which constitutes the major part of most children's speech, even the difficult ones. Friendly acts can be of very different natures and one of the most important subcategories is "friendly adaptive" which indicates an appreciation of and concern for the interests of other children (by suggesting shared interests, offering roles or help or comfort, approving another's appearance or activities). This can be distinguished from, for example, friendly boasting; challenging ("I bet you can't do that"); claiming ("I'm the driver");

attention-seeking ("Watch this", "See what I can do"); self (comments about one's own appearance or activity) or defining relationships ("You're my friend"). In *organizing,* adaptive, positive, negative, demanding and physical subcategories are similarly distinguished. A further qualification is that all utterances which contain additional material to make them more persuasive or interesting are marked by a (+) sign.

Although the results of this study are not yet complete, it is apparent that difficult children tend to show more contrary and annoying and less adaptive and (+) behaviour than well-adjusted children. Aggressive children score highly on attention-seeking, boasting, claiming and challenging among friendly acts and on negative, demanding and physical types of organizing. They seek to demonstrate their prowess, to compete, to control and to dominate. Dependent children often score highly on friendly claiming, and on defining relationships and on demanding types of organizing. They seek to be assured of friendship, attention, care, help and privilege. Thus while well-adjusted children usually enjoy developing co-operative interactions and treat all others as friends and partners in this (they seem able to take another's point of view from the start), difficult children more often appear to pursue other aims, which are centred on themselves and which involve the manipulation of others in ways which they may well resent. Hence difficult children cannot treat their peers as equals, nor closely consider their point of view and they may well come to regard others as hostile. In games too, the relatively few (+)s in their records suggest that they are not concerned with attracting interest or developing the game. They are not in games for the games' sake as are the well-adjusted children.

This study also revealed a further feature of a difficult child's behaviour which has been commented upon by many observers. This concerns its unexpected and often inappropriate qualities when considered from the point of view of the situation and the behaviour of the other children. As already described, Montagner (1978) talks of hostility arising for no obvious reason and of gratuitous violence in his aggressives; he also talks of unexpected aggression in his timid-dominateds (dependents). Manning sees the aggressives as teasers showing "out-of-the-blue" hostility, and the dependents as practising "games hostility" mainly in a game context (Manning *et al.,* 1978). In the former case it is the act itself which is unexpected. Teasing does not spring from a dispute or disagreement, often it seems like a sudden inspiration occurring to the child. He or she may dart from a solitary painting to tease another at the woodwork bench, splashing him with paint or tipping out his box of nails. Another may grab a toy in passing and flaunt it or hurl it to the ground. Herrmann also found that her two disturbed boys (unlike others) tended to be aggressive when alone or moving from place to place; their aggression was unpredictable and not related to any particular activity. Games hostility as practised by dependent children is unexpected often in its violence and roughness. Thus in a relatively friendly game of chasing between two loosely organized groups, one child may suddenly pounce on another, grip him round the neck and bang his head on the ground. Another may be unnecessarily intimidating in a game of monsters or robbers.

Bossy, organizing behaviour is likewise sometimes inappropriate both in its occurrence and in the intensity with which it is pursued. Thus Stephen outside, suddenly and for no apparent reason, insisted that Darren should put down the hood of his anorak and he hit him when he made a mild protest. The conversation went like this. "Darren put your hood down". "No, I don't want to. It keeps me warm". "It's not raining or something". Stephen then hits Darren. Montagner remarks that, in his "leaders", behaviour is usually related to the situation in an appropriate way. Stephen's behaviour is not. It suggests that Stephen is pushed by some motive within himself that does not allow him to accept Darren's reasons.

This does not mean that incidents such as these bear no relationship to a past happening. Manning has shown that teasing in particular, is, in some children (usually aggressives), significantly related to past happenings, reprimands or organizing by teachers, opposition or organizing by peers. But the incidents are not simply reactions, often they occur sometime after the event, when the connection is sometimes made explicit by remarks such as "You shouldn't have chucked me out of your game then". Moreover it is not always just the original offender who is persecuted. It is as if these happenings merely activate already existing grievances. The same conclusion may be drawn from observations that difficult children have "good" and "bad" days and that often good days with peers are also good days with adults, as if there is a global effect.

A final facet of unexpectedness in aggression concerns the nature of attacks in rough and tumble games. This has been noted by both Manning and Montagner. Well-adjusted children enjoy rough and tumble play just as much as do difficult children, but it is apparent that well-adjusteds tend to display or challenge their adversary before an attack as if they desire the fight to be on equal terms. The difficult children, particularly the aggressive ones, will more often launch completely unexpected attacks, grappling or pulling from behind, or knocking to the ground without warning. Montagner (1978) describes how his dominant-aggressive children are not at all responsive to their peers; when they make a threat they do not wait for the victim's reply but pass straight to aggression.

These two descriptions then agree in contrasting the fights of difficult children with those of more normal children, where rituals and rules are deployed to communicate the need for co-operation and to limit the extent and damage of the fight. They are equivalent to those described by Sluckin (1981) in primary school boys and by Marsh *et al.* (1978) for adolescents on football terraces. It is difficult to escape the impression that these different types of children are in it for different reasons. To the well-adjusted children it is an opportunity to enjoy physical competitiveness and balanced trials of strength, to the difficult children it may represent new opportunities for power, control and perhaps revenge. Many of them get carried away by the exciting, chaotic and apparently permissive atmosphere of a fight so as to become virtually "out of control".

Emotionalism

A marked feature of difficult children's behaviour concerns the emotionalism which they betray especially when opposed or frustrated. Well-adjusted children often cope with such occurrences with good humour and often much resourcefulness. Kate, returning after a diversion, to join her friend at the swing, found that the friend had been displaced by a much bigger girl. She quickly devised a new and more exciting game close by — which both children enjoyed immensely. Jennifer, whose friend did not immediately respond to her invitation to join in her "building", persistently returned with a new fantasy until at last she attracted him. At first she said, "Come on here. In the blue, blue car". Then it was, "I've got tickets on the bus". Finally, she said, "Yea, this is a house, eh? Now I'm going to cook the dinner". This worked and her friend came in and said, "Brrrr. I'm doing the washing machine". And Graham, whose friend was trying to force him to push a cart (with him in it) that was too heavy, finally said: "Well, I guess we're both tired. We'll have a rest". His friend liked this idea and called the Teacher. "You know, Miss . . . we're window cleaners and we're having a rest". Soon he helped carry the ladder.

These are all situations which would be likely to anger or distress difficult children, being pushed out of a favoured place, having one's invitation ignored, being ordered about. However, different types of difficult children tend to be angered at different circumstances and this seems to be an area in which one can most easily distinguish them. In general, aggressive, outgoing types seem most upset when their authority or leadership or general dominance is challenged. One became furious when a rival gang seized the football in a game that he was organizing; another stamped angrily out of a kicking game because his partner criticized his style of kicking and a third set up an intimidation episode to "punish" a rival who claimed to have won in a race. First the claim was hotly denied, "What do you mean you won? Don't you be so silly. You had to go over the bar, right?" (This was the first time the bar had been mentioned). Then our boy grabbed his rival, glared at him and said,

"Don't just stand there and look at me. Tell me a question or I'll kill you".

By contrast, the dependent children are more often upset when their friends leave them or when they feel no one will play with them. Their behaviour on such occasions has already been described. If active attempts to recall a companion fail, or sometimes after only minimal attempts, they may go to the teacher and say "So and so won't play with me" or they will sit and sulk or complain they don't know what to do. It is often after such withdrawals that harassment occurs. Alternatively, they may obtain some favour, a sweet or a cake from the teacher or a friend and display it to those by whom they feel rejected.

Dependent children also tend to become angry with teachers if help, praise, or assistance is not offered when they feel it is needed. Usually they seem to expect this of adults but not of their peers. Thus one girl was involved in prolonged, complicated attempts to put her coat on in the cloakroom. She laid it on the table, turned her back and tried to wriggle her way into it. She had little success but with her friends she joked about it with only an occasional "Oh, I can't do this", half-serious complaint. But when a teacher appeared on the scene her behaviour changed. She became sullen and angry and thrust her coat at the teacher as if in protest that she hadn't received attention earlier. From the teacher's remark, "Can't you do your coat? Are you getting cross about it again?" it would seem that such behaviour was not uncommon. Such children may also become quite hysterical if hurt even in a minor way. Again the appeal is to the teacher and if no attention is received the crying becomes increasingly angry and "outraged".

Relationships with adults

Since nursery school teachers see difficult children as those who present management problems, the nature of the relationship of these children with their teachers is bound to be affected by this, and in many cases the most dominant aspect of that relationship is controlling. In a pilot study, Manning, investigating eight difficult children in the same nursery, found the following proportions of organizing acts out of the totals directed by any teacher to the child: 21%, 33%, 35%, 48%, 52%, 52%, 55%, 57%. In a later study, when it had been suggested that teachers should show more friendly behaviour to difficult children, these proportions were reduced but they were still significantly higher than those for well adjusted children, i.e.

Difficult children   14,20,22,23,26,27,33,49%
Well-adjusted children   3,8,8,14,17,19,21,35%

This is not always the teacher's fault. Some try very hard to have friendly conversations with difficult children but many of the latter do not respond well and often seek to avoid the teacher's company. This is especially true of aggressive children who tend also to be non-compliant, uncooperative and sometimes defiant. Herrmann (1978) observed the relationship between her subjects and their mothers when the latter spent some time in the nursery. She found that one of her disturbed children (A) headed the rank order for non-compliance to his mother's orders. The other (E), headed the rank for disconfirmation (disregarding or contradicting the intentions of the mother) while (A) came third. Manning's observations also suggest that sometimes such children do not answer when teachers address a friendly remark to them. This is especially so when teachers try to "teach" them by setting up discussions about things of general interest. Then they will "dry up", refuse to answer or walk away.

Many of the actions of aggressive children relative to the teacher suggests a determination, sometimes explicit, not to be "bossed around". It has already been noted how aggressive or disruptive behaviour may follow upon teacher's reprimands or organizing. On other occasions such children may be openly defiant. An order to stop some exciting but disruptive behaviour, such as running wildly round the nursery or throwing sand, may be blandly ignored, as may an instruction to do some unwelcome act such as removing a coat. One boy even ran into the Wendy House and put his coat on again (in hiding) after the teacher had removed it for him.

In some moods difficult children may ignore any lead from a teacher however friendly. On one occasion, a teacher approached a group of boys who had been throwing stones down a drain. She talked to them about drains, how they worked and what happened if they were blocked. She did it well and most of the children were interested and asked questions, but the ring-leader spent his time on the outskirts of the group collecting more stones and awaiting the opportunity to resume his throwing.

Sometimes these acts seem to be personal affairs between the child and the teacher but sometimes there seems to be an attempt to get applause from onlookers. One boy, asked to carry a tape-recorder carefully and not switch it on, immediately operated the on-button, laughed excitedly and looked around for approval. In general, defiance of the teacher occurs very commonly in a situation where compliance means humiliation or loss of face. When, for example, a child is asked to apologize, for an act of teasing he or she may be very persistent and stubborn in refusal. If one interprets teasing as an attempt at "one-upmanship" in the first place, the requirement to apologize may well be doubly humiliating.

For dependent children the situation may be different. It has been described how these children are demanding of teachers and how they become angry if the demands are not met. They also seek the company of teachers and are outwardly very affectionate and chatty, but one often sees contrary behaviour, which is nevertheless hidden under a cloak of friend-liness. One girl played a lengthy "game" of this sort with a teacher who was trying to persuade her to finish her painting so as to give others a turn at the easel. She kept coming away, washing her hands at length, then dirtying them again but always insisting that her picture was not yet finished. Throughout she was very friendly but adamant. Her behaviour was very reminiscent of that of an eight year old boy observed with his mother by Manning *et al.* (1978). The mother, taking part in a structured play session, was trying to get the boy to play a card game before the skittles game which he preferred. He ignored her reasons and persuasions and started the skittles game regardless. However, he maintained a friendly atmosphere throughout and kept reporting his score and prowess with such enthusiasm that the mother was eventually won over.

These children also seem to indulge in a number of acts which can be contrasted as mischievous, playful and slightly cheeky but not really difficult or defiant. A child may continue to stir a bowl or blow a trumpet after everyone has been told to stop, another may call a teacher by a playful name, tug or pull at her clothes or even slap her bottom. Yet all is done with a smile and in a friendly way as if no manner of offence is intended. This behaviour is often interpreted as "limit testing", seeing how far one can go before being checked. It is assumed that this is part of some rule-making or ordering process of the child who will be happier once the limits are determined. While this may be true for well-adjusted children, nevertheless the children who tend to do this sort of thing most are always difficult or disturbed (not well-adjusted) and it seems possible that they are trying to express a hostility that they feel towards adults but which they dare not show openly. It is not therefore certain that they will be happier if checked.

Summary

The relationships of difficult children, both with peers and with adults are often poor in just those elements which seem to be the essence of the relationships of well-adjusted children. What is missing is the delight in sharing experiences, in doing things together, in learning about and adapting to another's point of view. Occasionally these qualities appear, they are not totally missing, but when they do it is usually in special circumstances, perhaps in one-to-one relationships with one particular person. More often they are overlain with behaviour which seems to have quite different intentions. Aggressives aim to display power, superiority and dominance; dependents want to attract interest, friendship and care. In both cases the children seem to be pursuing self-centred goals and take no interest in others as individuals, indeed they show hostility towards them. Some of this hostility is in immediate response to opposition or frustration but much of it is spontaneous and unexpected. Both types of child may become angry or discontented expecially when frustrated in their apparent aims. Both types seem always to be striving to interact and they cannot often settle to self-play.

Relationships with peers do not, in general, appear to be intimate or long-lasting. Those of aggressives are marked by quarrels and fights, those of dependents by tensions resulting from the difficult child's possessiveness. With adults, aggressives tend to be defiant and non-communicative, while dependents are demanding and contrary, although overtly friendly.

Theories about the Origin of Relationship Difficulties

There are a number of theories about the factors underlying the difficulties of problem children, and these have some considerable influence upon proposed remedies and treatments. There are some ideas common to all these theories but there are also some more fundamental differences reflecting different viewpoints of the development of peer relationships in general.

One group of theories centres on the constitutional contribution of the child. For example Thomas *et al.* (1968, 1977) showed that infants with certain clusters of temperamental characteristics (concerned with activity, adaptability, intensity, persistence, reactions to novel stimuli, distractability and rhythmicity) are more than usually likely to develop clinically recognizable behaviour disturbances later. Because these characteristics appear very early in life (i.e. within the first two years, and indeed the earlier they appear the more "predictive" they seem to be), it is assumed that although not immutable, they are manifestations of inborn differences of neuriphysiological functioning. Similarly, workers on hyperactive children (who present a somewhat similar syndrome of characteristics) also assume that these are constitutional features, intrinsic to the child (Ross and Ross, 1976; Safer and Allen, 1976). In support of this assumption, evidence is quoted of differences in, for example, automatic response patterns, electro-encephalic patterns and "biochemical individuality" which are recognizable at birth. However, it is not usually suggested, although it would seem reasonable to suppose, that complex temperamental differences like those described arise because much simpler organic differences tend to distort very early interpersonal relationships.

Nevertheless, these workers do not regard such constitutional difficulties as the sole cause of later disturbance. They see the development of disturbed (as of normal) behaviour as an interactional process and they see that early behavioural abnormalities are likely to affect both the mothers' behaviour and their relationships with their children (Campbell *et al.*, 1977). Herbert and Iwaniec (1977) describe hyperactive children as "hard to love", whilst Cunningham and Barkley (1979) have shown that mothers of hyperactive boys are less positive and more controlling than normal, although they become warmer and more tolerant if their sons are given drugs which increase their compliance and decrease their activity. However, most see this interactional process as one of associative learning and conditioning and they postulate distortions in this rather than emotional frustrations of goal-directed behaviour. Thomas *et al.* suggest that "the same motive, the same adaptive tactic will have different functional meaning in accordance with the temperamental style of the given child", and they conclude that "it is merely confusing to attribute elaborate psychological motivational mechanisms to the young child if a simpler explanation accounts for the facts".

A second group of theories puts more stress on the part played by environmental influences, especially those of the family, in promoting the development of problem behaviour. This is not surprising since many investigations have revealed an association between aggression, delinquency disturbance and poor home backgrounds (Rutter *et al.*, 1975; McCord *et al.*, 1961; Glueck and Glueck, 1962). The first of these theories is again dependent upon the idea that both mother-child and peer relationships develop by learning. The two are regarded as continuous and it is suggested that the tactics employed in peer relationships are often learned at home. It is believed that many children acquire antisocial and unadaptive techniques because of poor training. If tantrums, aggressive and demanding behaviour prove rewarding at home then the child will come to practise these techniques more and more. Many teachers tacitly assume such explanations to be true. They seem to see aggressive children as having been under-controlled; allowed to employ aggressive, demanding, bullying methods to get their own way; as having not been taught to share or see another's point of view and as having absorbed an ethos of violence and self-interest. On the other hand, dependent children are often viewed as spoilt and overindulged. It is assumed that all their needs and wishes have been satisfied on demand and hence they come to nursery with similar expectations and attempt to make slaves of their teachers and peers.

However, close examination of a difficult child's behaviour shows that it is not easily understood in these terms. In the first place, if the aggressive and demanding behaviour is to be regarded as tactical, as a means of dealing with the world, then one would expect it to be limited to those situations which give advantage. Instead we find constant, irrelevant and often inexplicable occurrences of such behaviour which suggest instead an underlying hostility.

The emotionalism expressed by difficult children is also a problem for such a learning theory. Well-adjusted children who employ a tactic which fails, will go on to try another, and do not normally become angry or distressed. We have seen that both these emotions are common in difficult children as is also excitement and pleasure expressed by the aggressives when they are admired and by the dependents when they are accepted into a game. Again this suggests strong underlying needs rather than the simple acquisition of social skills.

It is possible that much of the aggressive child's behaviour might be explained in terms of a learned ethos of violence and domination. In this sense any opportunity to prove one-upmanship or superiority would prove rewarding, but the children's aims do not seem as simple as this. Their desire for approval would seem to be as strong as their desire to dominate and their emotionalism suggests conflict rather than a unified aim.

The theories of affiliation developed by Mehrabian and Kzionsky (1974) and, in less extensive form, by Byrne, *et al.* (1963) also support the notion of a strong, learned component in social behaviour but go further than the idea of a learned ethos. In brief, the suggestion is that individuals derive from their interactions with the world a set of expectancies about people that they are likely to encounter and the treatment that they can expect at their hands. People may be seen in general as unfriendly, uncaring sources of negative experience or, alternatively, as warm, loving providers of positive and rewarding outcomes. Individuals adjust their affiliative behaviour accordingly and thus a child who expects hostility or indifference is unlikely to approach others in an open, friendly way. Instead he is likely to test out his expectations and in doing so he may well invoke reactions which seem to justify them. Such a child is doing more than simply employing techniques which he has found to "pay off" in his home environment; he is trying to prove that the world is as he thinks it is, or as he feels it is, relative to himself, so that he can be on his guard.

Such a theory would seem to explain much more about the behaviour and relationships of children as described above. It may be that expectancies are set up very early in life, during the child's first experiences with its mother and other caretakers and are relatively persistent. This would explain Montagner's (1978) findings of distinct styles of relationships in very young infants which persist. It might also explain why problem children do not very readily change their behaviour in the light of experience. The tactics of aggressive children in the nursery are rarely very rewarding; they are frequently reprimanded by teachers and opposed by peers. Yet they do not easily adjust their behaviour. Some temporary adjustment can be achieved in strong behaviour modification programmes (Brown and Elliott, 1965) but it does not normally happen. The same is true of dependent children. They typically approach others with the apparent expectation of hostility and rejection. They are suspicious and rarely seem able to approach with a smile and an invitation. They may be delighted if they receive welcome and warmth but this does not readily affect their behaviour on the next occasion.

Indeed, the inflexibility of a difficult child's behaviour is a characteristic that has often been noted. These children appear to be "in a rut" with their relationships and their strategies. They will meet the same situation, with the same person, again and again in the same way with the same, often disastrous, results. As an example, Peter often constructed railways, cars or buses out of blocks and proceeded to develop a fantasy game with them. Usually, within minutes, Paul would appear and tease him in some way, blocking his train, removing the car door or arranging a collision. Peter's reaction was always the same; he would become very angry, kick or hit Paul and violently destroy his construction, an activity in which Paul often joined. It could be argued that both these children were constrained to behave in this inflexible way because of the rigid beliefs each had about the other. This theory also perhaps explains the apparent inability of problem children to consider another's point of view. This may not be because they lack the intellectual capacity to do so (Paul Light, 1979, has shown that there is no close correlation between ability to "role-take" and IQ) but perhaps because they view others as hostile to their interests. In this respect Paul Light's findings about the mothers of good role-takers are perhaps also relevant. He describes them as permissive as regards cheekiness, attributing importance to the mother apologizing to the child, allowing him to do things for himself after initial explanation and being interested in the development of the child as an individual. These characteristics would seem to be the opposite of those found by Manning *et al.* (1978) in the mothers of her teasers. These manipulated and over-controlled their children in games, were insistent on rules and jobs at home and had ambitions for their children to be polite, good mannered, useful and to do well at school. Few considered the child's own interests. This would suggest that a coercive relationship had grown up between these mothers and their children rather than one of mutual understanding. The expectancy theory would also suggest that the children would, because of this, come to regard all people as insensitive oppressors. With such a belief, an aggressive child is unlikely to allow others to operate as independent persons; instead he will feel he must control them or be lost. Such a belief could also account for his defiant, non-cooperative behaviour with teachers. He acts as if he feels that any child of spirit will resist being bossed around; he even seeks applause for such acts.

However, while this theory explains much, it does not entirely account for the ambivalence, the tension, the unhappiness of difficult children. One might expect a child with stable expectancies to be relatively consistent in his behaviour, and because the process is regarded as cognitive, one would not expect strong associated emotions. Yet the behaviour of a difficult child is both contradictory and emotional. In the midst of defiant and disruptive behaviour, an aggressive child can sometimes be seen to be near to tears when he finds that a teacher is seriously displeased with him. Furthermore, dependent children appear to oscillate between attempts to court affection and sudden eruptions of teasing and hostility. In both cases behaviour appropriate to hostile expectations (defiance and teasing) appears to alternate with emotions and aims related to the need to be liked and understood. No theory which regards learning as the sole process involved in the development of relationships and omits all consideration of underlying motives and goals, seems adequate to explain all these phenomena. Perhaps theories about "needs" with their associated emotions as a driving force in social behaviour might make more sense.

The theory which expressed the growth of relationships between mother and child in these terms is Trevarthen's (1979) theory of intersubjectivity. It will be remembered that this asserts that an infant is both motivated and preadapted to seek and develop relationships concerned with mutual understanding, sharing and co-operation. However, associated with this instinctive mechanism are strong emotions. A baby strives to interact and to play with his mother; he is intensely delighted when he is successful and he becomes distressed, withdrawn and even hostile if something goes wrong. The development of a good relationship may become frustrated or distorted in many ways and for many reasons, by factors intrinsic to the child, to the mother, or to external circumstances. But, on this viewpoint, these factors do not merely interfere with a learning process, they frustrate and distort a highly motivated, goal directed behaviour system. Trevarthen suggests that the same forces which give the system power in normal circumstances may become destructive and pathological in abnormal ones.

Even without supposing pathological reactions, the idea of unsatisfied needs in a difficult child makes much sense of his ambivalence and distress. A dependent child possibly feels unsure of basic care and love (as described by Bowlby, 1969, 1979). He may feel frustrated by, and hostile to unfriendly, rejecting people but he still needs and strives to be loved. Hence the ambivalence, the overt friendliness, the unexpected and often concealed hostility, and hence the distress, specifically when he fails to fulfil the basic need, i.e. to be loved.

On the other hand, the aggressive child may feel secure about care, but he is unhappy about mutual understanding and reciprocity. He has been dominated and sees the world as caring but hostile to him and his needs as a person: hence his aggression and assertion of power, but at war with this is a need to be understood. Perhaps, examined more carefully, it may be seen that much of his anger is not so much about "not being the boss" or "being opposed" as at having his actions and intentions misunderstood and set aside. One bout of extremely difficult and disruptive behaviour in an aggressive boy, John, began after a teacher had checked him in somersaulting near the painting easels. She did it in a very friendly and reasonable manner, asking him to somersault elsewhere. But the boy had just, for once, established a friendly relationship with a girl and they were enjoying this mutual somersaulting together. The teacher broke it all up and did not even admire the somersaults. He seemed intensely hurt at a request that most children would find quite reasonable. For him it meant something very different.

A final important point can be made about interests and distractability. The idea of unsatisfied, interpersonal needs also explains the incessant search for interactions, the inability to settle to or concentrate on self-play, the lack of interest in others as persons, in objective things or in developing a game for its own sake. Perhaps only when one is satisfied that one is both loved and understood as a person can one properly explore one's own and others' interests and develop a truly balanced and reciprocal relationship with other people. Perhaps this is the real difference between being difficult and being well-adjusted.

Summary and Conclusion

In this chapter, the purely cognitive approach to the normal development of peer relationships in young children, stressing negotiations and learned tactics, has been contrasted with the idea of an inborn need and capacity to seek and develop social relationships, first with the mother and later with an increasing range of people. This does not eliminate learning as part of the process but it suggests unlearned capacities for understanding and expressing feelings or intentions and it stresses that there will be striving and goal-directed behaviour with strong associated emotions.

Where unsatisfactory relationships arise, these two viewpoints suggest different explanations. Cognitive theories suppose that the normal interactive learning process concerned in the development of mother–child relationships could be distorted by abnormal factors perhaps in the constitution of the child or mother, or perhaps in the environment. Thus poor social techniques, and perhaps also distorted expectations about people's natures and intentions may develop and be carried over to affect later peer relations. Alternatively, theories concerned with inborn needs and mechanisms suggest that the same factors will operate to distort and frustrate, not a simple learning process, but a highly motivated system with goals associated

with pleasure in success or with distress in failure. The emotional consequences of such frustration could of themselves lead to contradictory,
hostile and sometimes pathological (self-defeating) behaviour.

Observations of nursery school children highlight the poor relationships
of children whom teachers regard as difficult. They also highlight the aims
and emotions associated with the development of peer-relationships. Well-
adjusted children actively seek and enjoy friendly interactions and co-operative play. Because they enjoy shared interests they consider and show
interest in the viewpoint of their companions.

Problem children, by contrast, have relatively few friends, and their
relationships, although sometimes intense, tend to be unstable. Their interactions are often different in nature from those of well-adjusted children.
However, while maladaptive learned techniques and expectations, appear
to play some part in this, the behaviour of these children is more readily
understood in terms both of different aims and of conflict behaviour. Most
seem to be seeking either a demonstration of affection or a recognition of
personal identity and power. In pursuing such aims, they are manipulating,
rather than co-operating with, others and hence their interactions appear
self-centred with few adaptive qualities. However, their behaviour also
tends to be inconsistent and contradictory; there are oscillations between
attempts to solicit affection or understanding and hostile, dominating
behaviour which defeats these aims. Moreover their behaviour is often
unrelated to the situation in general as if "driven from within". All these
characteristics suggest conflict rather than stable tactics and expectations.
Finally problem children often seem to be tense and unhappy. There is a
constant striving for interaction, an inability to settle to self-absorbed play
and much emotionalism; sometimes exaggerated excitement, sometimes
anger, sometimes despondency and withdrawal. It is difficult to account for
such emotionalism in terms of purely cognitive processes and it is not
legitimate to leave it out of consideration; it is a marked feature of these
children's behaviour. In short, the emotionalism, the ambivalence, the
striving, all suggest, not a child dedicated to selfish aims, or schooled in
aggressive methods, but one frustrated in some important need. Two needs
— to be loved or to be recognized as a person — may be basically involved in
early mother–child relationships. If these are not satisfied, then the child
may continue to seek them but will also show hostile and conflict behaviour
resulting from his frustration.

These different views of the processes underlying the poor relationships of
problem children clearly have implications for those who have to deal with
and possibly help them. Short-term strategies to modify or contain difficult
behaviour may have little long-term effect if underlying needs remain unrecognized and unsatisfied.

Acknowledgement

The work quoted by Manning, and Manning and Sluckin was supported by grants from the Social Science Research Council.

CHAPTER 8

Friendship in Disturbed Adolescents

John J. La Gaipa and H. Diane Wood

If we seek to understand why many emotionally disturbed adolescents are lonely and withdrawn, with few, if any, close friends, then we must consider such questions as: what does it mean to an adolescent to have a friend? Why are disturbed adolescents rejected? And, what is the psychological importance of being rejected? The point here is a central one, namely that the meaning of friendship to the emotionally disturbed cannot be analysed separately from the developmental tasks faced by his peers (Bigelow and La Gaipa, 1980). Friendship plays a major role in the socialization process in integrating the individual into the culture. Feelings about sex and aggression can be explored with friends in an open manner unlikely to be achieved with parents. New social roles can also be learned, and help can be obtained in the development of a more adequate self-image (Fine, 1981). Kon (1981) also calls attention to the influence of friendship on various areas of development (such as changes in the structure of interpersonal relations, as well as cognitive and emotional development), and he comments on the importance of friendship in ego-development and the growth of self-awareness. It becomes, then, important to consider the extent to which disturbed adolescents are, on the one hand, capable of fulfilling such functions for their peers and are, on the other hand, capable of establishing peer relations which enable them to satisfy these functions for themselves.

An underlying theme of this chapter is thus to show the limitations of looking for the cause of isolation and withdrawal in the psychological "make up" of the disturbed adolescent. We suspect that much of the "cause" can be located in the observers and the peers with whom they interact— not just in the disturbed. For example, much consideration will be given to the possible effect of the label "emotional disturbance" on the establishment of friendship particularly since other adolescents are likely to use rather more offensive jargon to describe disturbed peers, such as "nuts" or "crazy". The basic assumption is that the stigma of being disturbed may exert a more profound influence on the social adjustment of teenagers than the various direct effects of mental or emotional impairments. Thus the central objective of this chapter is to try to explain some of the problems in establishing and maintaining friendships between the non-disturbed and the disturbed adolescent. Particular attention will be given to the nature of the interaction strains developing in such friendships.

The Social Consequences of Adolescence

Chronological age is of limited value in defining adolescence because of individual differences in biological development and the impact of culture. For instance, puberty is often used as the biological marker, but adolescence is a psychosocial phenomenon in both an individual and a societal response to puberty. The end of adolescence also has no specific age, no biological marker, and may continue far into what we call adulthood (Holzman and Grinker, 1974). For the purposes of this chapter, however, we have designated the age period of ten to twenty years as adolescence.

What differentiates adolescents from those in other chronological periods is the social tasks placed on them. The adolescent has to solve problems of ego identity and autonomy; there is a shift from childhood dependence to adult independence — a change from demanding of others to being demanded of, and from being provided for to providing for others. Many adolescents do not possess the adaptive techniques to cope with the task requirements, and the world is experienced as complex and confusing — indeed, some of the teenage misery reflects a sense of helplessness and vulnerability generated by feelings of incompetence as a result of which some adolescents develop "psychological problems" and are labelled "emotionally disturbed".

The essential point here is that whilst many forms of turmoil have been identified in adolescence (including the Eriksonian, 1968, major psychosocial crisis of identity versus confusion) emotional disturbance results in only a few cases. Whilst most adolescents report confusion, alienation, self doubt, feelings of unreality and a sense of strangeness, this does not go beyond the normal range except in a minority of cases (Framrose, 1977). Equally, although most adolescents report conflict with parents, it seems that it has been exaggerated as a cause of emotional disturbance, and the more satisfactory the relationships formed with *peers* the more successfully can the adolescents deal with autonomy issues in the family whilst retaining a positive relationship with their parents (Douvan and Adelson, 1966).

Thus although adolescent turmoil reflects many features of neurotic episodes, most adolescents do not experience clinical symptoms of psychiatric disorder, aside from some increase in anxiety and a moodiness that may approach depressive proportions for brief periods. It would be unwise to assume, however, that adolescents will necessarily "grow out" of their problems. The untreated or incompletely treated psychiatric disability of adolescence becomes the psychiatric disability of adulthood. An emotional disorder reflects a basic personality pathology rather than a developmentally induced, time-limited side effect of growth processes (Meeks, 1973).

Much of the research on psychological problems of adolescents has been done by psychiatrists using a medical model but, psychosocial illness, unlike physical illness, is less easily understood in terms of symptoms, diagnosis and causes. Psychosocial illness cannot be conceptualized in the same way as a medical disease and characterized by a common specific aetiology, a common set of observable signs, a known course and a known outcome (Trower 1980, 1981). Instead, for psychosocial illness, the causes are less definite, less tangible and often multiple. Moreover, assignment to a diagnostic category tells us little about the symptomatology of adolescence. Classification is based on the assumption that symptoms often "go together" to form syndromes, but individual differences are quite extensive and vary with demographic characteristics. There are, then, many inadequacies inherent in the classification system and difficulties are often encountered in the examination of the adolescent.

We recognize these difficulties but take the view that categorical concepts, however crude, are necessary for effective discussion of the issues. Therefore, some of the diagnostic classifications used with regard to disturbed adolescents will be described briefly in this section. The focus will be on the symptom of social withdrawal as this is part of syndromes characteristic of emotional disorders. Whilst a psychoanalyst would search for the meaning underlying withdrawal, and a behaviourist would treat the withdrawal as the disease itself and recommend treatment to remove the symptom; a social-psychological orientation, more consistent with our background, views such a symptom within a larger social context, and would focus on the responses to the disturbed adolescent which aggravate the existing condition.

Similarly, we are concerned with emotional disturbance as a cause of social withdrawal, although much can be written about other causes of adolescent social withdrawal (such as physical handicap, Dorner, 1975; Harper and Richman, 1978; hyperactivity, Hoy *et al.*, 1978; depression, Inamdar, *et al.*, 1979; schizophrenia, Kohn and Clausen, 1955; Siomopoulos, 1980; or "borderline cases", Gunderson and Kolb, 1978). Much research on these other topics has concerned the ways in which relationship disturbance may result from, or be an antecedent of, these other conditions but our concern in this chapter is with the aetiology of social withdrawal and emotional disturbance when such physical or clinical causes are *not* present to explain the abnormalities.

Some Aetiological Factors in Social Withdrawal

Social support

Increasing attention is being given to the social context in which individuals try to solve their problems. Social support can reduce one's vulnerability to stress by cushioning its impact: for instance, the greater the emotional support provided by their friends, the less likely were university students to report feelings of depression or inadequacy (Liem and Liem, 1976). However, an essential condition for maximizing the benefits from a support system is that of reciprocity (La Gaipa, 1981a); although a confiding relationship provides protection from stress, one-way disclosure is unlikely to have long-term benefits. Thus the effects of a confidant in mediating the influence of stress depend on the reciprocity of the relationship (Surtees, 1980), and disturbed adolescents may be affected by this because they lack the skills necessary to maintain reciprocal relationships.

The family is crucial in establishing basic trust in the child. Pollack and Bjork (1978) observed seriously disturbed adolescents during group therapy and their case histories revealed that 70% came from broken homes, characterized by abrupt separations and abandonments by the family. In the group sessions it was noted that these adolescent patients were quick to laugh and to strike out at each other; but they had little hope of ever being able to form a mutual bond with one another and there was little authentic communication of empathy towards one another. These adolescents, then, lacked the supportive situation needed to develop basic trust, hope, tolerance, and the capacity for intimacy.

There is also reason to believe that the level of success that adolescents experience in coping with the psychosocial conflicts of this period is influenced by the nature of "trust" experiences in childhood. For instance, the degree to which withdrawn pre-adolescents are egocentric or socio-centric depends on the trust level established in earlier stages of psychosocial development (Wood, 1976; Wood and La Gaipa, 1978). It may be the personal outlook of the socially withdrawn which is affected, and in a study in which pre-adolescents were asked to "make up a story" about the actions of children in vignettes, the normal girls were more likely to assign positive motives and tended to "see the good" in the situation whilst the withdrawn preadolescent girls were more pessimistic and viewed their social world as less friendly than the others (Klein and La Gaipa, 1978). Certainly, such a negative interpersonal orientation is related in some way to the social behaviour of the withdrawn (cf. Howells, this volume).

Personality

The self-report test scores of the emotionally disturbed can provide some clues as to the nature of their social inadequacies. As compared to normals, disturbed adolescents were found to have lower scores on nurturance and affiliation, and higher scores on succorance (Small *et al.*, 1979). These results were interpreted as indicating that the disturbed are less mature in the ability to give, and are primarily help-seekers rather than help-givers: this could help to explain the difficulties in maintaining reciprocal relationships. In a similar study, analysis of the MMPI profiles of disturbed adolescents suggested that they are immature, egocentric, resentful of authority and act in a self-defeating manner. Feelings of alienation and isolation were combined with thought confusion, though the nature of the impact of such deficits was not established (Archer *et al.*, 1979).

Some adolescents don't "get involved" with others because of low motivation for affiliation, whilst others avoid close relationships because of conflicts between the need for affiliation and fear of affiliation. Draper and La Gaipa (1980) examined TAT-type fantasy productions of university room-mates scored for affiliative conflict. Conflict scores were related to the quality of the relationship. High conflict dyads reported tension in the relationship, fewer mutual activities, and little effort toward maintaining the relationship. A distortion index was also calculated based on the difference between what each member of the pair reported giving and the other reported receiving. High distortion was associated with tension, lower trust and lower levels of friendship. It was concluded that affiliative needs and conflicts have an impact on the accuracy of self-monitoring of the exchange of rewards.

Cognitive structure

Social behaviour is influenced by the way the individual organizes and interprets his/her social world and the nature of the cognitive structure is related to behaviour. Hayden *et al.* (1977) assessed the cognitive structure of emotionally disturbed adolescent boys. Level of social adjustment was found to be related to the degree of construct differentiation and the accuracy in predicting the sequence of another's behaviour. Cognitive deficits that lead to reduction in accuracy of social perception, then, reduce the effectiveness of social encounters.

Friendship expectations are a component of a person's cognitive structure, and may have a significant impact on the nature of social relationships. An assumption underlying the construction of the La Gaipa (1977) Friendship Inventory was that individuals with interpersonal problems have atypical views of friendship. Since individuals diagnosed as psychiatric cases often have adjustment problems, we reasoned that their friendship expectations would differ from a so-called normal population, and the Friendship Inventory was administered to psychiatric patients undergoing treatment for schizophrenia or neurosis (Engelhart *et al.*, 1975). Overall, the psychiatric group placed much less value on similarity in friendship than was found in an early normative study. Perhaps this was due to the belief that similar psychiatric patients could not help them satisfy what they needed in friendship but an alternative explanation is that exposure to a "mirror-image" of themselves would be disturbing. Neurotics and schizophrenics differ from normals in the importance attached to strength of character in friendship, i.e. the possession of admirable character traits. The schizophrenics rated character as more important than did the normals, whilst the neurotics rated it as less important. Again, the underlying dynamics are not clear, but, for the schizophrenics, identification with a "superior" person might help them approximate their own high ideals and expectations.

The friendship expectations of neurotics appear to depend on gender differences. On several dimensions, the male neurotics are more like the female normals than like the female neurotics, suggesting a possible confusion of sexual role definition within the neurotic group. This is seen, for instance, in the greater importance attached to Self Disclosure by male neurotics and lesser importance assigned to disclosure by female neurotics. This finding suggests the presence of a tender, feminine-like receptivity in male neurotics in focusing on warmth, emotional and intimate qualities of friendship, whereas the female neurotics are focusing instead on their independence and self-sufficiency.

Eysenck and Claridge (1962) have made a distinction between introverted and extroverted neurotics, claiming that the label "neurotic" is too broad to make accurate predictions. La Gaipa and Engelhart (1977) found support for this position, but noted that sex differences again are important. For instance, when extroverted, neurotic males expect more self disclosure in a close relationship than do stable males. The opposite was found, however, for females. Only when they are introverted do neurotic females expect more self disclosure in a relationship than do stable females.

Behavioural disorders: withdrawal versus aggression

Little research has been done on behavioural disorders of adolescents, and what has been done has been quite atheoretical. We have conducted a series of studies to identify factors contributing to withdrawn and aggressive behaviour within the framework of Erikson's (1968) psychosocial theory of development. The initial task was to develop an instrument for identifying specific behavioural patterns in adolescents. The available techniques were effective in identifying the accepted and the rejected, but were less reliable in differentiating aggressives from the socially withdrawn. Results of a factor analytic study of preadolescents provided the basis for the construction of a "Guess Who" sociometric test (Wood, 1972; La Gaipa and Wood, 1973) from which emerged three behavioural patterns reflected in popular, aggressive and withdrawn dimensions. The Popular dimension characterizes children who are task-oriented leaders, but who are also high on socio-emotional activity, and show consideration and understanding. The Aggressive dimension characterizes persons who are disruptive and annoy others; are unco-operative, want things their own way, and are prone to quarrel with others. The Withdrawn dimension characterizes children who are self conscious; too shy to make friends easily; don't enjoy being with others, get embarrassed easily and do not appear to be noticed by their classmates. The withdrawn are treated with indifference, whereas the aggressives are actively rejected by their peers. Because problems may be faced in the use of a sociometric test, the "Guess Who" items were incorporated into a teacher rating format called the Behavioural Description Form (BDF).

Next, the Children's Friendship Expectancy Inventory (CFEI) was developed to tap social cognitions involving friendship in the form of conceptions, values and expectations (La Gaipa and Wood, 1976; Wood and La Gaipa, 1978; La Gaipa, 1981b). A basic assumption underlying the construction and standardization of the CFEI is that people having atypical conceptions of friendship are likely to encounter problems in establishing and maintaining friendships. The instructions in this inventory were to rate each statement in terms of its importance as a quality in a best friend. The scoring system derived from factor analysis taps four dimensions.

Conventional Morality taps the character traits of a potential friend rather than the quality of the relationship itself: for instance, does not lie or cheat; never gets me into trouble. The *Mutual Activities* dimension taps common interests and stimulation value: for instance, enjoy playing the same games and sports; have fun together. Again, the quality of the relationship is secondary. *Empathic Understanding* describes a friend that is sensitive to one's feelings and who demonstrates warmth, rapport and trust. One can talk about personal problems with such a person. *Loyalty and Commitment* describe a friend who will remain a friend regardless of the cost or sacrifice involved. It deals with the strength of the relationship or its resistance to dissolution.

The first study examined the relationship between behavioural patterns and friendship expectations. Do the socially withdrawn and the aggressive pre-adolescents differ from the popular children in what they consider important qualities in a best friend? The withdrawn personality rated Empathic understanding, and Loyalty and Commitment as less important qualities in friendship than the popular, but no difference was found between these two groups on Conventional Morality or Mutual Activities. This suggests a developmental interpretation, since Empathy and Loyalty scales tap abstract and internal dimensions of friendship, whereas Conventional Morality and Mutual Activities touch on the more external and more superficial aspects of a relationship. The withdrawns, then may be developmentally behind the populars, in so far as these more abstract dimensions are known to occur at later stages of social development (Bigelow and La Gaipa, 1975). An unexpected finding was that the aggressives rated Empathy at the same high level as did the populars and as more important to friendship than was expressed by the withdrawns. High aggressives differ also from low aggressives in assigning more importance to Conventional Morality, Empathic Understanding, and Loyalty and Commitment. Such findings pose some challenging questions for future research. If the socially withdrawn display little empathy and loyalty in their peer interactions, is this value orientation the "cause" or "effect" of their limited group exposure? Why is it that the aggressives "think" like the populars, but act in such a way as to evoke rejections? Do the aggressives lack the skills necessary for translating their beliefs about friendship into action?

The finding that pre-adolescents with different behavioural patterns vary in their conceptions of friendship raises the broader theoretical question regarding the role of social development in acceptance-rejection. A second study was conducted to determine if there are differences in behavioural type in the nature of psychosocial crisis resolution. Erikson (1968) posits eight psychosocial stages of development that can be viewed as evolving in a step-by-step fashion through a hierarchical arrangement of stages. A conflict or crisis comes into focus at each stage and how it is resolved leaves an impact on the resolution of crises at later stages. The specific developmental crisis for the first six stages are as follows: trust *vs* mistrust; autonomy *vs* shame and doubt; initiative *vs* guilt; industry *vs* inferiority; identity *vs* confusion; followed by intimacy *vs* isolation.

The Eriksonian model has generated relatively little research because of the lack of reliable instruments for testing the model, although Boyd (1964) developed a Picture Series Test for assessing this theory. We revised some of the TAT-type pictures and the coding instructions, so that the first four pictures tap the first four stages of Erikson's psycho-social stages and a fifth picture was added as an additional measure of the fourth stage, but based on the Sullivanian (1953) developmental notion of sociocentrism *vs* egocentrism. This was necessary because Erikson posits that interpersonal crisis occurs in late adolescence, whereas Sullivan focuses on pre-adolescence.

The socially withdrawn adolescent was found to differ quite dramatically from the populars in the adequacy of such resolutions. In their responses to the TAT pictures, the stories made up by the withdrawn had more themes denoting shame and doubt (stage 2); much less initiative and more evidence of guilt feelings (stage 3); and fewer themes touching on accomplishment (stage 4). The most striking differences were found on the Sullivanian sociocentric–egocentric dimension. The populars showed evidence of sociocentrism in describing story characters that were concerned with the need to establish interpersonal relationships; that viewed their group as friendly, sociable, and made up of persons with common interests. The stories of the populars expressed feelings of warmth and closeness, and an eagerness to join with others. The withdrawns were clearly more egocentric in that the story characters showed a preference to be alone; viewed the group as unfriendly; expressed indifference to others, and even a desire to disrupt the cohesiveness of the group. Overall, the aggressive pre-adolescents showed a similar pattern of poor conflict resolution, particularly in expressing more guilt feelings and more egocentricity than the popular children.

In conclusion, both conceptions of friendship and psycho-social development should be considered in explaining behavioural differences in pre-adolescence. The findings for the withdrawn are more clearcut than for the aggressives in that the atypical conceptions of friendship of the withdrawn are consistent with their nonacceptance. No difference was found between the withdrawn and aggressive preadolescents in psychosocial development: both groups were developmentally behind the populars. This finding supports the Eriksonian notion that social development is influenced by the quality of conflict resolution.

Sex differences were relatively minor in the Wood and La Gaipa studies on behavioural problems of pre-adolescence. The major sex difference was that females consider empathic understanding as more important than the males. Other investigators have found some differences in behavioural patterns as a function of gender. Achenbach and Edelbrock (1979) suggest that in adolescent years withdrawal is not the same for boys and girls. Among adolescent boys withdrawal was combined with enough aggressive and destructive behaviours to warrant the term hostile withdrawal but, by contrast, withdrawal in adolescent girls seemed accompanied by enough depressive features to be termed depressed withdrawal.

Douvan and Adelson (1966) identified some of the characteristics of adolescent females that were socially isolated from their peers. Essentially, the major factor appeared to be developmental lag. These isolated girls showed a general immaturity and were behind their peer group in establishing independence from their parents, being self-conscious, self-absorbed, insecure, disorganized and having low esteem.

The Social Context and Problems in Friendship

The stigmatized adolescent

The social and psychological environment of the emotionally disturbed is created to some extent by the attitudes of those with whom they come in contact. The attitudes toward the emotionally disturbed are not too unlike attitudes toward the disabled and Siller (1976) notes that the public, verbalized attitudes toward such persons are, on average, mildly favourable whilst indirect evidence suggests that the deeper, unverbalized attitudes are frequently hostile. Such attitudes, then, are typically unfavourable, despite what most people say when asked.

One source of prejudice toward any group is the negative behaviour of its members. The emotionally disturbed adolescents have a higher incidence of negative behaviour, but it appears to vary with the nature of the disturbance (Battle and Lacey, 1972). In research we have done, "moral character" was not an important dimension in the perception of the emotionally disturbed, but we have found that anti-social, deviant behaviour is an important cause of the termination of friendship in adolescence. After "disloyalty" the most important reason given by adolescents for breaking a relationship was such negative behaviour as fighting, lying, and the use of drugs (Bigelow and La Gaipa, 1980). The parents of adolescents also focus on the "sound character" of their children's friends rather than the more existential qualities such as authenticity and empathy (Clyne and La Gaipa, 1976).

Whether or not parents discourage their "teenagers" from associating with other emotionally disturbed adolescents has not been studied.

The label "emotionally disturbed" is a stigma that affects the perception of the disturbed adolescent by others and even by himself/herself. Stigma refers to an attribute that is deeply discrediting, and a stigmatized person is one who is thought to be not quite human or normal (Goffman, 1963). Expressions of repulsion, fear and anxiety, be they direct or indirect, are likely to have an impact on the self-concept of the emotionally disturbed adolescent (cf. Safilios-Rothschild, 1970). The negative feedback can evoke a view of self that is worthless, unreliable and despicable and this problem is made more serious by the tendency for the disabled to internalize views they perceive others to hold of them. Internalization of negative attitudes and stereotypes can then influence the quality of subsequent interactions.

The notion of the "negative mirror-image" may be useful in accounting for prejudice toward the emotionally disturbed adolescent. A person's self-concept can be said to include both an ideal image of what he/she would like to become and a negative image of what he/she fears becoming. The non-disabled person is fearful of disablement, disfigurement, loss of sensory capacity, loss of self control, being economically dependent and mentally disturbed (Gellman, 1959). The generalized fear is that of incompetence, in whatever form. People who possess those characteristics that dramatize what one fears becoming, then, are likely to cause intense discomfort and anxiety arousal. Thus a disturbed or handicapped person may provide an unwanted negative mirror-image of what we fear becoming. Neither the nature of the disturbance not its severity appear to be directly related to the intensity of the affective response to the disturbed person. Doctor and Sieveking (1970) observed that the more mildly impaired individuals are more psychologically threatening than the severely impaired individuals. Perhaps, the highest level of identification occurs with the less severe cases because the difference between self and other is not as great.

What we fear becoming can be understood in terms of its polar opposite as expressed in societal values. The ideal of wholeness is evident in social customs and norms that focus on wholeness, youth, and bodily perfection and health and these are an important source of prejudice towards the handicapped and disturbed (Gellman, 1959). Other social ideals besides wholeness and self competence that deserve consideration include kindness and charity to the less fortunate, and the ideal of authenticity as defined in terms of the relationship between inner thoughts and external actions. Disparities between the "ideal" and "real" create anxieties and guilt. The coping mechanisms used by both the disturbed and nondisturbed will be discussed shortly.

Interaction strains

The maintenance of "normal, smooth or unruffled" interactions with the emotionally disturbed is not always an easy task. Such interactions can be crippled both by the symptoms themselves and the reactions of the disturbed to the stigmatization. Any condition that makes communication difficult or involves unusual or unpredictable behaviour, can disrupt the customary pattern of social life, and is likely to be outside the accepted range for many adolescents. The non-disabled, then, are at a disadvantage because their ordinary social equipment is inadequate for coping with these new situations. Essentially, many adolescents lack the social skills to cope with the demands placed on them in such interactions. Friends and acquaintances either find it difficult to interact with disabled persons or they actually avoid or abandon them (Smith-Hanen, 1976).

Guilt feelings may have an impact on behaviour, such as to evoke excessive attention, or verbal avoidance of the problem or sugarcoating the reality of the disturbance or handicap. Self-awareness of inconsistencies between verbal response and negative, nonverbal behaviour may evoke attempts to be more reassuring that sometimes backfire into an oversolicitous and patronizing attitude.

The nondisturbed adolescent may seek to provide support and reassurance to a disturbed adolescent but often is not very convincing. Both role ambiguity and discrepancies in verbal and nonverbal behaviour towards a disturbed adolescent may evoke interactions characterized by uncertainty, awkwardness, hesitancy and tension. Attempts may be made for instance, to avoid topics that are really of concern to the disturbed adolescent. This evasion may be well motivated, but the disturbed adolescent may infer that others are not really interested in his/her feelings.

Tension is often generated by the role ambiguity involved in interactions with the disturbed. The role expectations for the nondisturbed are not sufficiently structured to permit smooth interaction, and the problem is complicated by the possible rejection of a "sick role" by the emotionally disturbed who may not take too kindly to being stigmatized. Assumptions, then, regarding appropriate behaviour are one source of the avoidance problem. Disparities between feelings and beliefs may create some problems in the relationship. While the feelings about the disturbed adolescent may be somewhat negative, the individual may believe that he/she should remain positive, optimistic and cheerful in their interactions. This conflict may result in behaviours which are unintentionally harmful to the disturbed leading to avoidance of open communication (Wortman and Dunkel-Schetter, 1979).

Feelings of inadequacy in dealing with an emotionally disturbed adolescent, then, can generate guilt. One way to reduce guilt feelings is to ridicule or imply that the disturbed adolescent is different — not quite human. This makes it easier to rationalize any reduced efforts to maintain a meaningful relationship with the disturbed person.

A more negative reaction involves derogation. Lerner (1970) theorizes that individuals are motivated to believe in a "just world" in which people "get what they deserve, and deserve what they get". If we can believe that people do not suffer unless something is wrong with them, or they did something wrong, it is possible to feel protected from undeserved sufferings. As applied to an emotionally disturbed adolescent, this would involve "explaining" the disturbance in terms of some negative behaviour, such as taking hard drugs. "He got what he deserved for taking cocaine." Any related drug-abuse would be seen as a cause rather than an effect of the disturbance.

The authenticity dilemma

In the adolescent value system the qualities of honesty and authenticity are at the top of the list as important qualities in people (Comeau, 1980) and in friends (La Gaipa, 1979). Certainly, authenticity is essential in building a relationship, but, perhaps, the nature of its contribution has been distorted. Authenticity reflects a self-oriented system and involves the fidelity of one's own self-expression regardless of its consequences to others. Trilling (1953) has observed that sincerity, not authenticity, is relationship-oriented: Authenticity does not imply a concern for people. Actually, this quality is relatively independent of other dimensions of friendship such as positive regard (La Gaipa, 1977). The significance of authenticity is in the filtering or information search process. Without authenticity, it is difficult to obtain the accurate information necessary for evaluating a candidate for friendship.

Behaviour that is constrained by social obligations or role relations is viewed by many adolescents as, by definition, deceptive and phony, so authenticity is critical also in friendship because it is supposedly free from prescriptions of role behaviour. The constraints or demands of a "sick role" can create a problem in maintaining friendship with a disturbed adolescent since a clinical relationship is quite different from a friendship and one does not take a *friend's* vulnerabilities into account, but rather assumes that the friend has the strength to take care of himself psychologically. "To do otherwise would be to change the relationship into a clinical relationship and thereby to destroy it as a friendship" (Douvan, 1974; p. 26). A friendship with a disturbed adolescent would create a conflict in some non-disturbed adolescents.

The Image of the Disturbed Adolescent

What teenagers feel and think about another adolescent labelled "emotionally disturbed" has received little attention. Since the literature review for this chapter isolated few studies specifically concerned with this stigma, we did our own study. The objectives were to determine the degree of acceptance–rejection; the dimensions used in the perception of the disturbed, and the relative contribution of each factor to acceptance–rejection.

A total of 105 students in their late adolescence were administered an 18-item questionnaire in which an "emotionally disturbed adolescent" was described as being 18 years old, still in school, of the same sex, and as visiting a counsellor once a week for help. The instructions were to indicate the likelihood that the disturbed adolescent would behave the same as a non-disturbed adolescent. The five-point scale of behaviour ranged from expect "much less" to "about the same" to "much more". The source of items included dimensions from the La Gaipa (1977) Friendship Inventory; discussions on the functions of friendship, particularly in Douvan and Adelson (1966), and studies on the social adjustment problems of the physically disabled.

The first objective on the degree of acceptance semed important because of the known hypersensitivity of teenagers to rejection that can approach a paranoid intensity. For instance, an adolescent girl fears that her friends will abandon her to social isolation. There is a fear that friends are talking about them or are out "to exclude, wound, and humiliate them" (Douvan, 1974, p. 181). The stigma of being emotionally disturbed should add to this anxiety already so prevalent. So are the emotionally disturbed adolescents justified in their fear of being rejected? An estimate of peer acceptance was obtained by a scale in which the students indicated the likelihood that a disturbed adolescent would become a full and accepted member of their group of friends. Twenty per cent indicated that such a likelihood was "the same" for a disturbed as for a non-disturbed adolescent. Three out of four reported that the likelihood was "much less" or "somewhat less". The paranoia, then, appears to have more than a "kernel of truth" to it.

The second objective was to specify the structure of the perception of emotionally disturbed adolescents. To identify the dimensions, the responses to the 18-items were subjected to factor analysis. Four factors were identified that were subjected to varimax rotation. The results of this analysis are presented in Table I. Each factor is presented along with the specific items loading on the factor and serving to define it. The percentage of the explained variance accounted for by each factor is presented in parentheses after the factor name.

TABLE I The image of the emotionally disturbed adolescent: dimensions and factor loadings

---

Instrumentality (65%)
  Peer acceptance (0·79)
  Social validation (0·55)
  Reciprocity (0·52)
  Stimulation value (0·51)
  Helping and support (0·44)
  Ease of communication (0·42)
  Identity (0·41)
Relationship-building (15%)
  Peer acceptance (0·02)
  Predictability (0·59)
  Genuineness (0·55)
  Loyalty and trust (0·56)
  Helping and support (0·47)
  Empathy (0·44)
Spontaneity (13%)
  Peer acceptance (0·17)
  Spontaneity (0·67)
  Mood: even tempered (0·65)
  Non-exploitative (0·55)
Similarity (7%)
  Peer acceptance (0·06)
  Similarity (0·70)
  Obligation-free (0·70)

The first factor, "Instrumentality", was so named because it seems to capture what friendship means to the typical teenager as was so aptly expressed by Douvan and Adelson (1966): "Friendship during the adolescent years carries much of the burden of adolescent growth, and is quite self-serving" (p. 174). Friendship can facilitate meeting such developmental tasks as consolidation of an ego identity, increasing one's social competence, developing communication skills, and so forth. These are the kinds of things that appear to be represented under the category of Instrumentality. It may be observed in Table I that the list is headed by Social Validation, followed by Reciprocity, Stimulation Value, Helping, Identity and Communication which are largely self-oriented gains of friendship. For instance, the identity *vs* confusion conflict, so important in adolescence, can be solved by one member of a dyad whilst the other member continues to experience diffusion.

The critical finding is that Peer Acceptance had a heavy loading on this dimension of Instrumentality. This suggests that the likelihood that a disturbed adolescent will gain acceptance varies with the perceived instrumentality of such a person for satisfying critical needs and functions. The mean ratings of the items categorized under each factor were also examined and the lowest mean scores were found for the instrumentality variables. This indicates that the emotionally disturbed are viewed as "different" from the non-disturbed regarding instrumentality. What is implied here is the view of the emotionally disturbed as being only minimally able to satisfy important needs of the adolescent such as developing an adequate identity and becoming more knowledgeable about the world around them.

A particularly important finding relates to the variable of Social Validation since this has received considerable attention in theorizing about friendship. This item was stimulated by Festinger's (1954) social comparison theory which emphasizes the importance for the individual of assessing the degree to which others share or accept his view of the world. In responding to the label of "emotionally disturbed", the students were asked to indicate how well such a person would be useful in comparing their view of the world to realistically check out impressions of the world and to help validate and verify them. The findings that social validation is an important aspect of instrumentality, and that the disturbed adolescent is rated low on potential for social validation can be interpreted in terms of Duck's (1977) predictive filter model. Duck posits that the appropriate method of validation is through social comparison with the cognitions of others. What this prerequires is an assessment of the value of the other person as a reliable model for comparing oneself. If the other person is not seen as potentially offering the right kind of support, he will not pass through the earlier phase of the filter process and will be ruled out as a more intimate associate. This model seems to describe quite accurately the reactions to the emotionally disturbed adolescent.

The second factor was labelled "Relationship-Building" because it is made up of elements that facilitate the growth of a relationship. The focus here is on interaction-maintenance instead of the self-maintenance represented by the first factor. The qualities included, for instance, predictability, essential in establishing stability in a relationship (see Morton and Douglas, 1981). Other attributes include Loyalty and Trust, Genuineness and Empathy — traits identified by La Gaipa (1977) as important requirements for a close friendship. But, it may be observed in Table I that Relationship-Building is independent of Peer Acceptance. One possible explanation is that the subjects were asked to evaluate the emotionally disturbed adolescent as a potential member of a larger group of friendship than as a "Best Friend". The variables important in early stages of friendship can be quite different than in later stages of friendship (Duck, 1975; La Gaipa, 1977). What Table I suggests is that such expressive variables as Genuineness and Empathy are assigned low priority in the screening phases of friendship formation, at least with regard to the assessment of disturbed adolescents. What the adolescent respondents appear to be saying is this: An emotionally disturbed person may be very honest and loyal, but if he distorts what he sees around him, he can hardly serve as a reliable guide. Honesty will help me to know him better, but not to know better the world around me.

The third factor "Spontaneity" was named after a rating scale with the same label. The opposite of spontaneity is evident when it is necessary to be "on guard" regarding what is said or done, and where there is concern over being misunderstood. The loss of spontaneity evokes an "interaction strain" when there is a need to engage in behaviour thought to be appropriate in the presence of a disturbed person. Goffman (1963) notes that signs of discomfort are evident in guarded references, for instance, certain words like "crazy" become taboo. Other signs of tension in the non-disturbed are evident in artificial levity, compulsive talking, and awkward solemnity. Davis (1961) has observed that one way to handle tension in such situations is to rely on the coping mechanism of superficiality. The lack of spontaneity in a relationship with a disturbed adolescent, then, might stimulate further efforts to keep the relationship at a superficial level, making it even more difficult for the disturbed person to gain genuine acceptance.

This study also suggests that freedom from exploitation is essential in a spontaneous relationship. A problem in friendship with a disturbed person arises from a conflict of roles. The disturbed person may request support that is inconsistent with the expected behaviour for the level of friendship that has been established. When demands are made on the basis of the "sick role", spontaneity is lost, the fear of exploitation increases, and both parties experience difficulty in interpreting the significance and meaning of any helping behaviour.

The fourth factor, "Similarity", is the weakest of the dimensions. It was named after the Similarity variable defined in terms of common interests, common attitudes and values, a compatible personality, and enjoyment of the same activities. We were surprised to find that this factor was independent of Peer Acceptance, as well as Social Validation and Identity. In prior research the relationship between similarity and attraction has been explained, in part, by the notion that similarity facilitates social comparison. The results of this study suggest that when such mediating variables are made explicit, similiarity plays a negligible role in attraction and similarity was found to covary, instead, with freedom from excessive obligations. This was defined as not feeling "duty bound" or "pressured" to come to the aid of the other person. The results suggest that the perception of the emotionally disturbed as dissimilar is associated with feelings of being pressured to provide instrumental aid. No simple explanation is suggested for this relationship. It appears, then, that similarity is a dimension used in the perception of the disturbed, but it makes a negligible contribution to acceptance–rejection.

The third objective of the study was to assess the relative contribution of each of the variables predicting peer acceptance. Multiple regression analysis was conducted on the seven variables significantly related to peer acceptance. A multiple r of 0·67 was obtained with four of these variables. Essentially, then, the best prediction of acceptance–rejection is possible with the following variables presented in order of importance, though of about equal weight: the best predictor was that of Stimulation Value. This was defined as having good times together, fun to be with and a good sense of humour. The second was Identity described in terms of helping to understand oneself better; getting a sense of who you really are, finding out more about oneself. The third variable was Helping and Support which was described as the behaviour of a person who is concerned with your welfare and helps to promote it; someone who acts in ways that show concern for your well being, and who comes to your aid when needed. The fourth variable was Ease of Communication. This is someone easy to talk to. No problem exists in maintaining a flow of conversation, and the relationship itself is free from tension. The variable of Ease of Communication is particularly important with regard to the emotionally disturbed. The nonverbal behaviours that occur when disturbed adolescents interact with non-disturbed adolescents is an area rich with research possibilities. Some clues are suggested by research on confrontations between able-bodied and handicapped individuals. The able-bodied often express their discomfort in such situations by more rigid and controlled motor activity, fewer smiles, greater interpersonal distance, and earlier exits than they demonstrated when interacting with other able-bodied individuals (Wortman and Dunkel-Schetter, 1979). Such disturbed interactions are characterized by being overcontrolled, inhibited and stereotyped (English, 1971). Information on nonverbal behaviour is essential for understanding the interactions between the disturbed and the non-disturbed, since nonverbal behaviours are likely to receive more attention than verbal behaviours in such dyadic relationships. This is because verbal behaviour becomes less credible as a source of information when the question of authenticity is salient.

The multivariate techniques used in this study have isolated four rather divergent areas of concern regarding decisions to interact or not to interact with the emotionally disturbed. Stimulation value is almost hedonistic in overtone. Identity is a more self or ego-relevant notion. Helping touches on the basics of instrumental aid and support. Ease of Communication, instead, focusses on the relationship itself, particularly freedom of tension, so essential in authentic communication. The criterion of instrumentality that dominates the thinking of the non-disturbed in responding to the emotionally disturbed can be defined largely in terms of these four characteristics.

The data we have collected on the emotionally disturbed, taps assumptions, beliefs and stereotypes, so the responses to the task probably reflect actual experiences to a very small degree. It is unwise to generalize about the operationalization of these dimensions in actual face-to-face relationships with the emotionally disturbed, but research in related areas of prejudice would suggest that direct experience with the emotionally disturbed would not necessarily make these "attitudes" more positive — indeed the opposite is as likely to occur. The relevance of such a cognitive map of responding to the emotionally disturbed is that the assumptions and beliefs may influence the likelihood of initial contact and serve to "filter" out emotionally disturbed individuals in the process of selecting from a pool of potential friends. Such stereotypes, of course, may also affect how adolescents behave in social interaction, and so influence how the emotionally disturbed react to others. Insofar as an emotionally disturbed adolescent thinks that others consider them "not much fun to be with" the adolescent may become more hesitant in seeking out friends.

Finally, it appears that adolescents, in assessing an emotionally disturbed person as a friend, assign high priority to the ability of such a person to satisfy important needs and problems they face during this period. Instrumentality seems to be the major factor. Perhaps, friendship, as defined existentially in terms of the higher human values, is a luxury that they feel they cannot afford at this time. Insofar as adolescents are looking for reliable support systems, the label that someone is "disturbed" may lead to a prejudgement that such a person lacks the competence to help solve some of the critical issues of adolescence. This may sound like a pragmatic point of view, except for the fact that we are dealing with stereotyped conceptions, and individual differences are likely to be ignored because of the stigma. Some disturbed adolescents can help others to find their way through this difficult period, but are not given the chance because of such assumptions.

Conclusions

We have tried to identify problems faced by disturbed adolescents in friendship. The early stages were emphasized because few studies exist on the development and termination of friendship in this group. Certainly, more research is needed, though we suspect that the problem for many disturbed persons is in the making of friends rather than in keeping them. The reluctance of some adolescents to form friendships with the disturbed obviously results in less freedom of choice and fewer friendship options so that the disturbed adolescents may have to make friends with others who lack essential characteristics. The disturbed, then, often have a poorer original selection from which to filter out undesirable friends and this is likely to contribute to the problems that they face in maintaining effective relationships.

There are several asymmetrical aspects in friendships with the disturbed that are a source of tension. There is asymmetry in the focal concerns of each party since the non-disturbed focus on friendship functions, relevant to the developmental tasks of the adolescent period, such as ego identity whilst the disturbed adolescents, on the other hand, focus on humanistic-existential considerations of personal worth and authenticity: for instance, does this friend show genuine acceptance or is the motivation based instead on kindness and sympathy. Each party emphasizes different criteria in assessing the other, the non-disturbed focusing on the abilities and competence of the disturbed person, while the disturbed is focusing on authenticity and other expressive needs.

Differences in vulnerability can have an impact on a relationship. The non-disturbed are concerned with interpersonal growth, whereas the disturbed are concerned with emotional stability. The problem of vulnerability is particularly serious for the disturbed insofar as he/she worries about the danger of psychosis: "Am I going crazy?" Such anxieties cannot be overlooked in trying to understand the course of friendship between the disturbed and the non-disturbed.

Asymmetry can occur also with regard to social exchange, especially the rules of exchange. The non-disturbed person is likely to be "cost-conscious" and apply a cost/benefit analysis: "What am I getting out out this relationship?" The disturbed person is likely to employ other equity considerations, and to stress "needs" rather than "input": "Since I am not well, I do need more help than most people, and I shouldn't be expected to give as much in return." Imbalances in the short-run are inconsequential, but in the long-run, they will provoke conflict.

Asymmetry is also reflected in the mirror-image that each party provides the other. The image received by the non-disturbed could be a source of discomfort and arousal, particularly if the non-disturbed already has existing doubts about his/her competency, and latent anxieties or concerns may be activated by interaction with the disturbed. There is some evidence also that the disturbed adolescent avoids other disturbed adolescents because the mirror-image provided by similar others accentuates and reinforces existing anxieties. In either case, the negative mirror-image operates to restrict still further the range of likely candidates for friends.

These aspects of asymmetrical elements in friendship facilitate tension and conflict in relationships, the resolution of which is difficult because each party is to some degree concerned with a different set of goals and need priorities. Such asymmetry, then, hinders the accommodations and negotiations essential for the maintenance and growth of a relationship, as well as for successful conflict resolution.

In conclusion, many adolescents think of the disturbed as being "different". The actual differences may have been exaggerated, but the problem remains in the "meshing" of divergent needs in critical areas of the relationship. Finally, it is not uncommon for an adolescent to find it difficult to form friendships. The psychological problems of the disturbed simply add an additional barrier to the achievement of friendship.

CHAPTER 9

The Relationships of Depressed Persons

Windy Dryden

To attempt a comprehensive review of the nature of relationships and relationship difficulties of a broad spectrum of persons experiencing psychological difficulties would be a monumental task, yet such a task is a necessary enterprise and the brave person who embarks upon it will ultimately produce a work of several volumes. The scope of the present chapter is, however, more modest and its aims limited. I have chosen to restrict myself to "depression as a focal form of psychological difficulty," because the research carried out on the relationships of depressed individuals, although modest in itself, is (in the author's opinion) richer than comparable research with other populations. Given this restriction, three tasks will be undertaken: (1) the exposition of three frameworks for understanding the relationships of depressed persons by means of the presentation of a review of relevant research literature; (2) the discussion of two attempts at integration of these different approaches; (3) the extraction of implications for the treatment of depressed individuals.

Most writers in the field of depression have stressed either cognitive, intrapersonal determinants (e.g. Beck *et al.*, 1979) or interpersonal determinants (e.g. Hinchcliffe *et al.*, 1978) in their quest to unravel the complicated processes which appear to be involved in the development and maintenance of depression. Adherents to the intrapersonal viewpoint stress the

191

cognitive factors involved and, although acknowledging that interpersonal processes have some relevance, tend to de-emphasize their influence in theory building. A "middle" perspective on depression is one developed by Lewinsohn and his colleagues (e.g. Libet and Lewinsohn, 1973, 1974; Youngren and Lewinsohn, 1980). This perspective emphasizes the depressed person's presumed lack of social skills which lead them to the types of interpersonal settings (both impoverished and conflictual) where depression is maintained. The adherents of the truly interpersonal viewpoint, however, argue that the depressed person has the kind of impact on *other* people that diminishes the quality of their interpersonal experiences and their consequent interactive styles.

The result of these parallel activities in the research is that we now have a reasonably detailed understanding of how depressed persons construe the world and the errors that they commit in making these constructions. We also have an increasingly clearer picture of the interpersonal settings in which a patient's experience of depression develops and/or is maintained. Very few writers have attempted to give *both* intrapersonal *and* interpersonal factors sufficient consideration in a more comprehensive view of depressive phenomena. However, two sets of theorists (Feldman, 1976; Rush *et al.*, 1980) have done this and I shall accordingly give their work attention in some detail in a later section. In the following section I will first review the research that relates to three other perspectives on the relationships of depressed persons.

Three Perspectives on the Relationships of Depressed Persons

In this section I shall review three particular perspectives (*viz.* the cognitive, the social skill and the interpersonal approaches) that are specifically directed at the explanation of the relationships of depressed persons. The reader is again reminded that the review is selective.

The cognitive perspective

The cognitive perspective on depression holds that people become depressed as a result of the ways in which they process information about themselves, about other people, and about the world in general. Two major proponents of this view are Ellis (1962) and Beck *et al.* (1979). Beck *et al.* postulate three major concepts to explain depressive phenomena. The first ("the cognitive triad") consists of three components. The depressed individual tends to view himself, his present experiences and his future in an idiosyncratic and negatively distorted manner. The second concept ("cognitive schemata") holds that the depressed individual organizes his negative cognitions in structured and stable patterns which may be activated in the right circumstances. The third concept ("faulty information processing") describes the errors in the depressed person's thinking which serve to perpetuate the person's negative views in the face of contradictory evidence. Examples of such faulty thinking styles include "overgeneralizing", (that is, the generalization of fallacious rules on the basis of single instances), "arbitrary inference" (drawing a specific conclusion when evidence to support such a conclusion is absent or contradictory) and "black and white thinking" that is, over rigid and simplistic categorization of events).

Ellis's (1962) cognitive view of depression overlaps with that of Beck *et al.* but places more emphasis on the role of irrational beliefs in depression. Irrational beliefs are characterized by demands made by depressed persons on themselves, others and the world. If these demands are not met, evaluative conclusions are made to the effect that (a) the person, the other or the world is no good, (b) it's awful and (c) the person cannot stand the resulting conditions, Empirical evidence supporting the cognitive view of depression (e.g. De Monbreun and Craighead, 1977; Hammen and Krantz, 1976; Krantz and Hammen, 1979; and Nelson and Craighead, (1977) exists but some studies have failed to confirm this theory (e.g. Frost *et al.*, 1979). However, research linking depressogenic cognition to the relationships of depressed persons is lacking. Thus the present analysis must necessarily be speculative in nature.

The view that depressogenic cognitions underlie the way depressed persons interact with others in their life space is one that has been implicit in the writings of the cognitive theorists rather than one that has been systematically studied. Consider an example. One of the frequent themes that depressed patients present in therapy is the theme "I am helpless". In relationships with significant persons in their life, such patients often place the other in the role of "rescuer", so that the other carries out certain activities on behalf of the patient. Such a relationship may or may not be characterized by resentment. When anger is absent both partners are relatively unambivalent with the roles which they have come to adopt. The patient's depressive symptoms in this scenario often increase when the other (through absence or incapacity) is unable to continue to rescue the patient. When anger is present, one or both persons are ambivalent with the role system that has developed between them. There the patient often devalues himself for having the helpless self-image and is simultaneously pleased and resentful that the other is rescuing him. However as McPartland and Hornstra (1964) note, when a patient's request for help in this manner is not satisfied, primarily because (for the patient) the veracity of the motives of others is doubted, the patient's request becomes more diffuse, aimed less at a specific audience; his symptoms become more severe, associated with a more debasing self-image and others in his life space respond more and more negatively (as a result of his despair) so a dire cycle of increasing alienation is established.

One cognitive theme often neglected in writings on depression is that of "poor me". "Poor me" thinkers often sulk when their "needs" are considered unmet. Sulking is a behavioural style which in addition to reflecting "poor me" thinking also serves to punish the other who is viewed as depriving the person of what he considers he must have. Sulking as a behavioural style often elicits one of two major responses to the other. Firstly the other person may increase caring-type responses which has the unfortunate effect of reinforcing sulking behaviour since the depressed person learns that sulking is a good way of getting the caring which may be denied to him through other means. On the other hand, the other person may increase rejecting-type responses which may serve to increase the depressed person's resentment and/or feelings of low self-worth.

The above two examples reflect the role of others as serving as unwitting "accomplices" in perpetuating the patients cognitively based interactive styles (Wachtel, 1977). As Wachtel notes "this process of 'distorted' perception leads to a skewing of responses from others and hence to a 'confirmation' of the problematic way of experiencing" (p. 54). This of course reflects the self-fulfilling prophecies with which academics and clinicians are so familiar (e.g. Trower, this volume).

The picture of the depressed person holding a self-image with a complementary image held of the other person which serves as a blue-print for the interactive arena is much more complicated in reality. A detailed exploration of a depressed patient's phenomenal view of the world and behavioural styles reveals a complicated matrix of self and other images where the person moves from one state to another depending upon responses from others and changing circumstances ("state" being defined by Horowitz, (1979) as "a recurrent pattern of experience and of behaviour that is both verbal and non-verbal").

One important variable that intervenes between the depressed person's cognitive view of the world and the quality of his relationships is his defensive style (Freud, 1936). Take for example, a person with low self-worth. Such patients often believe that they are "worthless", "bad", "evil", etc. However, while for some patients these cognitions are readily accessible, for others their beliefs are sheltered behind a variety of strategies which are designed to protect the individual from his own feelings of inadequacy. Such strategies are often manifested in the interpersonal realm and determine the quality of relationships that the depressed person has. A common strategy employed by some depressed patients to protect themselves from feelings of low self-worth is to criticize others. Transactional analysts call such a strategy "blemishes". Finding blemishes in others helps distract the individual from his own blemishes. Such a strategy often leads to interpersonal friction which is often a feature of depressed women's close interpersonal relationships (Weissman and Paykel, 1974). Another strategy that is used by other depressed patients is withdrawal. For these patients rejection leads to activation of self-devaluing cognitions and this rejection is to be avoided at all costs. One way of doing so is to withdraw from relationships altogether which leads to depression based on a sense of isolation. Another, perhaps less extreme method, is to keep relationships superficial or to ensure that one is the first to end relationships which start to develop. While an acute sense of depression is warded off by such strategies the person is not entirely successful since he still experiences a sense of depression because his relationships are lacking in richness and intimacy. Other people within such a person's life space are often heard to remark that they hardly know the person. Thus an understanding of the depressed person's preferred defensive styles is an important key to understanding his relationships. Unfortunately in their zeal to depart from a psychoanalytic perspective on depression the cognitive theorists have tended not to emphasize defence mechanisms in their explanation of depressive phenomena and the depressed person's relationships.

The social skill perspective

A consideration of social skill factors in depression originated from Lewinsohn's view (1974), that an individual's depression stems from that individual's low rate of response-contingent positive reinforcement. This low rate may stem from the fact that (a) few events are reinforcing for the individual, (b) reinforcing events are unavailable in the individual's life space and (c) the individual due to social deficits, does not emit responses that would be reinforced (Blaney, 1977). Lewinsohn's view has led to studies being carried out in all three areas, but it is the last area with which we are concerned here. While Lewinsohn has argued that possession of poor social skills is an antecedent to depression in that it leads to a low rate of positive reinforcement from others, Heiby (1979) has noted that no studies exist where depression has been induced by a reduction in social skill and she concludes that it is thus difficult to ascertain whether possession of poor social skills precedes the onset of depression.

The evidence which exists in this area is correlational in nature and much of the work that has been done on that topic has compared verbal and nonverbal aspects of social skill for depressed and non-depressed subjects.

Hinchcliffe *et al.* (1970) in a semi-structured ten-minute dyadic interview pertaining to the patient's symptoms found that depressed patients maintained less eye contact that did non-depressed (surgical) patients. In a later study these authors found that depressed subjects exhibited a lower rate of speech during verbal interchanges (Hinchcliffe *et al.* 1971a), a finding confirmed by both Shaffer and Lewinsohn (1971) and Libet and Lewinsohn (1973).

Other experimenters have found that depressed persons show less predictable timing of interpersonal responses (Rosenberry *et al.* 1969) and show more ambiguous non-verbal communication (Prkachin *et al.* 1977) than do non-depressed persons. It appears that the experience of depression does interfere with the person's social functioning but the conclusion that depressed persons are thereby deficient in social skills may not be entirely warranted; since it has yet to be shown that such persons also exhibit poor social skills when they are not depressed.

The picture becomes even less clear when we consider Youngren and Lewinsohn's (1980) study. In comparing depressed and non-depressed patients' verbal and non-verbal behaviour in group and dyadic interactions it was found that while self-, peer-, and observer-rated deficiencies in interpersonal style in group interactions were identified in the group condition, no deficits uniquely associated with depression were identified on the verbal and non-verbal behaviour measures in both the group and dyadic interaction settings.

Furthermore different interpretations can be made when even positive results are found. In the Libet and Lewinsohn (1973) study cited above the experimenter had depressed and non-depressed subjects, interacting in group settings. In addition to exhibiting smaller amounts of speech, depressed subjects (1) talked to fewer people in the group than did non-depressed subjects, i.e. they restricted their interpersonal range, (2) took longer to respond than did non-depressed subjects (poor timing) and (3) emitted fewer positive reactions than did non-depressed subjects. Coyne (1976a) has argued that since Libet and Lewinsohn also found a high correlation between rate of positive reactions emitted and rate of positive reactions elicited, while it may be that their depressed subjects did display poor social skills; it could also be that fewer people were willing to interact with the depressed persons because of the negative mood induced in the non-depressed in such an interaction. This might lead the non-depressed subjects to emit fewer positive responses to the depressed subjects thereby reducing the positive responses elicited from the latter. Coyne (1976b) argues that if the behaviour of the depressed person induces negative affect in others which leads others to interact less with the depressed person, then that person may well require a special set of social skills to enable them to maintain social relationships despite such disruption.

This complicated picture of the role of depressed persons' social skills in determining the quality of their relationships is further complicated by other findings. For example, Youngren and Lewinsohn (1980) note that such social skill deficits are likely to be situation specific. In their study when depressed and non-depressed subjects were asked to interact in a group setting (to introduce themselves for three minutes and continue conversing for another 25 minutes) their verbal and non-verbal behaviour patterns (at least on the measures used) were similar. Yet Libet *et al.* (1973) found that depressives are less skilful than non-depressed controls when interacting in less structured therapy groups and in their homes. Unfortunately we do not know what Youngren and Lewinsohn's subjects talked *about* in the ensuing 25 minutes in the group condition. Perhaps they did not continue to talk about themselves which may have made the observable skill variables less apparent since it may only be when depressed subjects focus on their own personal experiences that such factors become salient. Youngren and Lewinsohn also found that the depressed students did not show deficits in social skill in the dyadic condition, which did not confirm earlier findings concerning depressed persons' deficits in frequency and duration of eye contact (Hinchcliffe *et al.* 1971b) and facial expression (Waxer, 1974). Unfortunately again Youngren and Lewinsohn give little information about the content of what was discussed in the dyadic condition making meaningful comparisons difficult.

Whatever it was that made observer and participants comment negatively on the interpersonal style of the depressed subjects in the group condition, this was not tapped in the Youngren and Lewinsohn design. It may be again that in some way depressed persons induce negative mood in their peers and observers, as Coyne (1976b) has argued, but the precise manner in which this is done awaits to be determined in skills-based studies.

Two fruitful areas which are hinted at in the literature on social skills in depressed persons deserve future elaboration. Firstly behavioural observations carried out by the Lewinsohn group in the homes of depressed patients (e.g. Lewinsohn and Shaw, 1969) indicate that social skill deficits are also exhibited by other members of the patient's family. Coyne (1976a, pp. 32–33) argues that "the most useful conceptualization of social interaction involving depressed persons would specify the lack of social skills of all participants as evidenced by their inability to alter the contingencies offered or received. Behavioural interventions in the depressed person's marital and family relationships would therefore involve training all participants in these social skills and go beyond simply altering the contingencies available to the depressed person". Such an approach could be best implemented as part of a more comprehensive approach where the assumptions and beliefs of participants are also made focal.

The second area which deserves more attention is the patterns of self-disclosure employed by depressed patients. Coyne (1976b) carried out a study where non-depressed subjects conversed on the telephone with either a depressed patient, a non-depressed patient or a normal control in an open-ended fashion. In listening to the tapes from the study, Coyne formed the impression that depressed patients were very willing to discuss very personal issues (such as marital infidelities, death and family strife). This suggests that depressed patients display patterns of self-disclosure that are inappropriate to the situation and which may, as Chaikin and Derlega (1974) have shown, lead to the patients being regarded as maladjusted and treated accordingly.

In conclusion, the role of social skill factors in depression and the relationships of depressed patients require further elaboration. Social skill deficits are unlikely to be a universal difficulty for all depressed persons (Lewinsohn *et al.*, 1976). In addition, social skill deficit plays an unclear role in relation to severity of depression since most studies were conducted with moderately depressed persons. Furthermore, the interaction of this factor with the other major factors associated with depression remains unexplored as does the question of how changes in depressive symptomatology may covary with changes in social skill. However, sufficient evidence exists for social skill factors not to be ignored in any framework purporting to clarify depressed patients' relationships.

The interpersonal perspective

The interpersonal perspective on depression focuses on the impact that depressed persons have on others, the quality of relationships that ensue, and the interactive styles that depressed individuals commonly exhibit. In this section, the emphasis will be on both the theoretical and the empirical work that has been done in this area.

(1) The work of the "New Haven" group (USA)

The New Haven group (Myrna Weissman and her colleagues) studied the social relationships of 40 depressed American women between the ages of 25 and 60 who lived in the New Haven area of Connecticut, USA. Initially the women were studied over a 20-month period (Weissman and Paykel, 1974) but the group was followed up four years after the acute depressive episode (Bothwell and Weissman, 1977). All the depressed women (who were mainly drawn from the middle and lower social classes) were clinically depressed for at least two weeks prior to the start of the study. A comparable control group of forty non-depressed women was assessed at the beginning of the study and was also followed up four years later. Subjects' social relationships were assessed by interview on a 48-item Social Adjustment Scale (SAS) which aimed to determine the quality of subjects' relationships in six role areas (work, social and leisure, extended family, spouse, parental and marital family unit).

During the initial twenty-month period in which the depressed women were interviewed on six occasions, the New Haven group found that depression produced far-reaching and lasting social impairments and that specific interactional problems persisted even when the women were symptom-free (Weissman and Paykel, 1974).

Acutely depressed phase. When they were acutely depressed, the women's social impairments extended into all roles (as wife, mother, worker and community member) but were most marked in marital relationships, and parent and worker roles. During this period the patient's subjective distress about role performance was more marked than her objective impairment. While the depressed women tended to withdraw from the *extended* family framework, overt friction in this area was not marked — although the women did harbour unexpressed feelings of resentment and guilt. This somewhat harmonious withdrawal is contrasted with the friction and tension that were a feature of the women's relationships with spouse and children.

The depressed woman's relationship with her spouse was marked by overt friction, poor communication and increased dependency. She might strive to exercise overt control in this relationship through her symptoms and by controlling sexual behaviour, which was reduced in frequency and satisfaction. Women whose marriages were poor prior to the onset of acute depression tended to blame the spouse for their depression, and hostility in these marriages was more marked than in marriages which were adaptive prior to onset. In those marriages, the wife tended to withdraw more from her husband to protect him from the effects of her depression: husbands in the adaptive marriages were more protective than those in the poor marriages.

Relationships with children were also impaired, the type of impairment depending on the age of the children. When offspring were infants, the depressed woman tended to act in an overconcerned, but helpless manner and was sometimes overtly hostile. When the mother had younger school-age children then conflict was less marked than with adolescents although with the former the woman was either emotionally detached or irritable. However there was much conflict with adolescents who tended to be unsympathetic and exploit the mother's helplessness.

Recovery from depression. As the woman became less depressed then the quality of her social relationships improved albeit more slowly than symptomatic improvement. Social adjustment improved most rapidly in the first two months of symptomatic recovery, slowed down during the next two months and then became static. Social improvement, although marked, was not complete, social adjustment was poorer than that of normals. Work performance and relationships improved most rapidly; the woman also began fairly quickly to become less dependent on her family. However the poor communication and interpersonal friction improved much more slowly and the improvement remained incomplete. Even after recovery, relationships with friends and close family were still characterized by interpersonal friction, resentment and arguments.

When depressive symptoms returned, this was accompanied by a quick deterioration of social functioning. Work performance and relationships became worse and the woman's dependency and family attachment increased.

As part of the study, some of the depressed women received individual psychotherapy and were closer to the normals in social functioning than those who did not receive therapy. Weissman and Paykel (1974) argued that psychotherapy had its greatest impact by reducing friction and improving communication. However, as is often the case, those with most marked social adjustment were the women who displayed poorest motivation for treatment.

Four-year follow-up. Bothwell and Weissman (1977) report a follow-up study of both the depressed and control group's social functioning. The findings showed that only a third of the depressed group were free of depressive symptomatology, which, though mild, was accompanied by some social impairments. Such impairments were present in work, marriage, family and extended family units and on three of the six factors examined in the study — work performance, interpersonal friction and anxious rumination. Impairments were not found on the other three factors — inhibited communication, submission dependency and family attachment — and performance in the social and leisure and the parental roles did not differ between the depressed and non-depressed groups.

In the sub-sample of depressed women who were free of symptoms and were considered to have recovered, social impairments were still found on the interpersonal friction factor and in the marital role as compared to the normal group. Such a tendency has distinct implications for clinical practice (see below).

Limits of the study. The New Haven study represents a major contribution to our understanding of the quality of depressed female patients' relationships and the extent of social impairments that is associated with clinical depression. The study is, however, descriptive in nature and can only point to associations between severity of depressive symptomatology and disordered social relationships. The study's findings must be further viewed in the context that only women were studied and thus generalization to the relationships of depressed men may not be warranted. Indeed studies carried out by Norman Kreitman and his colleagues on the marital relationships of neurotic men indicate that depressed men may have a different pattern of relationships at least in the marital area (e.g. Collins *et al.*, 1971). Finally, the data were collected from the woman's perspective only, thus the degree to which this perspective validly represents the actual relationships of depressed women and not their perception of such relationships remains unclear.

(2) *The social context approach*

The social context approach to understanding the relationships of depressed persons is one that has been developed by McPartland and Hornstra (1964) and by Coyne (1976a). It is a perspective which seeks to explain depressive symptoms in terms of message value and intended audience. Thus an understanding of the social context is important to understanding depression. McPartland and Hornstra (1964) hypothesized that critically depressed persons present themselves in ways that are intended for a specific audience i.e. specific people in the depressed person's life space. Such self-presentation tends to take the oblique form of withdrawal from interaction by irritability and agitation, by self-preoccupation or by slowing. The interactive burden is thus thrown on other people since these oblique communications are difficult to ignore. The next set of interactive messages are more diffuse and less answerable and tend to take the form of helpless and hopeless communication. The patient shows lack of energy and vitality and is less able to perform socially necessary acts for physical reasons. The intended audience here appears to be less specific. Next in McPartland and Hornstra's hypothetical order are depressive messages of worthlessness, badness, and evil. These messages tend to be unanswerable for the others in the depressed person's social context and they often respond by calling in outsiders (e.g. physicians). If this depressive drift continues social relationships are often broken off altogether and the person withdraws completely from interaction. Such a psychotic message is too diffuse for comprehension and the intended audience is undifferentiated. McPartland and Hornstra's (1964) view is (a) that depressive themes increase in stridency and become progressively baffling to other people and (b) that the intended audience becomes less differentiated and obscure. Thus a set of interactive stalemates is established, with other people in the social context becoming increasingly impotent in their attempts to alleviate the person's suffering. McPartland and Hornstra (1964) by analysing the clinical records of patients hospitalized for depression, found some evidence for their views by categorizing depressive themes (as those identified above) and relating them to patient diagnosis and degree of patient life space disruption. However they did not study whether patients progress along their continuum of depressive drift as hypothesized; yet this would seem an important test of their theory.

Coyne (1976a) drawing on McPartland and Hornstra's (1964) analysis conceptualized depression as a self-perpetuating interpersonal system. He sees depressive symptoms as being congruent with the developing inter-personal context of the depressed person and as having a mutually maintaining relationship with responses from others in the depressed person's life space. The depressed person and others in this social context combine to create a system in which feedback cannot be received and various attempts to effect change serve only to maintain the system.

While McPartland and Hornstra's (1964) analysis did not provoke much research, perhaps because their ideas were put forward when systems theory was not in vogue, Coyne's (1976a) approach was more successful in stimulating research. This research has tended to be laboratory based, using depressed college students as subjects and to be focussed on the response of others to the depressed person in initial short interactions between the depressed person and a stranger.

Coyne (1976b) carried out the first of these studies. Students were asked to take part in a study of the acquaintance process and conversed on the telephone for twenty minutes with either a depressed patient, a non-depressed patient or a normal control. All target individuals were female. Interacting with the depressed patients induced negative affect in the students. They were more depressed, anxious, hostile and less willing to engage in future interaction after speaking with the depressed patient than when speaking with the non-depressed patient or normal control. Depressed patients were seen as making less of an effort than the other target individuals to present themselves in a socially desirable manner, they were viewed as being more depressed in reality and were not seen as deliberately seeking sympathy.

Three studies have looked at the differential effect of male and female depressed persons on others. In Hammen and Peters' (1977) study (which did not involve interaction) subjects were asked to read stimulus materials portraying either a male or a female student with reactions of depression, anxiety or blurred affect in response to an identical stressor. Depressed men were evaluated more negatively than were depressed women. Such differences were not found when anxiety or blurred affect reactions were portrayed. A discriminant analysis suggested that males were rejected for departing from a typical male role. Such a suggestion was subsequently explored by Hammen and Peters (1978). Students were asked to take part in a study of first impressions in same sex or opposite sex pairs. They had a five minute telephone conversation with a student who enacted either a depressed or a non-depressed role. Depressed persons were more strongly rejected than non-depressed persons particularly by persons of the opposite sex. Significantly more feminine traits were attributed to depressed than non-depressed persons, a finding which confirmed Hammen and Peters' (1977) previous suggestion. Males may thus learn to express their distress in more socially acceptable ways, which may account for the greater incidence of depression in women than men. Sex differences however, were not found on mood induction measures. Coyne's (1976b) finding was replicated here. Interactions with a depressed person induced more depression in the listener than did interactions with the non-depressed person.

None of the studies on responses of others to depressed persons reviewed so far, has attempted to study the subject's behaviour while interacting with depressed persons. Howes and Hokanson's (1979) study was designed to examine behavioural aspects of a subject's response. Student subjects were left alone for seven minutes with a same-sex confederate (who assumed a depressed role, a non-depressed role, or a physically ill role) on the pretext of waiting together for an experiment to begin. Subjects who waited and talked with the "depressed" person spoke less, made more directly negative comments and responded with a higher proportion of silences. As in the three aforementioned studies, subjects were more rejecting of their "depressed" partners and described them in more negative terms and as having greater interpersonal impact than partners in other roles. However, unlike the other studies, no induced mood differences were found — which suggests that differential responses to depressed persons may not be based solely on induced negative affect. Expressions of direct support to "depressed" partners were equivalent to those made to the "physically ill" partner and greater than those made to the normal partner. Thus both positive and negative responses to depressed persons were found in this study which provides support for Coyne's (1976a) description of a double message given by others, consisting of reassurance and rejection. This may make it difficult for the depressed person to believe in the sincerity of the other's reassurance, a frequently repeated claim by depressed patients.

It is clear then, that in such initial interactions, depressed persons have a negative impact on others. However, the contents of such interactions were not studied. This was the major focus of a study by Hokanson *et al.* (1980), where three groups of subjects (depressed, other psychological problems, and normal) interacted with a same-sex normal partner in a modified two-person prisoner's dilemma game in which each player's relative power was manipulated. Partners were also allowed to communicate with one another by previously-devised one sentence statements. When depressed persons were in the high power role they were exploitative and noncooperative but also communicated high levels of self-devaluation, sadness and helplessness. This set of interpersonal responses elicited extrapunitiveness, noncooperation and helplessness in their partners. Depressives in the low-power role while not differing from the other psychological problem and normal group in game behaviours did send more helpless and self-devaluation messages. They also blamed their partner for their low-power position. This pattern led to more ingratiating behaviours in their partners. Thus low-power depressives may elicit responses which may reinforce their interpersonal style. However the fact that low-power depressives blamed the other for their conditions may then lead them to be rejected by those who were once ingratiating.

In the Hokanson *et al.* (1980) study, while participants interacted from position of unequal power — a situation reflecting the unequal relationships that depressed persons are often involved in — they were not involved in face to face interaction. Participants could communicate only by pressing buttons or by sending a restricted and pre-designed set of one-sentence statements. Thus only tentative suggestions can be made relating these findings to every day interactions of depressed persons.

While the social context view is one that has made predictions concerning the developing relationships of depressed persons and those with whom they are involved, the research stimulated by this model has been laboratory-based and thus has not tested these predictions, one notable exception being the work carried out by Hinchcliffe *et al.* (1978) which we will consider in the next section.

(3) *The work of the "Bristol" group (England)*

Hinchcliffe *et al.* (1978) report on a large-scale study designed to test the view that depressive symptoms are indicative of an interpersonal system that has reached a state of pathological homeostasis. Hinchcliffe's research group expected to find indices of this pathological equilibrium, and in order to examine this view they asked patients who were hospitalized for depression to interact with their spouse and a stranger when in hospital. The task of the dyad was to attempt to reach agreement or "agreed disagreement" on two or three issues where they held initially different views. Twenty minutes of the interaction were videotaped. The depressed patient interacted with their spouse again on recovery. As a control, patients hospitalized for non-psychiatric reasons (surgical) interacted with their spouses while in hospital.

The group expected to find significant differences in the communicative style of the depressed and non-depressed couples and that such differences would be reduced with the recovery of the patients. They also anticipated the finding that the communicative style of the depressed patient and spouse would be significantly different from that of the patient and stranger. Communication styles were assigned on four dimensions: (1) Expressiveness (the interactive content as reflected in speech); (2) Responsiveness; (3) Disruptions in communication, and (4) Power (how the participants attempt to control the interaction). When "expressiveness" was considered, marked differences were found in the expressive style of depressed men as compared with depressed women. The males showed high levels of tension and hostility when they were depressed, their wives showing tense and anxious behaviour. On recovery the men had returned to their usual instrumental role, negative tension was significantly reduced and their wives displayed more relaxed behaviour. The depressed women and their spouses showed high levels of negative tension (anxious and hostile behaviour) and this negative expressive style was maintained at recovery. This finding confirms Weissman and Paykel's (1974) findings that interpersonal friction was a feature of the relationship between their sample of depressed women and their spouses even when the women were not symptomatically depressed. These differences between male and female patients' expressiveness must be tempered by the group's view that the females had poorer premorbid marital adjustment than did the males.

The negative expressive styles of the depressed couple was not a feature of the patients' interaction with the stranger confirming that the marital system is important in determining negative expressiveness. The control couple's interaction was marked by their ability to disagree with one another but yet compromise their differences amicably.

When "responsiveness" was considered, the picture emerged that the depressed couple were responsive to one another. They showed more formality of style than the control couple especially when the patient was female. This formality was reduced at the time of recovery. The depressed couples were seen to be more self-centred than the surgical couples, relating the topics to their own situation more than the control couple who were happy to discuss the situation more objectively. In general male patients were more able to focus on the task than female patients at the time of their depressive episode indicating that depressed women may disrupt everyday task-centred communication by focussing on non-task issues. An interesting finding emerged when depressed male patients were compared with their male non-patient counterparts. At the time of their hospitalization they showed greater preoccupation with their wife's opinions than on recovery, indicating increased dependency. Male non-patients were more preoccupied with their own opinions when their wives were depressed than when their wives had recovered. This indicated that one major difficulty in the female patient marriage is that their husbands (through emotional detachment) had become insensitive to their wife's opinion.

When "communication disruption" was considered, depressed couples exhibited a great deal of negative tension release i.e. tense emotional outbursts (at the time of the depressed episode) which were not a feature of depressed patients' interaction with strangers at the same time. Here pause rate was halved and laughter doubled, indicating that speech disruptions were generated by interaction and were not just a feature of a depressed state. On recovery, depressed men's rate of overall tension release (which was the highest at the time of hospitalization) was markedly reduced, while that of depressed women did not change on recovery. Furthermore on recovery the male patients and their wives showed a clearcut increase in their use of positive tension releasers (increased humour) which again suggests that depressed men in this study had a better premorbid marital adjustment than depressed women.

When "power" variables were considered, the picture that emerged could not be simply interpreted. When interruptions were considered the results suggested that wives in the depressed marriage (both the patient and spouse) used interruptions as a control strategy more often and more successfully than husbands. This technique was employed less often on recovery of the patient. With regard to questioning as a control strategy, the most striking finding was that the wives of depressed men showed a sharp increase in questioning at recovery. This suggested the return to a more traditional role system in the depressed male marriages at recovery, as indicated when expressive communication was considered. When eye contact was considered the traditional view that depressed patients do not engage in much eye contact was not found. Male depressed patients engaged in more eye contact with their wives when they were depressed than at recovery. Depressed women engaged in a lot of eye contact both at recovery and when they were depressed. These findings when taken with the fact that slightly higher speech rate was found in depressed patients at the time of depression indicates, argue Hinchliffe *et al.* (1978), a picture very diferent from the dejected powerless and subordinate depressed spouse.

The results of Hinchcliffe *et al.'s* (1978) imaginative study indicates that men when they are depressed adopt an expressive stance. They quite easily become dependent and their wives respond by offering a nurturing maternal role. At recovery the couple appear to revert easily to their more traditional roles with the husband adopting his accustomed instrumental role. Women on the other hand, when they are depressed appear to take up a regressive passive-aggressive position which makes it difficult for their husbands to respond with nurturance. An atmosphere of emotional alienation is established in which disturbed patterns of communications become fixed. At recovery these marriages are still characterized by negative affect as described by Weissman and Paykel (1974). However as Hinchcliffe *et al.* (1978) point out, these findings may have been biased by the premorbid marital adjustment which seemed to be poorer in the female patient marriages. These marital systems contrast markedly with that of the surgical couples. The latter were able to maintain a productive balance between challenge and support in their interactions. They used tension release and humour, and supported one another while developing and maintaining an open, problem-focussed communication pattern.

While the "Bristol" study focussed on the marital system, the authors do speculate on the impact of the depressed patient on the family. Hinchcliffe *et al.* (1978) hypothesize three major patterns of family organization when one of the patients is depressed. First, the depressed patient may be protected and shielded. Secondly, the patient may be labelled as the "sick" person in the family and excluded as an important member in the family organization. In this pattern the depressed person may become the "identified patient", a status that may be reinforced by helping agencies. Thirdly, the depressed patient may deny feelings of depression and blame family members for their expressions of frustration and powerlessness. This blame may take the form of defensive hostility and even paranoid ideation (see Orford and O'Reilly, this volume).

These patterns have been suggested from clinical cases and while they have face validity, more data are needed to confirm or deny the existence of these and other patterns. Perhaps the home observation methods of Lewinsohn and his colleagues (e.g. Lewinsohn and Shaw, 1969) would present a promising methodology here, if practical problems can be overcome.

(4) *The instrumental view*

The instrumental view of depression holds that there is a depressive type in which depressive self-punitive behaviours have secondary gain features in that they serve to elicit attention and sympathy or ward off interpersonal threat. Such behaviour then is seen as an attempt to control the behaviour of other people in the depressed person's life space. More specifically self-harming responses of the depressed person acquire arousal-reducing properties if these responses help the individual to avoid more intensely aversive responses from another person. Forrest and Hokanson (1975) attempted to test this hypothesis in an experimental two-person interaction shock-reward paradigm. Depressed or non-depressed college students placed in a booth in the laboratory interacted with a confederate who was in another booth. The confederate was primed to act aggressively by administering periodic electric shocks. The subject could choose from three responses (shock, friendly gesture or self-shock). The results showed that when faced with their partner's aggressive behaviour depressed subjects made significantly more self-punitive responses than did non-depressed subjects. The physiological data strongly suggested that greatest arousal-reduction occurred in the depressed group when a self-punitive or friendly response was made to their aggressive partner. These findings (and the fact that depressed subjects established a higher rate of self-punitive behaviour quickly in the baseline period) suggest that while non-depressed subjects have learnt to retaliate aggressively to aggression from other people, depressed subjects have learnt to respond to aggression by making friendly overtures to the aggressor or by making self-punitive responses. This study indicates that the interpersonal context is an important factor in accounting for the self-punitive behaviour of some depressed persons (see also Howells, this volume). Attention should be paid to the responses from others that such behaviour is designed to elicit or ward off. Thus, the instrumental view is promising and deserves further study in situations more closely approximating to every day life.

The interpersonal perspective has generated interesting research and the seeds have been sown for future study particularly in areas when actual interaction sequences are tracked over time. This is particularly important when the social context views of McPartland and Hornstra (1964) and Coyne (1976a) are considered. Indeed, such work, and such a discussion in the foregoing review, place us in a position to consider attempts that have been made to integrate the three perspectives (cognitive, social skills and interpersonal) that have been outlined in this chapter.

Integrating the Three Perspectives

To gain a more comprehensive view of depressive phenomena it is important to bring together the three perspectives reviewed so far. Emphasizing one or even two of the perspectives gives us a distorted view of the total picture. Two recent attempts to integrate cognitive and interpersonal factors associated with depression have marked an advance over the more common unidimensional view. However as we shall see they do not go far enough since they tend to de-emphasize the social skill dimension.

(1) The cognitive approach utilizing the "couples system"

Rush *et al.'s* view (1980) is rooted firmly in Beck's cognitive view of depression where the patient's depressive experience is viewed as stemming from one or more cognitive distortions. As we have seen, such distortions do have interpersonal implications in that the patient reacting to her own phenomenal field behaves accordingly to people in her social sphere. Thus if a wife is operating according to an "overgeneralization" distortion that "men are not to be trusted" then she may act towards her husband as if he were untrustworthy — such actions having decided implications for the marital system. His responses to the wife's distortion-based actions are important to consider in determining the wife's future responses. Rush *et al.* note that the spouse's behaviour may serve to reinforce and thereby perpetuate those cognitive distortions which are claimed to contribute to depression. They recognize the importance of the spouse's role in determining the possible course of treatment and this has led them to experiment with a cognitive therapy of depression with couples. As they say "neglecting the spouse may mean missing an opportunity to engage an ally or to disarm an inadvertent enemy of treatment" (p. 104).

The view then, that Rush *et al.* hold is that it is crucial to determine the spouse's response to the distortion-based actions of the depressed person since it has reinforcing properties. In addition, they take the view that the spouse's response itself may be based on cognitive distortions held by the spouse. Communication problems and relationship difficulties are considered, in the main, to arise from a couple's pattern of idiosyncratic distortions. Table I illustrates one couple's dysfunctional interaction sequence based in the couple's inaccurate cognitions.

In this couple's case, communication improved as they learned about each other's distortion style. However, communication skills do not necessarily improve once a couple become aware of each other's thinking style. Rush *et al.'s* model, although representing a distinct advance over a traditional cognitive perspective of depression could be improved by giving a more central role to the communication and social skills of both partners.

(2) Family-systems model of depression

Drawing from family-systems theory, Feldman (1976) has advocated a model of depression which attempts to integrate the intrapsychic concept of cognitive schemata with the interpersonal concepts of social reinforcement and social stimulation. He argues that homeostasis in the interpersonal system is perpetuated by negative feedback while changes in the system are affected by positive feedback.

TABLE I An illustration of a couple's interaction difficulties and related cognitive distortions (from Rush et al., 1980)

Situation	Wife's responses		Husband's responses	
	Affect	Cognition	Affect	Cognition
She wants to go shopping. He agrees but starts to work on another project.	Anger	First he promises to go shopping and then he lets me down. He doesn't really care.	Happiness	I'm glad she is feeling good today. I'll finish up this job and then we'll handle the shopping.
She withdraws to the bedroom. He continues working.	Sadness	Nobody cares about what I want. I don't really deserve to go because he has more important things to do. I shouldn't make requests of him. I'm too selfish.	Anxiety	She's going into one of her moods again. I wonder what upset her? I'd better leave her alone or she'll lose her temper.
She sits upstairs. Having finished the other job he makes coffee for the couple.	Guilt	I don't deserve to be his wife. I'm just a burden on him. It would be better if I were dead.	Anxiety	I'd better make the dinner tonight to take off some pressure.
He makes dinner.	Sadness	He doesn't even need me to cook any more. The kids didn't even notice I wasn't around. I'm totally useless to my family.	Anger	Well, if she's going to pout all night, I'm going out for a beer.

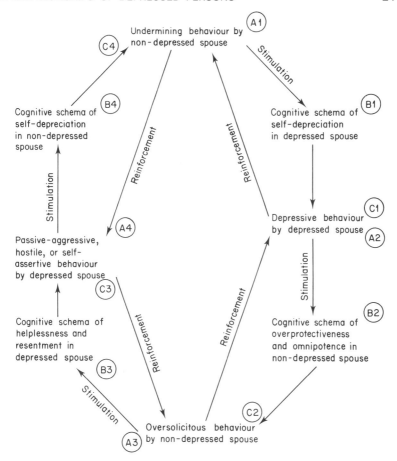

Fig. 1. Patterns of reciprocal stimulation and reinforcement in depression (from Feldman, 1976)

An example taken from Feldman (1976) illustrates his model (Fig. 1). In the example mutual causality is stressed indicating that the process is seen as circular rather than linear — a prominent feature of the systems-based approach to understanding depression. The model emphasizes the triggering of complementary cognitive schemata in both spouses (in this marital system) which in turn leads to patterns of reciprocal stimulation and reinforcement which are repeated. In this circular interaction pattern each spouse'sbehaviour serves (1) as a trigger to the succeeding cognitive schemata and behavioural response of the other spouse; (2) as a response to one's own cognitive structure and to the foregoing behaviour of the other spouse; and (3) as a reinforcement of the preceding sequence of behaviours by self and the other spouse.

The undermining behaviour of the non-depressed spouse (at Al in Fig. 1) may appear to be an innocent remark that "unfortunately" serves to hit a sensitive chord in the depressed spouse's shaky sense of self-esteem. However, Feldman argues that such a remark is purposeful in that it serves to protect the non-depressed spouse's own sense of self-depreciation (B4). This undermining remark of the non-depressed spouse leads to a depressive response in the depressed spouse (C1) via the activation of the cognitive schema of self-depreciation in the depressed spouse (B1). This depressive response serves (A2) to stimulate cognitive schemata of overprotectiveness or omnipotence in the non-depressed spouse (B2) which triggers over-solicitous behaviour on his part (C2). When the depressed spouse experiences her husband's oversolicitous behaviour this serves (A3) to remind her of her own helplessness which she resents (B3) and thus she may attempt to assert herself constructively or she may show her hostility overtly or passive-aggressively (C3). Once she has done so (A4), she succeeds only in conjuring up self-depreciating cognitions in her husband (B4) which he, as we have already seen, tries to dispel by undermining her attempts at self-assertion (C4). The cycle is then repeated and the process may start up again at any of the points on the circle.

Thus from this viewpoint, the symptoms of depression are considered to be

> "an important aspect of homeostatic process that is functioning all too well. It is only when the system can be moved away from the existing homeostasis and toward a process of morphogenesis that the depressive symptoms lose their system-maintenance function and begin to change" (Feldman, 1976, p.394).

As do Rush *et al.* (1980), Feldman tends to omit the social skills dimension in his model. Thus the depressed spouse in Fig. 1 (point A4) may not have the appropriate skills in her repertoire to assert herself constructively even though other changes in the system may have been effected. Indeed the execution of poor social skills at various points on the circle may serve as negative feedback which may return the system to the familiar level of homeostasis.

Despite the fact that both models seem to neglect social skill factors, they do begin to suggest treatment interventions which make the presence of both partners (in the case of a marriage) highly desirable when one member presents with depression. Treatment implications derived from the preceding sections will now be considered.

Implications for Therapeutic Practice

Depressed persons who present for psychological treatment often talk about their problematic relationships with family and friends (Weissman and Klerman, 1973). The stance taken in this chapter suggests that therapists could profitably explore the cognitive determinants of such relationship difficulties, possible social skill deficits that might be involved in such difficulties and the ways in which significant people respond to the patient and the dysfunctioning interactive cycles that might be involved. This implies that effective therapy with depressed patients should be multi-modal in nature (Lazarus, 1976).

With regard to cognitive factors, therapists would do well to identify, challenge and help change the faulty inferences and irrational beliefs that patients may hold with respect to their relationships. This has traditionally been done in individual therapy but, as Rush *et al.* (1980) have shown, can also be carried out in the context of couples therapy, particularly where the spouse holds faulty cognitions which may exaggerate an already disturbed relationship. Here therapists would attempt to modify the cognitions of the spouse. Helping depressed patients to improve poor social skills is less easily achieved in individual therapy. The social skills that the depressed person might exhibit in the clinical context may be a poor predictor of social skills manifested in relationships with significant people. Thus it may be more profitable for therapists to involve those significant others so that more reliable information on the patient's social skills is obtained. Also Coyne's (1976b) points need to be re-iterated here. First, if social skills training is to be effective from a long term perspective then therapists may need to teach all significant people in the depressed person's life space more adaptive social skills. Secondly, depressed patients may need to be taught a special set of social skills to help them cope with the negative responses from others that have commonly been found in a variety of studies. The nature of these special skills has yet to be identified.

From the interpersonal perspective, therapists are advised to make more attempts to involve significant others in the therapeutic context on the grounds that lasting changes in interaction patterns are better effected when those involved in the relevant social context are present than when most of them are absent. This is particularly relevant at the present time when family therapy models are becoming increasingly influential (cf. Orford and O'Reilly, this volume). Lewinsohn's (1974) view that therapists should observe depressed patients in their naturally occurring environments to gain relevant data concerning dysfunctional interaction patterns is an equally challenging one for therapists who in the main see patients in their office.

The question whether depressed patients who are in relationships should be seen alone and/or conjointly with their partner is a central issue. Therapists have provided different answers according to their theoretical orientation. As has already been mentioned, therapists adhering to an intrapsychic model of disturbance would be more likely to see the patient in individual therapy while those advocating an interpersonal or systems view of disturbance would seek to see the patient in the context of the couple or family. The present author advocates a more flexible approach with both individual and conjoint interviews taking place over the course of treatment. Just how this may be organized in the treatment of a given patient is dependent on a number of factors. Hinchcliffe *et al.* (1978) suggest that individual therapy be conducted where contact with the spouse is limited where "personality difficulties predominate for one individual or where it is clear that the couple do not wish to change the equilibrium which they have established between themselves" (p. 85). Where the couple do wish to change such equilibrium, then conjoint interviews are called for and are often more effective then individual therapy (Gurman and Kniskern, 1978). In this situation, individual interviews with the depressed partner might also be held, particularly where that partner's personality difficulties would lead to depression in any context. Conjoint treatment is particularly called for when there is a negative response by the spouse to the depressive episode of the patient. Vaughn and Leff (1976) found that when such a response is found, relapse among hospitalized married partners is much more likely to occur than when such a response is absent. Rounsaville *et al.* (1979) moreover found that most women who were receiving individual treatment (eight months duration) for depression failed to effect substantial improvements in their marriages when marital disputes were a feature of such relationships.

This situation often leads to a paradox: conjoint therapy becomes more important in situations where a negative response on the part of the spouse is found, however such a partner is often reluctant to come for joint treatment believing that "the depression of my wife or husband is nothing to do with me other than being an inconvenience" (Hinchcliffe *et al.*, 1978, p.86). Interestingly enough, McLean (1976) reports from his own experience that wives of the depressed person are more easily involved in a joint treatment programme than husbands. Whether this is due to practical or emotional obstacles needs further clarification. Clearly therapists need to develop more effective strategies in involving the reluctant spouse when this is indicated, but also need to be mindful of the rights of the reluctant person. However, as is clearly indicated in the central arguments of this chapter, the efficacy of conjoint and individual therapy in the treatment of depressed patients (and the conditions under which such modes of treatment might be productive) are crucial areas for empirical enquiry.

CHAPTER 10

Social Relationships in Violent Offenders

Kevin Howells

This chapter reviews psychological and social studies relevant to under-standing the role of personal relationships and interactions in the genesis of violence in violent offenders. There will thus be little discussion of experimental laboratory studies of aggression, except to the extent that laboratory derived theories have directly influenced field studies. Further, this discussion is subject to three limitations: (1) It is restricted mainly to extreme and statistically unusual acts of violence, such as homicide and life-threatening assaults. (2) The discussion focuses on studies and research findings that have some clinical relevance, and, in particular, some implications for treatment though the use of the words "clinical" and "treatment" here should not be taken to imply the acceptance of a medical model. (3) Most of the studies reviewed, though not all, have been conducted with offenders — persons convicted, and often incarcerated, for their violent acts. Such persons obviously form a highly selected, and to some extent, unrepresentative group, being the end-product of a long sequence of judicial decisions and filters. A substantial proportion of violent acts go unreported and do not lead to convictions. It is intended that the conclusions drawn from the studies be seen as applicable to serious violent behaviour in general, rather than as restricted to that labelled as criminal. Here, it is acknowledged that the definitions of aggression and violence are problematic and closely bound to value judgements (Tedeschi *et al.*, 1974; Rule and Nesdale, 1976) so that noxious stimulation or harm-doing prescribed by society (e.g. judicially approved executions, injuries inflicted by the military) are much less often considered as examples of violence than are the actions of those whose behaviour infringes the criminal code. Attempts to understand, and perhaps, modify the violent behaviour of convicted violent offenders may, then, be useful activities, but offer only partial solutions to the problem that violence poses.

The following discussion can be divided into five sections: (1) the nature and background of violent offending is described; (2) Megargee's theory is described and evaluated; (3) studies of social interaction and social skills are reviewed; (4) attention is drawn to the role of social cognition; and (5) implications of the studies for treatment and policy are suggested.

The Nature of Violent Offending

Quinney (1970) has suggested that "wherever the concept of crime exists, images are communicated in society about the meaning of crime, the nature of the criminal, and the relationship of crime to the social order". We possess little empirical information about the nature and accuracy of images of violent offences, but informal observation suggests that public images do exist (derived, perhaps, from the mass media and from sensationalized accounts of unrepresentative offences) and that they may be discrepant with reality in some key respects. For instance, possible components of public mythology about violence are the beliefs that members of the public are most at risk from strangers, and that these strangers are invariably crime and violence prone. Social studies reveal, on the contrary, two facts which not only contradict these beliefs, but also are important to a psychological understanding of violent behaviour, since they emphasize the significance of relationships in such behaviour. These two facts are: that violence is often committed on victims known to the aggressor; and that in such cases a previous history of violent behaviour is frequently absent.

(1) Serious violence shows considerable situational specificity, occurring predominantly in intimate domestic relationships. Blom-Cooper and Morris (1962) commented with regard to England and Wales: "In this country murder is overwhelmingly a domestic crime in which men kill their wives, mistresses and children, and women kill their children". This assertion is supported by Home Office studies (1961, 1975) which show, for example, that nearly 60% of adult female victims of murder are the wife or girlfriend

of the aggressor. Less than 20% of adult male and female victims are killed by strangers. The proportion of victims who are relatives or intimates is even higher for offenders who are classified as "mentally abnormal" or who subsequently commit suicide. In West's (1965) sample of murder/suicides (i.e. those who murder others and then kill themselves), only 7% of offenders killed someone not related to them. In the United States, a similar pattern is found, although the proportion of strangers is larger. Mulvihill *et al.*, (1969), in their report to the American Crime Commission, estimated that 1 in 4 homicides occurred between family members, and that one third involved primary group relationships (husband, wife, lover, close friend, family). More recent studies (Wolfgang, 1978) confirm these findings. In general, less "serious" violent assaults, which do not lead to the death of the victim, more often involve strangers than do homicides, but, even here, a substantial proportion involve family members and persons who know one another (McClintock, 1963).

The importance of these findings lies in the demonstration that violence frequently occurs as an event in an established *relationship*, rather than as a spontaneous unprovoked attack on a stranger. This raises the possibility that the relationship between offender and victim (or their previous social interactions) are important determinants of the violent incident. The importance of previous interactions is also suggested by findings that victims are intimately involved in the sequence that culminates in the violent act. On the basis of police reports, Mulvihill *et al.*, (1969) concluded that in 22% of homicides and 14% of aggravated assaults, victim participation was such that the victim was the first to use physical force against the subsequent aggressor. Typically the violence follows from an argument or disagreement between the participants. Family quarrels, petty jealousies and disputes are more frequent precipitants of violent incidents than are financial or sexual acquisitiveness. Approximately half of the homicides studied by the Home Office (1961, 1975) were attributed to motives of "quarrel or violent rage", though, clearly, the imputing of motives is subjective and probably unreliable. McClintock (1963) also emphasizes disagreements with neighbours and workmates, petty jealousies and arguments as precipitants of lesser forms of assault. In summary, serious violence often occurs between people who are intimately related and appears to occur following angry disputes and altercations.

(2) Not all persons who commit serious violent offences, such as homicide, are violence prone, in the sense of having previous convictions for violence. McClintock (1963) found that 80% of convicted violent offenders had no history of violent offences, though half had previous convictions for non-violent offences, and the 1975 Home Office study of homicide found that

only about 26% of offenders had previous convictions for violent offences. Where murder is followed by suicide, the individual is likely to have even fewer previous convictions, thus confirming the notion that they are ordinary people driven to acts of desperation; for example, West (1965) found that only 13% of murder/suicides (i.e. those who kill others and then kill themselves) had previous convictions compared to 47% of convicted murderers. In all of these studies, of course, the "dark figure" of unreported violence is unknown, but even so, the evidence does suggest that explanations are not best sought solely in terms of internal, individual factors, but perhaps by reference to interpersonal and relational factors.

Typologies of Violent Offenders: Megargee's Theory

Given the evidence that relationships are important determinants of, and outlets for expression of, violence, it is particularly important to evaluate theories of aggression in terms of the stress which they place on the violent person's relationships with others. Whilst many theorists in this area distinguish the criminal from the non-criminal aggressor, Megargee has developed a larger typology, whose importance is precisely its emphasis on interpersonal friction over long periods of time. However, we start by distinguishing the criminal aggressor (for whom violence forms part of a pattern of social deviance, often with several previous instances of violent behaviour) from the non-criminal aggressor (whose behaviour is generally conforming and controlled, who does not habitually break the law and whose act of violence — often homicide — seems utterly uncharacteristic of the person). Wolfgang (1958b) and West (1965) identify murder/suicides as the clearest example of the non-criminal aggressor, and describe them as persons "of relatively normal character development (super-ego), acting under the stress of acutely frustrating circumstances, usually severe conflict with an individual to whom the offender is very attached".

Megargee (1966, 1971) has elaborated this distinction and attempted to provide a basis for it in empirical work. His starting point was the clinical observation that many murderers do not conform to the popular stereotype of an aggressive offender, and he quotes an example of a typical assaulter who was a "meek, mild-mannered, deferential person", suggesting that many such aggressors show these traits rather than being aggressive, hostile and abrasive. Megargee then tries to provide a model of how such a paradoxically controlled person might commit an act of extreme violence. He starts by making three assumption: (1) that inhibitions against violence are as important as instigators, (2) that the degree of violence is proportional to the strength of instigation, and (3) that people with high levels of inhibition will respond aggressively only to extreme provocation. Megargee conceives of a threshold of inhibition of violence (in which individuals vary) which may be exceeded, in the case of people with a high level of inhibition, only by extreme levels of provocation. Individuals with low levels of inhibition find their threshold exceeded easily by relatively low levels of provocation. In this way, Megargee makes a distinction between "overcontrolled" aggressors and "undercontrolled" aggressors. The model predicts that when overcontrolled offenders do offend they will tend to use an extreme degree of violence, as the degree of violence is proportional to instigation. Megargee proposes that the overcontrolled person's threshold is exceeded only when there has been a "temporal summation of frustration" over a long period of time. This appears to refer to a prolonged period of interpersonal friction. A man may be constantly goaded and humiliated by his wife over many years, for example, until he finally explodes into violence. From his model Megargee predicts that more overcontrolled aggressors will be found amongst offenders who have committed extreme assaults (EAs) than amongst offenders who have committed moderate assaults (MAs). This prediction has received some, though not total support from empirical studies (Megargee, 1966; Molof, 1967; Blackburn, 1968, 1971; Crawford, 1977; McGurk, 1978; McGurk and McGurk, 1979).

In the present context, the value of Megargee's theory lies in its stress on an understanding of violence largely in terms of long-term relationships and (implicitly) the behaviours necessary to conduct them. However, Megargee's theory, and the work stemming from it, are open to a number of criticisms, both theoretical and methodological. The theory is relatively divorced from contemporary models of the control of aggression (e.g. Novaco, 1978) and utilizes concepts whose validity has been questioned. The concept of summation of frustration, for example, is essentially hydraulic. It is assumed that the expression of aggression reduces aggressive drive within the person in a cathartic manner, and that the overcontrolled person builds up frustration through not discharging it behaviourally. Recent work (Quanty, 1976) casts some doubt on the validity of catharsis. There is also little apparent empirical support for the assumption that frustrative states persist over long periods of time within the person, independently of external stimulation or internal cognitive activity. The strength of the theory might be improved by the inclusion of behavioural and cognitive processes with the affective aspects of aggression stressed by Megargee. Behaviourists might emphasize, for example, that the "meek", overcontrolled person may be prone to occasional extreme violence because he is incapable of acting sufficiently assertively to stop the provocation from another person. Persons unskilled in behaviour which might enable them not to be "picked on" are likely to be constantly re-exposed to a high, and perhaps escalating, level of provocation. Intervening cognitive processes might also explain the sudden change from overcontrolled to explosively violent behaviour. The overcontrolled person may, over a period of time, change his constructions and interpretations of events, other people, relationships and of himself to such an extent that anger or other violence-generating affects increase and precipitate an incident. West (1965), for example, draws attention to the frequency of "depressive" views of the world in murder/suicides. The mother who kills her child to protect it from a world she now perceives as too horrible to live in, is impelled to violence by her changed perceptions of the world and of her child. The gradual evolution of "paranoid" cognitions might also explain drastic changes in behaviour (see below).

Aspects of violent offenders' constructions of self, significant other people and victims have recently been studied by the author, using Repertory Grid technique (Kelly, 1955; Fransella and Bannister, 1977). This work is reported in detail elsewhere (Howells, 1981) but will be briefly summarized here because such constructions obviously feed into and influence relationships and their conduct. Individual grids were administered to groups of "one-off" (overcontrolled) and "multiple" (undercontrolled) offenders from an English Special Hospital (the same source used by Blackburn, 1968, 1971). Significant differences in personal construing were found, some of which were consistent with Megargee's theory. Overcontrolled offenders were shown to produce more "biased" construct systems. They were more intropunitive in their judgements, and were more oriented to the positively evaluated poles of constructs in their judgements of other people. Victims of the overcontrolled offenders were construed in a more "idealized" way than those of the undercontrolled. The author interpreted these results as indicative of a "repressive" mode of social perception in the overcontrolled. Hostile evaluations of others (including victims) may be "submerged" (Kelly, 1955) until, under stress, a shift is made to these submerged, highly hostile evaluations. These newly emerging hostile cognitions legitimize violence towards the victim and precipitate the homicide. Subsequently the offender reverts to the repressive mode. Such a cognitive view of over-control has many similarities to Megargee's theory, but locates the important change as being in the cognitive appraisal of the world (and the people in it) by the offender, rather than in a physiological build-up of frustration. There would be considerable overlap in the therapeutic strategies suggested by the affective and cognitive perspectives, both seeing the therapeutic task as being to teach homicides, paradoxically, to break down excessive inhibitions, perhaps by encouraging a more central focus on relationships and their conduct.

The term "overcontrol" perhaps gives a greater clinical flavour to the behaviours involved than is warranted by the evidence. Most of the comparisons reported (Megargee, 1966, 1971; Blackburn, 1968, 1971) are between EA and MA offenders rather than between EAs and normals, which would be required to demonstrate that homicides are overcontrolled rather than controlled (McGurk and McGurk, 1979). It should also be noted that most of the data quoted in support of the theory are psychometric, often deriving from the MMPI, an instrument not designed for the analysis of hostility and susceptible to biases induced by extreme response styles in highly unusual testing enviroments. It would be useful for future research to devote more effort to establishing that overcontrolled aggressors actually *behave* more inhibitedly and less aggressively following experimental or real-life frustrations. Finally, research of this type is conducted with groups exposed to the processes of judicial selection. The possibility that observed group differences are artifactual cannot be ruled out. Social class or criminal record-based biases in arrest or hospitalization policy (Hood and Sparks, 1970) would artificially depress the frequency of overcontrolled assaulters in the MA group. Intuitively, it seems highly likely that overcontrolled persons who commit a moderately assaultive crime are less likely to get to court, be convicted, and sent to a prison or security hospital than are undercontrolled persons committing the same offence. The overcontrolled person is more likely to be viewed by the police, the courts, psychiatrists and other decision-makers as non-criminal, conforming, and unlikely to re-offend, and as not needing a custodial-type sentence. The same bias is unlikely to apply for more serious assaults, such as homicide, which are more visible and less likely to be hidden by police or court discretion. The effect of such biases would be to produce an unrealistically higher incidence of overcontrolled persons in EA than in MA groups. This difficulty points to the necessity for future research to assess the extent of hidden, non-homicidal violence occurring in domestic circumstances (husbands assaulting wives) which is not reported and does not feature in criminal statistics. Violence has been found to be common, for example, in divorce-prone and other families (Levinger, 1966; O'Brien, 1971; Gelles, 1974). More detailed studies of the behavioural histories of apparently "one-off" overcontrolled homicides might help to establish whether such acts are, in fact, explosions following long periods of inhibition, or whether the homicide has been preceded by lesser violent assaults. In any case it is clear that greater attention needs to be paid to the relationships that preceded the violence and the ways in which they may have contributed to its manifestation. We therefore turn to specific consideration of the social behaviour of violent offenders.

Social Interaction and Social Skills in Violent Offenders

There are two lines of research that emphasize strongly the relational and interactional aspects of violent behaviour. These are: the work of Hans Toch, and recent work on Social Skills and assertiveness training. They are based broadly within the behavioural tradition, offer interesting possibilities for future research into the therapeutic modification of violence and also they manifest some degree of theoretical convergence.

The research of Hans Toch

Toch's contribution (1969) to the study of violence is unique and of major importance. Its uniqueness lies in its closeness to "real-life" aggressive behaviour and in the detail of its analysis of violent episodes. Toch's approach follows naturally from what is known about violent crime, as discussed above, and is consistent with its situational specificity and interactional quality. As indicated above, violence does not occur indiscriminately, but occurs more frequently in the context of a prior relationship (e.g. domestic disputes) and is usually the result of an interaction with the victim that "gets out of hand". Toch attempts to "focus on the chain of interactions between aggressor and victim, on the sequence that begins when two people encounter each other — and ends when one harms, or even destroys, the other" (Toch, 1969, p.9). For instance, in the United States, violence often occurs when a suspect is stopped and questioned by a police officer. Toch's research focusses particular attention on the chain of interactions that precede such incidents, deriving his data from the transcripts of violent offenders (interviewed by other offenders) and of policemen (interviewed by other policemen). This method is open to methodological criticisms, as is Toch's analysis of his data, but a wealth of interesting observations amenable to a more scientific analysis, are presented. In one typical violence-engendering sequence:

"The officer starts an interaction with a civilian by means of an order, a demand, a suggestion, a question, a request, or some other communication. Usually no serious offence has been committed by the civilian and the contact is classifiable either as preventative police work or as an effort to cope with a nuisance act. A group of boys are 'told to move', or 'questioned as to what they are doing', an errant driver is 'told to stop' or 'notified of his violation', a person who is engaged in an altercation is questioned as to 'what the problem was' or is 'instructed to be quiet' or 'told to go home'. A request for name, address or identification may also provide the opening spark of the sequence. The violence may occur as early as immediately after the initial approach but more often does not materialize until one or two further exchanges have taken place. Most typically, the civilian just fails to cooperate with the officer" (Toch, 1969, pp. 76–77).

Typically the sequences involve abuse and threats on the part of the suspect and a series of escalating exchanges, until the point of violence is reached. Toch suggests that both participants show longitudinal consistency in their behaviour, that the police officer and the suspect involved in a violent incident often have a history of being assaulted and being an assaulter respectively. The police officer, for example, may show a long-term disposition to react to minor provocation in a particular way. He may consistently react to being sworn at in the street by attempting to arrest the offending person. The latter resists noisily, feeling unjustly apprehended, and thereby attracts a crowd of onlookers. The police officer is now faced with the embarrassing task of having to arrest a resisting suspect in front of an audience, and may find he has to resort to violence to carry out the arrest. The suspect may show a similar consistency over time, typically reacting in a threatening manner in situations in which he feels "picked on" in a bullying manner. Toch summarizes: "The incident, therefore, represents the collision of two violence-prone modes of response to violence-prone modes of provocation - each characteristic of the man involved" (p.161).

Toch describes a series of modes of approach to relationships which might make violent outcomes more likely. The "self-image promoter" values toughness and masculine status and seeks confirmation of this image by provoking violence. Demeaning insults and threats to masculinity in group contexts are likely to be the precipitating stimuli. This form of violence is clearly similar to the subcultural violence described by Wolfgang (1958a, 1978) and by Wolfgang and Ferracuti (1976). Wolfgang, in his early study of homicide in Philadelphia, explained the subcultural and sex differences for homicide in terms of "quick resort to physical combat as a measure of daring, courage or defence of status. . . [this appears to be] . . . a cultural expectation, especially for lower socio-economic class males" (Wolfgang 1958a, p.188). This hypothesis, that some violent offenders have differing values concerning toughness and masculine status, is eminently testable by empirical research, though preliminary attempts to test it have provided little support (Ball-Rokeach, 1973; Poland, 1978).

Toch's "social skills deficient" aggressors, on the other hand, "use violence as an expression of helplessness or as a last-minute effort to obliterate siutations in which they are unable to respond" (p.194). There are some similarities between this type and Megargee's overcontrolled homicide, though Toch's account emphasizes behavioural skill deficiencies rather than emotional (anger) inhibition. This aggressor is seen as possessing insufficient verbal skills to deal with difficult situations, and as having to resort to violence to terminate the altercation and "remove pressure". Amongst other types described by Toch is the "self-defender" who uses violence to neutralize perceived danger. For this person there is either something about his behaviour which induces others to behave dangerously towards him, or his subjective evaluation of the social environment is biased (see discussion of paranoia below). This typological system, and Toch's observations in general, remain in need of empirical validation. It has still to be demonstrated, for example, that the social skills deficits described are in fact more frequent and intense in violent than in non-violent offenders.

Toch's work, again, points to the significance of relationships and to a number of aspects of violent interactions that rehabilitation programmes would need to accommodate: (1) programmes would need to be based on a detailed assessment of the aggressor's role in the sequence of social interactions that precede violent incidents; (2) those components of the aggressor's relational behaviour which precipitate violence would need to be specified. Toch's analysis stresses verbal components in the main. Attention has been drawn elsewhere (Trower, 1979) to the non-verbal and paralinguistic components which would need to be included in a comprehensive analysis; (3) role-playing methods would be needed to deal with real-life problems in restricted institutional settings:

> "There must be clear relevance and transferability in the trial situations that we are able to devise. These must be subjectively equivalent to temptations and threats, goadings and pressures encountered in the tavern, the back alley, the home and the prison cell". (Toch, 1969, p.278)

Such a programme would have many similarities to those developed for therapeutic purposes in the mental-health field, under the rubric of social skills training (see Trower's chapter in the present volume for a discussion of this training in other contexts).

Social skills and assertiveness training

Given its specific emphasis on inadequacy in the conduct of social relationships, the development of social skills and assertiveness training in recent years provides a theoretical framework (and a source of assessment, research and treatment methods) suited to a more precise application and evaluation of the observations of Toch. The literature in this area has been comprehensively and critically evaluated in a recent volume (Bellack and Hersen, 1979) and also in this book (Trower, Chapter 4). Social skills training arose from observations that, for many individuals, social relationships are problematic, as a result of deficiencies in social skills. Such deficits may be the result of a failure to acquire skilled behaviours, or a failure to *perform* skilfully because of interference by emotion (anxiety) or the learning of incompatible responses. Social skill deficiency has been shown to be associated with psychopathology, and there has been a large scale application of social skills training to a variety of types of psychological and psychiatric disturbance, including schizophrenia, alcoholism, sexual deviation and social anxiety (Hersen, 1979). Social skills training is subject to definitional problems, and a variety of methodological issues remain unresolved in its evaluation (Curran, 1979) but it has made significant inroads in the modification of social difficulty. Assertiveness training overlaps considerably with social skills training, though its roots in the work of Wolpe (1954,1969) were different. The problems in defining assertiveness have become increasingly clear (Linehan and Egan, 1979), but the term encompasses behaviours such as the expression of feelings and wants, standing up for one's rights, and being able to disagree appropriately with others. Both social skills and assertiveness training involve analysis and modification of molecular and molar psychological processes, including verbal and non-verbal elements. Both methods involve a range of therapeutic procedures, typically including rehearsal, feedback, *in vivo* practice, modelling and simple instruction.

Some specific studies

There are a small number of published studies in which training programmes have attempted to modify violence. Ivey (1973) describes working with a client who became "hostile and belligerent" when discussing topics related to authority relationships. Therapy sessions involved video-taping typical social interactions and identifying behaviours that created the impression of hostility — in this case, rate of speech and tone of voice. Sarason and Ganzer (1973) compared a modelling-with-feedback procedure and a problem-oriented discussion group with conventional institutional treatment in improving the adjustment of male delinquents. The goals of treatment were broader than attempting to change violent behaviour, including the teaching of skills in areas such as applying for jobs and resisting peer temptation. Both modelling and problem-oriented discussion proved superior to conventional treatment in terms of attitude and behaviour change, and subsequent recidivism. Sarason (1978) has reported that many of those improvements were still found at a five-year follow-up.

Rimm *et al.* (1974) report a study aimed to help the person who gets into trouble because he is unduly belligerent, rather than under-assertive. These authors used feedback and modelling of appropriate ways to deal with anger-inducing situations with male volunteers who had difficulty in controlling their tempers. Feedback and modelling were more effective in producing appropriate assertiveness than a "discussion of angry feelings" control group. Foy *et al.* (1975) treated a man with "inappropriate explosive outbursts". This person suffered "chronic difficulties in behaviourally complying with what he felt were the unreasonable demands of others until he released anger in a verbally abusive and often assaultive manner". Frederiksen *et al.* (1976) used social skills training to reduce aggressive behaviour in two hospitalized patients, and demonstrated some generalization of behaviour change to real-life aggression-eliciting situations.

However, as noted earlier, these treatments are not aimed directly at preventing violence so much as improving the violent person's relational behaviour to the point where violence becomes an unnecessary means of achieving desired goals. To this end, the present author has described a social skills group for violent offenders in an English Special Hospital (Howells, 1976), emphasizing the need to distinguish types of violent behaviour requiring different treatment strategies. The first type described was of an overcontrolled homicide who reacted with self-aggression and intense internal anger to teasing and provocation, whilst responding with a low voice volume, smiling, no eye-contact, and an absence of criticism of the provoking person. The second type was a Toch-style "self-image promoter" who became involved in a series of fights. A violence-engendering pattern was described which included loud voice volume, threatening posture and facial expression, and hostile verbal comments. The third type was a person convicted of violent sexual assaults, where poor social skills made sexual partners inaccessible and induced instrumental violence. Crawford and Allen (1979) have reported in more detail on a social skills programme with this latter group, and Crawford (personal communication) has found social skills training to produce significantly better improvements than a psychotherapy control group.

Ollendick and Hersen (1979) compared social skills training and discussion controls as a treatment for delinquent adolescents whose offences included assaults, robbery and rape. Social skills training proved superior to discussion on a variety of self-report and behavioural measures, though the follow-up period was short. This study involved a wider range of treatment components than the comparable study of Sarason and Ganzer (1973). Finally, a recent study by Rahaim *et al.* (1980), though an uncontrolled single-case study, is of interest in the similarity of the case described to those studied by Toch (1969). The client was a 30-year-old police officer who had difficulty in controlling his aggressive behaviour at work. He had sought treatment as a result of complaints from several citizens from the community and a reprimand from his superior officer, following an incident in which he had broken the arm of a man he had arrested for reckless driving. Assertiveness training produced behavioural changes and modified cognitions concerning anger. Apart from suggesting that behavioural procedures have effects on the cognitive realm, this study alerts the reader to the possibility of using social skills programmes with a wider variety of clients than convicted offenders.

The above studies indicate that a promising start has been made in the application of social skills and assertiveness training to the problem of making violent people better at maintaining relationships and hence potentially reducing their resorts to violent behaviour. This research, however, is at a very preliminary stage. The problems of definition, interpretation, evaluation and assessment which beset social skills training in general (Curran, 1979; Hersen, 1979) exist equally strongly in this particular field of application. These forms of training, and particularly assertiveness training, do have a strong face validity when applied to problems of aggression. Assertiveness training, for example, is directly concerned with the very area of relating which is problematic for both overcontrolled and under-controlled violent offenders — that of appropriate non-violent self-assertion. The widespread use of assertion training with violent offenders, however, must await more detailed evaluation of the interpersonal effects of assertive behaviour. It is assumed that assertive social styles enhance positive social outcomes for the person and reduce negative outcomes, and this would be the rationale for teaching an overcontrolled homicide to be more assertive. It is, as yet, however, not entirely clear that assertive responses always have positive consequences for relationships, even though short-term personal effectiveness may be improved (Falbo, 1977; Marriott and Foster, 1978; Linehan and Egan, 1979). Linehan and Egan (1979) quote an unpublished study by Ford and Hogan who reported that high voice volume and direct eye contact (behaviours usually assumed to be components of appropriate assertiveness) resulted in the assertive person being seen as "aggressive" and "authoritarian". Similarly, Page and Balloun (1978) found that an interviewee with a high voice volume was rated as more aggressive, less mature, less sincere and less desirable as a work partner than an interviewee with a low voice volume. It would, clearly, be inappropriate to teach an overcontrolled aggressor to speak louder if it was likely to produce a social image of greater aggressiveness. It is likely that, in the case of voice volume, a curvilinear relationship exists between volume and perceptions of appropriateness, with intermediate volumes perceived as appropriate, and both extremes as inappropriate.

Future work in this area will need to differentiate assertiveness and aggression (Hollandsworth, 1977; De Giovanni and Epstein, 1978) more stringently, and to assess which assertive interpersonal verbal and non-verbal behaviours might, in fact, be provocative of counter-aggression from the other person. The selection of verbal and non-verbal processes for attention in assertiveness training on the basis of face validity alone is unacceptable. Current assessment procedures used in assertiveness training, as indicated by the review of De Giovanni and Epstein (1978), have poor discriminant validity for assertiveness and aggression, a weakness illustrated by the inclusion of items such as "Anyone attempting to push ahead of me in a line is in for a good battle" in assertion inventories. Behavioural assessments of assertiveness, similarly, often code instances of threat and insult as indicators of assertion. Future work of this sort with violent offenders obviously depends on being able to differentiate assertion and aggression in the areas of verbal content, non-verbal and para-linguistic behaviour.

A recent study by Kirchner *et al.* (1979), however, indicates that assertiveness and aggression *can* be distinguished in offender groups. In this study assertion and aggression showed some, though not complete, independence, and significant differences were found between offenders and non-offenders for aggressive, but not for assertive, behaviours. It should not be impossible for future studies to correlate the specific verbal and non-verbal content of a person's interactional style (in both violent and "normal" groups) with observers' perceptions (based on video-taped recordings) of what styles are "threatening", "provocative" or "likely to provoke a fight" as opposed to those that are appropriately self expressive.

Given such work and its emphasis on the possible mediating effects of relational and social incompetence in the genesis of violent behaviour, it is encouraging that results indicate the general value and productiveness of that style of approach. However, the theme can be extended and developed by attention to the cognitive and organizational principles by means of which people — particularly violent people — prepare themselves for, and create beliefs about personal relationships. Social skills approaches as detailed above, have perhaps understressed this important area of study, to which we now turn.

The Role of Cognitive Variables in the Genesis of Violence

In the last ten years the importance of cognitive factors as determinants of social difficulty has been increasingly recognized. Workers have begun to concern themselves with what might be labelled issues of psychological epistemology, of how persons know and construct reality (including the social world of other persons and relationships), and how these constructions affect their behaviour. Attribution theory, for example, has concerned itself with how people make causal inferences about events, with how they answer questions beginning with "why?" (Kelley, 1973). Personal Construct Theory (Kelly, 1955) has similarly focussed on what Heider (1958) called "naïve psychology", the "lay" person's attempts to understand and predict his world. Research arising from attribution theory, in particular, has affected our understanding of violence, by means of its clarification of the ways in which people perceive and construct models of social causality.

The perception of social causality

Bandura's (1971a, 1971b) social learning theory of aggression describes two pathways for the learning of aggressive responses. Aggressive behaviour may be learned as a non-emotional, non-angry response through reinforcement and imitative learning, or it may be learned as a way of coping with negative arousal states. This distinction approximates to that often made between instrumental and angry aggression. Angry aggression is one possible reaction to the negative arousal engendered by a wide range of aversive stimuli. Attribution processes are likely to be very relevant to angry aggression, and might be thought of as intervening between aversive environmental events and subsequent internal and overt behaviours. The attributions made to explain an aversive event will determine the label attached to the arousal state and also the ensuing behaviour. Many of the aversive stimuli that precipitate violence in real-life situations will be frustrating actions on the part of other persons (see above). Such actions must be attributed and causal inferences made, in order to explain the occurrence of the action. Heider (1958) draws attention to three classes of causative factors — self, the other person, and the environment. The selection of one particular locus of causality leads to the ascription of some "dispositional property" to that source. Severe criticism from another person may be attributed, for example, to one's own "inadequacy", to "bad temper" on the part of the other person, or to situational factors. Significant biases in attributional styles have been described in clinical groups, for example, the tendency of neurotics to ascribe such incidents to personal inadequacy rather than to external, situational forces has been noted in the literature (Valins and Nisbett, 1971; Storms and McCaul, 1977). Such intropunitive attributional biases would seem, intuitively, to be unlikely to provoke violence, and would require therapeutic re-attribution of the unpleasant event (criticism) to an external source. The contra-typical bias, the tendency to attribute negative events to others, rather than to the self, has received much less attention, and is likely to be found amongst individuals that others will describe as "hostile" and "extrapunitive" rather than as self-critical and "suffering from feelings of inadequacy". That such hostile evaluations have some relationship to aggressive behaviour has been demonstrated by Loew (1967).

The attribution of malevolent intent

The origin of violence in social inferences and beliefs is most clearly demonstrated in the case of one particular subclass of "other person" attributions — the attribution by a recipient of a particular aversive behaviour, that the behaviour was specifically directed at harming him. If the other person's harm-doing was deliberately intended to harm me, rather than a product of carelessness, environmental pressure or inadequacy on his part, then it is clearly more of an "offence" (Beck, 1972) and requires self-defending on my part. A person with a marked bias towards such attributions would be expected to be characteristically "resentful" (social difficulties in his life would have been attributed to other people's attempts to "put him down") and also "suspicious" (because his attributions of malevolent intent would cause him to predict and expect such intentions in the future). The importance of the attribution of intent for aggressive behaviour has been suggested by the experiments of Epstein and Taylor (1967), Greenwell and Dengerink (1973), Nickel (1974) and Dyck and Rule (1978). The latter study demonstrated that consensus and foreseeability information are also important, in that retaliatory aggression to perceived malevolent intent is greater when there is low consensus for the provocation, and when the attacker has knowledge of the negative consequences of his actions. There are few studies of attributional bias in aggressive offenders themselves, though Nasby *et al.* (1980) did investigate the link between violence and attributional bias in adolescents. In this study violence was associated with a generalized bias to infer hostility from social stimuli. These authors draw attention to the possibility of a bi-directional reciprocally deterministic relationship existing between hostile attributions and aggressive behaviour (Novaco, 1978); that is, attributions may mediate aggressive behaviour, but behaving aggressively may also maintain the attribution bias. A person who is repetitively aggressive may inadvertently organize other people to be hostile towards him, making his hostile attributions realistic.

Paranoia

If there is a continuum of extrapunitive bias in the attribution of social events and a consequent influence on social relationships, an extreme point on this continuum would be occupied by the person clinically labelled as "paranoid". For the paranoid individual, events that most people consider unimportant may be attributed to some hostile, malevolent and even conspiratorial intent on the part of other persons. It is very difficult to assess the incidence of paranoid states and ideas amongst violent offenders, as such information is rarely available in studies. It is known, however, that a substantial proportion of persons committing crimes such as homicide, in the United Kingdom, are classified as "mentally abnormal" (Home Office, 1975). Amongst such persons diagnoses of "paranoia", "paranoid state" or "paranoid schizophrenia" are not uncommon. Paranoid delusions are a common feature of schizophrenic symptomatology, and schizophrenia is a very frequent diagnosis amongst mentally abnormal violent offenders (Black, 1973). Similarly, Blackburn (1971) identified a "paranoid aggressive" type in his homicide typology. The violent behaviour of such persons is comprehensible only with reference to their delusional interpretations of social reality. A changed interpretation of the world, such that other people are suddenly seen as agents of some organization or group intent on harming, or even killing, the individual, may be sufficient to induce retaliatory aggression in an otherwise controlled person. As indicated above, paranoid cognitions may become self-fulfilling and no longer an indication of bias. Cameron (1959), for example, has discussed how the hostile behaviour of the paranoid person "unintentionally organizes. . . (other people) . . . into a functional community, a group unified in their supposed reactions, attitudes and plans with respect to him".

If paranoid aggressors do show extrapunitive and "malevolent intent" attributional biases, then several avenues for attributional therapy suggest themselves. If a bias exists toward "other person" attributions for negative events, then paranoid individuals might be trained to perceive the self as causal, perhaps through use of video-taped social interactions to demonstrate the role of the client himself in producing the aversive outcome. Alternatively, if the client is biased toward malevolent intent interpretations of the behaviour of others, he might be encouraged to make more appropriate use of contextual information in his judgements about other people (Kelley, 1973). It would appear, for example, that the incorrect attribution that the other person is intent on harming me often reflects a failure on my part to use "distinctiveness" information appropriately (Kelley, 1973). The noxious behaviour of the other person is assumed to be directed at the self ("taking everything personally") without observing that this behaviour may also be shown to other persons in the environment. It is plausible that paranoid aggressors could be systematically taught to seek out and use such information. Before concluding this discussion of paranoia, it is worth pointing out that there may be correspondences between paranoia at the individual level and paranoid beliefs in relations between groups (Storr, 1978).

Cognitive aspects of psychopathic relating

There is a small, though significant, area of overlap between violent

behaviour and "psychopathic" states. Psychopathic disorder is a classi-
ficatory label frequently applied to abnormal violent offenders in England
and Wales, under the 1959 Mental Health Act. This medico/legal category is
heterogeneous, but includes a small proportion of violent offenders who
show characteristics supposed to be typical of the classic "psychopath"
(Cleckley, 1964; Blackburn, 1971, 1975; Hare and Schalling, 1978; Smith,
1978). Studies of psychopathic offenders are of value in understanding
"normal" aggression insofar as they isolate important psychological
processes (for example, lack of empathy) which may play a role in facili-
tating the expression of aggression in many non-psychopathic persons. The
nature of the psychopath's relationships to significant others is an area of
experimental research which is surprisingly undeveloped, given the fact that
the very definitions of psychopathy most commonly used emphasize
variables that are clearly *interpersonal*, such as emotional coldness, avoidance of close relationships and insensitivity to others (Smith, 1978). Gough
(1948) has, however, outlined a cognitive/interpersonal theory of
psychopathy which has received some empirical support. Gough's basic
thesis is that the psychopath has a "role-taking" deficiency. Whereas the
normal child learns to see himself/herself as a social object for others, and is
able to see the self as others observe it, the psychopath is unable to identify
with significant others and fails to take their viewpoint. Such a failure has
dire consequences: his prediction of other people's behaviour is impaired,
he is not sensitive, in advance, to the reactions of others, and he is genuinely
surprised at the negative social reactions to his transgressions. This theory
has received some support from a repertory grid study (Widom, 1976a)
which compared the individual's construction of situations with his construction of how *other people* would construe them, and also with how a represen-
tative group of other people *actually did* construe the situations. A group of
violent primary psychopaths assumed that other people saw the situations as
they themselves did, but this assumption was unfounded in reality. These
results would support the hypothesis that violent psychopaths misperceive
others' perceptions. Another study by the same author, using the prisoner's
dilemma, however, failed to find such misperceptions (Widom, 1976b).
Schalling (1978) has also reviewed work which suggests that role-taking
deficiency (as measured by socialization scales) has some relationship to
psychopathic behaviour. Further work on this variable will need to distinguish between the cognitive and the affective understanding of other people
in the psychopath. It is possible to know that one's aggressive behaviour will
distress another person, without that knowledge producing a negative
emotional reaction. Whether psychopaths are deficient in both areas is, as
yet, unknown. Finally, some persons labelled as psychopaths may have
perceptions of other people, and of the social world, which differ

dramatically from those of the majority in society. Howells (1978) has demonstrated the existence of an extreme, unusual and highly idiosyncratic construct system in a person diagnosed as suffering from a psychopathic disorder. The explanation of violent behaviour which is so extreme that it attracts the label "psychopathic" may require such a detailed investigation of the person's cognitive framework, particularly since it is clear that such frameworks are the very stuff of the predispositions upon which social relationships are based.

The biases in social cognition discussed in this section would require that any therapeutic programme should include efforts to encourage the violent person's cognitive restructuring of social events and his relationships with other people. The most comprehensive attempt to provide such therapy can be found in the work of Novaco (1975, 1976a, b, 1977a, b, 1978) who also draws attention to the complex bi-directional causal relationships existing between social cognitons, affective state and violent behaviour itself.

Implications for Treatment and Policy

In this chapter I have attempted to sketch out an approach to the under-standing of violent behaviour and I have placed major emphasis on the long-term interpersonal origins of acts of violence. It represents a change of focus in that it centres so forcefully on the relationships that form the context of the violent acts and on the violent person's views of relationships and of other people. The work outlined in previous sections amounts, perhaps, to little more than a promising beginning in the task of explaining and changing (where appropriate) the interpersonal behaviour of violent persons. Large scale, tightly controlled studies of the effects of treatment interventions, with long-term follow-ups, remain to be done. Nevertheless, the work already completed does indicate the potential utility of a *social* psychological perspective on violence, as an alternative to the biological, psychodynamic and narrowly behavioural perspectives which often inform attempts at therapeutic intervention in this field.

The vast majority of persons who engage in serious violent behaviour, whether formally labelled as offenders or not, receive little by way of psychological assistance in understanding and changing their behaviour in relationships or their views of them. The application of the therapeutic methods deriving from social skills research, and from the work of Novaco, requires that certain conditions be met in the therapeutic situation. First, it needs to be recognized that not all violent persons will share the definitions of their violent behaviour made by the potential therapist. There will be many persons whose violent behaviour is ego syntonic and perceived as a legitimate, and even necessary, form of action. It is inappropriate, and perhaps unethical, to attempt psychological intervention in such cases. There will also be, on the other hand, very many people who, in a manner which they only dimly understand and feel incapable of controlling, find themselves precipitated into unforeseen and personally unacceptable violence against wives, children, acquaintances and strangers briefly met. The latter group might be regarded as a legitimate target for the interventions described.

The second requirement is for a trusting and non-authoritarian relationship between client and therapist. Clients would need to feel able and willing to discuss behavioural histories of aggression, internal affective states, and personal interpretations and meanings. Such a relationship is not easily established in custodial settings, or in contexts in which the client fears that his disclosure of violent, and perhaps illegal, acts might have adverse consequences.

The third requirement is for a treatment environment which approximates to the environment in which violent behaviour occurs. Many persons who have acted violently will, in fact, be found in "secure" environments, such as prisons and security hospitals. A major obstacle to the use of social psychological methods in these environments is the fact that the offender may be effectively removed from the very interpersonal events which provoke him to violence. A man, who cannot cope non-violently with aspects of his relationship with his wife or family, may find himself himself entirely removed from such situations, for a long period of time, by virtue of his incarceration. Such methods are only fully practicable in settings which can reproduce the richness and complexity of real-world interactions and relationships.

Finally, almost all of the work described above stresses the importance of the role of the victim, particularly when the victim and the aggressor are known to one another. The bi-directional relationship between victim's and aggressor's behaviour suggests that dyads, and even larger groups, ought to be seen as the appropriate unit for future assessment and treatment efforts.

References

ACHENBACH, T.S. and EDELBROCK, C.S. (1979). The child behaviour profile: II. Boys aged 12 – 16 and girls aged 6 – 11 and 12 – 16. *Journal of Consulting and Clinical Psychology*, **47**, 223-233.

AHRONS, C.R. (1979). The binuclear family: Two households, one family. *Alternative Lifestyles*, **2**, 499-515.

AINSWORTH, M.D.S. (1967). "Infancy in Uganda: Infant Care and the Growth of Love", Johns Hopkins University Press, Baltimore.

AINSWORTH, M.D.S., BELL, S.M. and STAYTON, D.J. (1974). Infant-mother attachment and social development: Socialisation as a product of reciprocal responsiveness to signals. *In* "The Integration of a Child into a Social World" (Ed. M.P.M. Richards), Cambridge University Press, Cambridge.

ALDEN, L. and SAFRAN, J. (1978). Irrational beliefs and nonassertive behaviour. *Cognitive Therapy and Research*, **2**, 357-364.

ALLAN, L.J. (1978). Child abuse: a critical review of the research and the theory. *In* "Violence and the Family" (Ed. J.P. Martin), Wiley, Chichester.

ALTMAN, I. and TAYLOR, D.A. (1973). "Social Penetration", Holt, Rinehart and Winston, New York.

ANDREYEVA, G.M. and GOZMAN, L.J. (1981). Interpersonal relations and social context. *In* "Personal Relationships 1: Studying Personal Relationships" (Eds. S.W. Duck and R. Gilmour), Academic Press, London and New York.

ANTAKI, C. and FIELDING, G. (1981). Research on ordinary explanations. *In* "The Psychology of Ordinary Explanations of Social Behaviour" (Ed. C. Antaki), Academic Press, London and New York.

ARCHER, R.P., WHITE, J.L. and ORVIN, G.H. (1979). MMPI characteristics and correlates among adolescent psychiatric inpatients. *Journal of Clinical Psychology*, **35**, 498-504.

ARGYLE, M. (1969). "Social Interaction", Methuen, London.

ATHANASIOU, R. and SARKIN, R. (1974). Premarital sexual behaviour and postmarital adjustment. *Archives of Sexual Behaviour*, **3**, 207-225.

ATHANASIOU, R., SHAVER, P. and TAVRIS, C. (1970). Sex (a report to *Psychology Today* readers). *Psychology Today*, **4**, 37-52.

ATHENS, L.H. (1980). "Violent Criminal Acts and Actors: A Symbolic Interactionist Study", Routledge and Kegan Paul, London.

ATKINSON, V.C. (1981). Selective Group Formation in Pre-school Children. Unpublished Ph.D. thesis, University of Edinburgh.

AVERILL, J.R. (1973). Personal control over aversive stimuli and its relationship to stress. *Psychological Bulletin*, **80**, 186-303.

BACH, G.R. and WYDEN, P. (1971). "The Intimate Enemy: How to Fight Fair in Love and Marriage", Avon Books, New York.

BALL-ROKEACH, S. (1973). Values and violence: a test of the subculture of violence thesis. *American sociological Review*, **38**, 736-749.

BANCROFT, J. (1979). Treatment of deviant sexual behaviour. *In* "Current Themes in Psychiatry" (Eds. R. Gaind and B. Hudson), Macmillan, London.

BANCROFT, J., DAVIDSON, D.W., WARNER, P. and TYRER, G. (1980). Androgens and sexual behaviour in women using oral contraceptives. *Clinical Endocrinology*, **12**, 328-340.

BANDURA, A. (1971a). Social learning theory of aggression. *In* "Control of Aggression: Implications from Basic Research" (Ed. J. Knutson), Aldine—Atherton, Chicago.

BANDURA, A. (1971b). "Aggression: A Social Learning Analysis", Prentice Hall, New York.

BANDURA, A. (1977). "Social Learning Theory", Prentice Hall, Englewood Cliffs, New Jersey.

BANE, M.J. (1979). Marital disruption and the lives of children. *In* "Divorce and Separation" (Eds. G. Levinger and O.C. Moles), Basic Books. Inc., New York.

BARBACH, L.G. (1974). Group treatment of preorgasmic women. *Journal of Sex and Marital Therapy*, **1**, 139-145.

BARLOW, D.H. (1976). Assessment of sexual behaviour. *In* "Handbook of Behavioural Assessment" (Eds. A.R. Ciminero, K.S. Cachoun and H.E. Adams), Wiley, New York.

BARLOW, D.H. and WINCZE, J.P. (1980). Treatment of sexual deviation. *In* "Principles and Practice of Sex Therapy" (Eds. S.R. Leiblum and L.A. Pervin), Tavistock, London.

BARRY, W.A. (1970). Marriage research and conflict: An integrative review. *Psychological Bulletin*, **73**, 41-54.

BART, P. (1972). "Portnoy's Mother's complaint", Atherton, New York.

BATESON, G., JACKSON, D.D., HALEY, J. and WEAKLAND, J.H. (1956). Towards a theory of schizophrenia. *Behavioural Science*, **4**, 251-264.

BATTLE, E. and LACEY, B. (1972). A context for hyperactivity in children over time. *Child Development*, **43**, 757-773.

BECK, A.T. (1972). Cognition, affect and psychopathology. *In* "The Cognitive Alteration of Feeling States" (Eds. H. London and R.E. Nisbett), Aldine, Chicago.

BECK, A.T. (1976). "Cognitive Therapy and the Emotional Disorders", International Universities Press, New York.

BECK, A.T. and EMERY, G. (1979). "Cognitive Therapy of Anxiety and Phobic Disorders", Centre for Cognitive Therapy, Philadelphia.

BECK, A.T., RUSH, A.J., SHAW, B.F. and EMERY, G. (1979). "Cognitive Therapy of Depression", Wiley, New York.

BEE, L.S. (1959). "Marriage and Family Relations", Harper and Bros, New York.
BELLACK, A.S. and HERSEN, M. (Eds.) (1979). "Research and Practice in Social Skills Training", Plenum Press, New York.
BELSKY, J. (1978). Three theoretical models of child abuse: A critical review. *Child Abuse and Neglect*, 2, 37 – 50.
BEM, D.J. and ALLEN, A. (1974). On predicting some of the people some of the time: The search for cross-situational consistencies in behaviour. *Psychological Review*, 81, 506 – 520.
BEM, S.L., MARTYNA, W. and WATSON, C. (1976). Sex typing and androgyny: Further explorations of the expressive domain. *Journal of Personality and Social Psychology*, 34, 1016 – 1023.
BENJAMIN, L.S. (1977). Structural analysis of a family in therapy. *Journal of Consulting and Clinical Psychology*, 45, 391 – 405.
BENTLER, P.M. and NEWCOMB, M.D. (1978). Longitudinal study of marital success and failure. *Journal of Consulting and Clinical Psychology*, 46, 1053-1070.
BERGER, C.R. (1979). Beyond initial interaction: Uncertainty and understanding, and the development of interpersonal relationships. *In* "Language and Social Psychology" (Eds. H. Giles and R.N. St. Clair), Blackwell, Oxford.
BERGER, C.R. (1980). Self consciousness and the adequacy of theory and research into relationship development. *Western Journal of Speech Communication*, 44, 93-96.
BERGER, C.R. and CALABRESE, R.J. (1975). Explorations in initial interactions and beyond: toward a developmental theory of interpersonal communication. *Human Communication Research*, 2, 33-50.
BERGER, C.R., GARDNER, R.R., PARKS, M.R., SCHULMAN, L. and MILLER, G.R. (1976). Interpersonal epistemology and interpersonal communication. *In* "Explorations in Interpersonal Communication" (Ed. G.R. Miller), Sage, Beverley Hills.
BERGER, P.L and KELLNER, H. (1964). Marriage and the construction of reality. *Diogenes*, 46, 1-23.
BERNE, E. (1964). "Games People Play", Penguin, Harmondsworth.
BIGELOW, B.J. and LA GAIPA, J.J. (1975). Children's written descriptions of friendship: a multidimensional analysis. *Developmental Psychology*, 11, 857-858.
BIGELOW, B.J. and LA GAIPA, J.J. (1980). The development of friendship values and choice. *In* "Friendship and Social Relations in Children" (Eds. H.C. Foot, A.J. Chapman and J.R. Smith), John Wiley and Sons Ltd., New York.
BILLINGS, A. (1979). Conflict resolution in distressed and nondistressed married couples. *Journal of Consulting and Clinical Psychology*, 47, 368-376.
BIRCHLER, G.R. and WEBB, L.J. (1977). Discriminating interaction behaviour in happy and unhappy marriages. *Journal of Consulting and Clinical Psychology*, 45, 494-495.
BLACK, D.A. (1973). A decade of psychological investigation of the male patient population of Broadmoor. *Special Hospitals Research Reports, No. 8*, Special Hospitals Research Unit, London.
BLACKBURN, R. (1968). Personality in relation to extreme aggression in psychiatric offenders. *British Journal of Psychiatry*, 114, 821-828.
BLACKBURN, R. (1971). Personality types among abnormal homicides. *British Journal of Criminology*, 11, 14-31.
BLACKBURN, R. (1975). An empirical classification of psychopathic personality. *British Journal of Psychiatry*, 127, 456-460.

BLAIR, M. (1970). Divorcees' adjustment and attitudinal changes about life. *Dissertation Abstracts*, **30**, 5541-5542.

BLAKE, J. (1961). "The Family Structure in Jamaica", Free Press, Glencoe, Illinois.

BLANEY, P.H. (1977). Contemporary theories of depression: critique and comparision. *Journal of Abnormal Psychology*, **86**, 203-223.

BLOM-COOPER, L. and MORRIS, T.P. (1962). "A Calendar of Murder", Michael Joseph, London.

BLOOD, R.O. and BLOOD, M.C. (1979). Amicable divorce: A new lifestyle. *Alternative Lifestyles*, **2**, 483-498.

BLOOM, B.L., ASHER, S.J. and WHITE, S.W. (1978). Marital disruption as a stressor: A review and analysis. *Psychological Bulletin*, **85**, 867-894.

BLUMER, H. (1969). "Symbolic Interactionism: Perspective and Method", Prentice-Hall, Englewood Cliffs, New Jersey.

BOHANNON, P. (1970). "Divorce and After", Doubleday and Co., Garden City, New York.

BOHMER, C. and LEBOW, R.D. (1978). Divorce comparative style: A paradigm of divorce patterns. *Journal of Divorce*, **2**, 157-173.

BOTHWELL, S. and WEISSMAN, M.M. (1977). Social impairments four years after an acute depressive episode. *American Journal of Orthopsychiatry*, **47**, 231-237.

BOWLBY, J. (1951). "Child Care and the Growth of Love", W.H.O., Geneva.

BOWLBY, J. (1969). "Attachment and Loss, Vol.1: Attachment", Hogarth Press, London.

BOWLBY, J. (1979). "The Making and Breaking of Affectional Bonds", Tavistock, London.

BOWMAN, C.C. (1975). Loneliness and social change. *American Journal of Psychiatry*, **112**, 194-198.

BOYD, R.D. (1964). Analysis of the ego-stage development of school-age children. *Journal of Experimental Education*, **32**, 249-258.

BRAIKER, H.B. and KELLEY, H.H. (1979). Conflict in the development of close relationships. *In* "Social Exchange in Developing Relationships" (Eds, R.L. Burgess and T.L. Huston), Academic Press, New York and London.

BRENNAN, T. and AUSLANDER, N. (1979). "Adolescent Loneliness: An Exploratory Study of Social and Psychological Pre-disposition and Theory". Behavioural Research Institute, Boulder, Colorado.

BRIGGS, J.L. (1970). "Never in Anger: Portait of an Eskimo Family". Harvard University Press, Cambridge, Mass.

BROCKNER, J. and HULTON, A.J.B. (1978). How to reverse the vicious cycle of low self-esteem: The importance of attentional focus. *Journal of Experimental Social Psychology*, **14**, 564-578.

BROWN, G.W. and HARRIS, T. (1978). Social origins of depression: a reply. *Psychological Medicine*, **8**, 577-588.

BROWN, G.W., MONCK, E.M., CARSTAIRS, G.M. and WING, J.K. (1962). Influences of family life on the course of schizophrenic illness. *British Journal of Preventive and Social Medicine*, **16**, 55-68.

BROWN, P. and ELLIOTT, R. (1965). Control of aggression in a nursery school class. *Journal of Experimental Child Psychology*, **2**, 103-107.

BROWN, R. (1979). The rewards of solitude. Paper presented at the UCLA Research Conference on Loneliness, Los Angeles, California, May 1979.

BRYANT, B.M. and TROWER, P.E. (1974). Social difficulty in a student sample. *British Journal of Educational Psychology*, **44**, 13-21.

BRYANT, B.M., TROWER, P.E., YARDLEY, K., URBIETA, H. and LETEMENDIA, F. (1976). A survey of social inadequacy among psychiatric outpatients. *Psychological Medicine*, 6, 101-112.
BUKSTEL, L.H., ROEDER, G.D., KILMANN, P.R. and SOTILE, W.M. (1978). Projected extramarital sexual involvement in unmarried college students. *Journal of Marriage and the Family*, 40, 337-340.
BURGESS, E.W. and LOCKE, H.J. (1953). "The Family", American Book Co., New York.
BURGESS, E.W., LOCKE, H.J. and THOMES, M.M. (1963). "The Family from Institution to Companionship", American Book Co, New York.
BURGESS, R.L. and HUSTON, T.L., (Eds.) (1979). "Social Exchange in Developing Relationships", Academic Press, New York and London.
BURR, W.R. (1970). Satisfaction with various aspects of marriage over the life cycle: A random middle class sample. *Journal of Marriage and the Family*, 32, 29-37.
BYRNE, D., McDONALD, R.D. and MIKAWA, J. (1963). Approach and avoidance affiliation motives. *Journal of Personality*, 31, 21-37.
CAMERON, N. (1959). Paranoid conditions and paranoia. *In* "American Handbook of Psychiatry" Vol. 1, (Ed. S. Arieti), Basic Books, New York.
CAMPBELL, S., SCHLEIFER, M., WEISS, G. and PERLMAN, T.A. (1977). A two-year follow-up of hyperactive preschoolers. *American Journal of Orthopsychiatry*, 47, 148-162.
CARR, J. (1975). "Young Children with Down's Syndrome", Butterworths, London.
CARTER, H. and GLICK, P.C. (1976). "Marriage and Divorce: A Social and Economic Study", Harvard University Press, Cambridge, Mass.
CATTELL, R.B. and NESSELROADE, J.R. (1967). Likeness and completeness theories examined by sixteen personality factor measures on stable and unstable married couples. *Journal of Personality and Social Psychology*, 7, 351-361.
CHADWICK, B.A., ALBRECHT, S.L. and KUNZ, P.R. (1976). Marital and family role satisfaction. *Journal of Marriage and the Family*, 38, 431-440.
CHAIKIN, A.L. and DERLEGA, V.J. (1974). Liking for the norm-breaker in self-disclosure. *Journal of Personality*, 42, 117-129.
CHANDLER, M. (1972). Egocentrism in normal and pathological child development. *In* "Determinants of Behavioural Development" (Eds. F. Monk, W. Hartup and I. Dewit), Academic Press, London and New York.
CHANDLER, M. (1973). Egocentrism and antisocial behaviour: the assessment and training of social perspective-taking skills. *Developmental Psychology*, 9, 326-332.
CHIRIBOGA, D.A. (1979). Marital separation and stress: A life course perspective. *Alternative Lifestyles*, 2, 461-470.
CHIRIBOGA, D.A. and CUTLER, L. (1977). Stress responses among divorcing men and women. *Journal of Divorce*, 1, 95-106.
CHIRIBOGA, D.A., ROBERTS, J. and STEIN, J.A. (1978). Psychological well-being during marital separation. *Journal of Divorce*, 2, 21-36.
CHOWN, S.M. (1981). Friendship in old age. *In* "Personal Relationships 2: Developing Personal Relationships" (Eds. S.W. Duck and R. Gilmour), Academic Press, London and New York.
CLARK, J.V. and AWKOWITZ, H. (1975). Social anxiety and self-evaluation of interpersonal performance. *Psychological Reports*, 36, 211-221.
CLAUSEN, J.A. and YARROW, M.R. (1955). The impact of mental illness on the family. *Journal of Social Issues*, 11, 3-65.

CLECKLEY, H. (1964). "The Mask of Sanity", C.V. Mosby, Saint Louis.

CLEMENTS, W.H. (1967). Marital interaction and marital stability: A point of view and a descriptive comparison of stable marriages. *Journal of Marriage and the Family*, **29**, 697-702.

CLYNE, S. and LA GAIPA, J.J. (1976). The measurement of level of moral reasoning of parents with their children. Unpublished Manuscript.

COLE, C.A. (1976). A behavioural analysis of married and living together couples. Unpublished doctoral dissertation, University of Houston.

COLLINS, J., KREITMAN, N., NELSON, B., and TROOP, J. (1971). Neurosis and marital interaction: III. Family roles and functions. *British Journal of Psychiatry*, **119**, 233-242.

COMEAU, H. (1980). Changes in reported self-values among students in grades 9-12. *Adolescence*, **15**, 143-147.

COTTON, N.S. (1979). The familial incidence of alcoholism; A review. *Journal of Studies on Alcohol*, **40**, 89-116.

COULTHARD, M. (1977). "An introduction to Discourse Analysis", Longman, London.

COYNE, J.C. (1976a). Toward an interactional description of depression. *Psychiatry*, **39**, 28-40.

COYNE, J.C. (1976b). Depression and the response of others. *Journal of Abnormal Psychology*, **85**, 186-193.

CRAWFORD, D.A. (1977). The HDHQ results of long-term prisoners: relationships with criminal and institutional behaviour. *British Journal of Social and Clinical Psychology*, **16**, 391-394.

CRAWFORD, D.A. and ALLEN, J.V. (1979). A social skill training program with sex offenders. *In* "Love and Attraction" (Eds. M.Cook and G. Wilson), Pergamon Press, Oxford.

CROCKETT, W. and FRIEDMAN, P. (1980). Theoretical explorations of the processes of initial interactions. *Western Journal of Speech Communication*, **44**, 86-92.

CUNNINGHAM, C.E. and BARKLEY, R.A. (1979). The interactions of normal and hyperactive children with their mothers in free play and structured tasks. *Child Development*, **50**, 217-224.

CUNNINGHAM, M.R. (1977). Personality and the structure of the nonverbal communication of emotion. *Journal of Personality*, **45**, 564-584.

CURRAN, J.P. (1977. Skills training as an approach to the treatment of heterosexual-social anxiety: A review. *Psychological Bulletin*, **84**, 140-157.

CURRAN, J.P. (1979). Social skills: methodological issues and future directions. *In* "Research and Practice in Social Skills Training", (Eds. A.S. Bellack and M. Hersen), Plenum Press, New York.

CUTRONA, C.E. (in press). Transition to college: Loneliness and the process of social adjustment. *In* "Loneliness: A sourcebook of Current Theory, Research and Therapy" (Eds, L.A. Peplau and D.Perlman), Wiley-Interscience, New York.

DANZIGER, C. (1976). Unmarried heterosexual cohabition. Unpublished doctoral dissertation, Rutgers University.

DAVIS, F. (1961). Deviance disavowal: The management of strained interaction by the visibly handicapped. *Social Problems*, **9**, 120-132.

DAVIS, H. (1979). Self-reference and the encoding of personal information in depression. *Cognitive Therapy and Research*, **3**, 97-110.

DEAN, G. and GURAK, D.T. (1978). Marital homogamy the second time around. *Journal of Marriage and the Family*, **40**, 559-570.

DeGIOVANNI, I.S. and EPSTEIN, N. (1978). Unbinding assertion and aggression in research and clinical practice. *Behaviour Modification*, **2**, 173-192.

DEIKER, T.A. (1974). A cross-validation of M.M.P.I. scales of aggression on male criminal criterion groups. *Journal of Consulting and Clinical Psychology*, **42**, 196-202.

DeMONBRUEN, B.G. and CRAIGHEAD, W.E. (1977). Distortion of perception and recall of positive and neutral feedback in depression. *Cognitive Therapy and Research*, **1**, 311-329.

DENZIN, N.K. (1970). Rules of conduct and the study of deviant behaviour: some notes on the social relationship. *In* "Social Relationships" (Eds. G.J. McCall *et al*), Aldine, Chicago.

DERLEGA, V.J. and CHAIKIN, A.L. (1976). Norms affecting self disclosure in men and women. *Journal of Consulting and Clinical Psychology*, **44**, 376-380.

DERLEGA, V.J., WILSON, M., and CHAIKIN, A.L. (1976). Friendship and disclosure reciprocity. *Journal of Personality and Social Psychology*, **34**, 578-582.

DICKENS, W.J. and PERLMAN, D. (1981). Friendship over the life cycle. *In* "Personal Relationships 2: Developing Personal Relationships" (Eds. S.W. Duck and R. Gilmour), Academic Press, London and New York.

DIL, N. (1972). Sensitivity of emotionally disturbed and emotionally non-disturbed elementary school-children to emotional meanings of facial expressions. *Dissertation Abstracts International*, **32**, 4448A.

DION, K.K., BERSCHEID, E. and WALSTER, E.H. (1972). What is beautiful is good. *Journal of Personality and Social Psychology*, **24**, 285-290.

DION, K.K. and DION, K.L. (1978). Defensiveness, intimacy and heterosexual attraction. *Journal of Research in Personality*, **12**, 479-487.

DOCTOR, R.M. and SIEVEKING, N.A. (1970). Survey of attitudes toward drug addiction. *Proceedings of the Annual Convention of the American Psychological Association*, **5**, 795-796.

DOMINIAN, J. (1979). Choice of partner. *British Medical Journal*, 8 Sept, 594-596.

DORNER, S. (1975). The relationship of physical handicap to stress in families with an adolescent with spina bifida. *Developmental Medicine and Child Neurology*, **17**, 765-776.

DOUVAN, E. (1974). Commitment and social contract in adolescence. *Psychiatry*, **37**, 22-36.

DOUVAN, E. and ADELSON, J. (1966). "The Adolescent Experience", Wiley, London.

DRAPER, M. and LA GAIPA, J.J. (1980). The role of need affiliation in the social exchange of friendship rewards. Unpublished Manuscript.

DUCK, S.W. (1973a). Personality similarity and friendship formation: Similarity of what, when? *Journal of Personality*, **41**, 543-558.

DUCK, S.W. (1973b). "Personal Relationships and Personal Constructs: A Study of Friendship Formation", Wiley, London.

DUCK, S.W. (1975). Personality similarity and friendship choices by adolescents. *European Journal of Social Psychology*, **5**, 70-83.

DUCK, S.W. (1976). Interpersonal communication in developing acquaintance. *In* "Explorations in Interpersonal Communication" (Ed. G.R. Miller), Sage, Beverly Hills.

DUCK, S.W. (1977a). "The Study of Acquaintance", Teakfields-Saxon House, Farnborough.

DUCK, S.W. (1977b). Inquiry, hypothesis and the quest for validation: personal construct systems in the development of acquaintance. *In* "Theory and Practice in Interpersonal Attraction" (Ed. S.W. Duck), Academic Press, London and New York.

DUCK, S.W. (1977c). Tell me where is fancy bred: some thoughts on the study of interpersonal attraction. *In* "Theory and Practice in Interpersonal Attraction" (Ed. S.W. Duck), Academic Press, London and New York.

DUCK, S.W. (1980). Personal relationship research in the 1980s: towards an understanding of complex human sociality. *Western Journal of Speech Communication*, **44**, 114-119.

DUCK, S.W. (in press, a) A topography of relationship dissolution, *In* "Personal Relationships 4: Dissolving Personal Relationships" (Ed. S.W. Duck), Academic Press, London and New York.

DUCK, S.W., (Ed.) (in press, b) "Personal Relationships 4: Dissolving Personal Relationships", Academic Press, London and New York.

DUCK, S.W. and CRAIG, R.G. (1978). Personality similarity and the development of friendship: a longitudinal study. *British Journal of Social and Clinical Psychology*, **17**, 237-242.

DUCK, S.W. and GILMOUR, R., (Eds) (1981a) "Personal Relationships 1: Studying Personal Relationships", Academic Press, London and New York.

DUCK, S.W. and GILMOUR, R., (Eds) (1981b) "Personal Relationships 2: Developing Personal Relationships", Academic Press, London and New York.

DUCK, S.W. and GILMOUR, R. (1981c). Preface. *In* "Personal Relationships 1: Studying Personal Relationships" (Eds. S.W. Duck and R. Gilmour), Academic Press, London and New York.

DUCK, S.W. and MIELL, D.E. (in preparation). Towards a comprehension of friendship development and breakdown. *In* "The Social Dimension: European Perspectives on Social Psychology" (Ed. H. Tajfel), Cambridge University Press, Cambridge.

DUCK, S.W., MIELL, D.K. and GAEBLER, H.C. (1980). Attraction and communication in children's interactions. *In* "Friendship and Social Relations in Children" (Eds. H.C. Foot, A.J. Chapman and J.R. Smith), Wiley, London.

DUNN, J. (1977). "Distress and Comfort", Fontana/Open Books, London.

DUVAL, S. and WICKLUND, R.A. (1972). "A Theory of Objective Self-Awareness", Academic Press, New York and London.

DYCK, R.J. and RULE, B.G. (1978). Effect on retaliation of causal attributions concerning attack. *Journal of Personality and Social Psychology*, **36**, 521-529.

EDDY, P.D. (1961). Loneliness: A discrepancy with the phenomenological self. Unpublished doctoral dissertation, Adelphi College.

ELLIS, A. (1962). "Reason and Emotion in Psychotherapy", Lyle Stuart, New York.

ELLIS, A. (1971). Rational-emotive treatment of impotence, frigidity and other sexual problems. *Professional Psychology*, **2**, 346-349.

ELLISON, C. (1972). Vaginismus. *Medical Aspects of Human Sexuality*, August, 34-54.

ENGELHART, R.S., LOCKHART, L.M. and LA GAIPA, J.J. (1975). The friendship expectations of psychiatric patients. Paper read at meeting of the Southeastern Psychological Association, Atlanta, Georgia.

ENGLISH, R.A. (1971). Combating stigma toward physically disabled person. *Rehabilitation Research and Practice Review*, **2**, 19-27.

EPSTEIN, S. and TAYLOR, S.P. (1967). Instigation to aggression as a function of degree of defeat and perceived aggressive intent of the opponent. *Journal of Personality*, **35**, 265-289.

ERICKSEN, J.A., YANCEY, W.L. and ERICKSEN, E.P. (1979). The division of family roles. *Journal of Marriage and the Family*, **41**, 301-313.

ERIKSON, E.H. (1968). "Identity: Youth and Crisis", W.W. Norton, New York.

ESPENSHADE, T.J. (1979). The economic consequences of divorce. *Journal of Marriage and the Family*, **41**, 615-625.

EYSENCK, H.J. and CLARIDGE, G. (1962). The position of hysterics and dysthymics in a two-dimensional framework of personality description. *Journal of Abnormal and Social Psychology*, **64**, 46-55.

FALBO, T. (1977). Multidimensional scaling of power strategies. *Journal of Personality and Social Psychology*, **8**, 537-547.

FARINA, A. and HOLZBERG, J.D. (1968). Interaction patterns of parents and hospitalized sons diagnosed as schizophrenic or non-schizophrenic. *Journal of Abnormal Psychology*, **73**, 114-118.

FARINA, A., MURRAY, P.J. and GROH, T. (1978). Sex and worker acceptance of a former mental patient. *Journal of Consulting and Clinical Psychology*, **46**, 887-891.

FELDMAN, L.B. (1976). Depression and marital interaction. *Family Process*, **15**, 389-395.

FERREIRA, A.J. and WINTER, W.D. (1968). Decision-making in normal and abnormal two-child families. *Family Process*, **7**, 17-36.

FESTINGER, L. (1954). A theory of social comparison processes. *Human Relations,* **7**, 117–140.

FINE, G.A. (1981). Friends, impression management and preadolescent behaviour. *In* "The Development of Friendship" (Eds. S.R. Asher and J.Gottman), Cambridge University Press, Cambridge.

FOA, U.G. and FOA, E.B. (1974). "Societal Structures of the Mind". Thomas, Springfields, Illinois.

FOOT, H.C., CHAPMAN, A.J. and SMITH, J.R., (Eds) (1980). "Friendship and Social Relations in Children", Wiley, London.

FORGUS, R.H. and DE WOLFE, A.S. (1974). Coding of cognitive input in delusional patients. *Journal of Abnormal Psychology*, **83**, 278-284.

FORREST, M.S and HOKANSON, J.E. (1975). Depression and automatic arousal reduction accompanying self-punitive behaviour. *Journal of Abnormal Psychology*, **84**, 346-357.

FOY, D.W., EISLER, R.M. and PINKSTON, S.G. (1975). Modelled assertion in a case of explosive rage. *Journal of Behaviour Therapy and Experimental Psychiatry*, **6**, 135-137.

FRAMROSE, R. (1977). A framework for adolescent disorder: Some clinical presentations. *British Journal of Psychiatry*, **131**, 281-288.

FRANK, E., ANDERSON, C. and RUBINSTEIN, P. (1978). Frequency of sexual dysfunction in "normal" couples. *New England Journal of Medicine*, **299**, 111-115.

FRANKEL, A.S. (1970). Treatment of multisymptomatic phobia by a self-directed, self-reinforced technique. *Journal of Abnormal Psychology*, **76**, 496-499.

FRANSELLA, F. and BANNISTER, D. (1977). "A Manual for Repertory Grid Technique", Academic Press, London and New York.

FREDERIKSEN, L.W., JENKINS, J.O., FOY, D.W. and EISLER, R.M. (1976). Social skills training in the modification of abusive verbal outbursts in adults. *Journal of Applied Behaviour Analysis*, **9**, 117-125.

FREUD, A. (1966). "The Ego and the Mechanisms of Defence", Hogarth Press, London.

FROMM-REICHMANN, F. (1959). Loneliness. *Psychiatry*, **22**, 1-15.

FROST, R.O., GRAF, M., and BECKER, J. (1979). Self-devaluation and depressed mood. *Journal of Consulting and Clinical Psychology*, **47**m 958-962.

FURSTENBERG, F.F. (1979). Premarital pregnancy and marital instability. *In* "Divorce and Separation" (Eds. G. Levinger and O.C. Moles), Basic Books, Inc., New York.

GALE, A. (1979). Problems of outcome research in family therapy. *In* "Family and Marital Psychotherapy" (Ed. S. Walrond-Skinner), Routledge and Kegan Paul, London.

GARDINER, J. (1975). Women's domestic labour. *New Left Review*, **89**, 47-58,

GELLES, R.J. (1974). "The Violent Home: A Study of Physical Aggression Between Husbands and Wives", Sage, Beverly Hills, California.

GELLMAN, W. (1959). Roots of prejudice against the handicapped. *Journal of Rehabilitation*, **25**, 4-11.

GERSICK, K.E. (1979). Fathers by choice: Divorced men who receive custody of their children. *In* "Divorce and Separation" (Eds. G. Levinger and O.C. Moles), Basic Books, Inc., New York.

GERSON, A.C. and PERLMAN, D. (1979). Loneliness and expressive communication. *Journal of Abnormal Psychology*, **88**, 258-261.

GILFORD, R. and BENGSTON, V. (1979). Measuring marital satisfaction in three generations: Positive and negative dimensions. *Journal of Marriage and the Family*, **41**, 387-398.

GILGER, K. (1976). Loneliness and the holidays. Holidays News Story No.19, Department of Agricultural Communications, University of Nebraska-Lincoln.

GIVENS, D. (1978). Greeting a stranger: Some commonly used nonverbal signals of aversiveness. *Semiotica*, **22**, 351-367.

GLASER, B. and STRAUSS, A. (1967). "The Discovery of Grounded Theory", Aldine, Chicago.

GLENN, N.D. and WEAVER, C.N. (1977). The marital happiness of remarried divorced persons. *Journal of Marriage and the Family*, **39**, 331-337.

GLICK, P.C. and NORTON, A.J. (1971). Frequency, duration, and probability of marriage and divorce. *Journal of Marriage and the Family*, **33**, 307-317.

GLUECK, S. and GLUECK, E.T. (1962). "Family Environment and Delinquency", Kegan Paul, London.

GOFFMAN, E. (1955). On facework: An analysis of ritual elements in social interaction. *Psychiatry*, **18**, 213-231.

GOFFMAN, E. (1959). "The Presentation of Self in Everyday Life", Doubleday Anchor, New York.

GOFFMAN, E. (1961). "Encounters", Bobbs-Merrill, Indianapolis.

GOFFMAN, E. (1963). "Stigma", Prentice-Hall, Englewood Cliffs, New Jersey.

GOFFMAN, E. (1967). "Interaction Ritual", Allen Lane/The Penguin Press, London.

GOFFMAN, E. (1972). "Relations in Public: Microstudies of the Public Order", Penguin, Harmondsworth.

GOODE, W.J. (1956). "After Divorce", Free Press, New York.

GOODE, W.J., HOPKINS, E. and McCLURE, H.M. (1971). "Social Systems and Family Patterns: A Propositional Inventory", Bobbs-Merrill, Indianapolis.

GOODWIN, D.W. (1971). Is alcoholism hereditary? A review and critique. *Archives of General Psychiatry*, **25**, 545-549.

GORDON, S. (1976). "Lonely in America", Simon and Schuster, New York.

GOTTMAN, J., MARKMAN, H. and NOTARIUS, C. (1977). The topography of marital conflict: a sequential analysis of verbal and nonverbal behaviour. *Journal of Marriage and the Family*, **39**, 461-478.

GOUGH, H.G. (1948). A sociological theory of psychopathy. *American Journal of Sociology*, **53**, 359-366.

GREENWELL, J. and DENGERINK, H. (1973). The role of perceived versus actual attack in physical aggression. *Journal of Personality and Social Psychology*, **26**, 66-71.

GUBRIUM, J.F. (1974). Marital desolation and the evaluation of everyday life in old age. *Journal of Marriage and the Family*, **36**, 107-113.

GUNDERSON, J.G. and KOLB, J.E. (1978). Discriminating features of borderline patients. *American Journal of Psychiatry*, **135**, 792-795.

GURMAN, A.S. (1973). The effects and effectiveness of marital therapy: A review of outcome research. *Family Process*, **12**, 145-170.

GURMAN, A.S. and KNISKERN, D.P. (1978). Research on marital and family therapy: Progress, perspective and prospect. *In* "Handbook of Psychotherapy and Behaviour Change" (Eds. S. Garfield and A. Bergin), Wiley, New York.

HAFNER, R.J. (1977). The husbands of agoraphobic women and their influence on treatment outcome. *British Journal of Psychiatry*, **131**, 289-294.

HALEY, J. (1972). Critical review of the present status of Family Interaction Research. *In* "Family Interaction: A Dialogue Between Family Researchers and Family Therapists" (Ed. J.L. Franco), Springer, New York.

HAMMEN, C.L. and KRANTZ, S. (1976). Effect of success and failure on depressive cognitions. *Journal of Abnormal Psychology*, **85**, 577-586.

HAMMEN, C.L. and PETERS, S.D. (1977). Differential responses to male and female depressive reactions. *Journal of Consulting and Clinical Psychology*, **45**, 994-1001.

HAMMEN, C.L. and PETERS, S.D. (1978). Interpersonal consequences of depression: responses to men and women enacting a depressed role. *Journal of Abnormal Psychology*, **87**, 322-332.

HARE, R.D. (1970). "Psychopathy: Theory and Research", Wiley, New York.

HARE, R.D. and SCHALLING, D. (1978). "Psychopathic Behaviour: Approach to Research", Wiley, Chichester.

HARLOW, H.F. (1961). The development of affectional patterns in infant monkeys. *In* "Determinants of Infant Behaviour, Vol. 1" (Ed. B.M. Foss), Methuen, London.

HARLOW, H.F. (1963). The maternal affectional system. *In* "Determinants of Infant Behaviour, Vol. 2" (Ed. B.M. Foss), Methuen, London.

HARLOW, H.F., and HARLOW, M.K. (1965). The affectional systems. *In* "Behaviour of non-human Primates" (Eds. A.M. Schrier, H.F. Harlow and F. Stollnitz), Academic Press, New York and London.

HARPER, D.C. and RICHMAN, L.C. (1978). Personality profiles of physically impaired adolescents. *Journal of Clinical Psychology*, **34**, 636–642.

HARRÉ, R. (1974). The conditions for a social psychology of childhood. *In* "The Integration of a Child into a Social World" (Ed. M.P.M. Richards), Cambridge University Press, Cambridge.

HARRÉ, R. (1977). Friendship as an accomplishment: an ethogenic approach to social relationships. *In* "Theory and Practice in Interpersonal Attraction" (Ed. S.W. Duck), Academic Press, London and New York.

HARRÉ, R. (1979). "Social Being", Basil Blackwell, Oxford.

HARTMAN, C.M. (1980). The interface between sexual dysfunction and marital conflict. *American Journal of Psychiatry*, **137**, 576-579.

HARTOG, J., AUDY, J.R. and COHEN, Y.A. (Eds.) (1980). "The Anatomy of Loneliness", International Universities Press, New York.

HARVEY, J.H., WELLS, G.L. and ALVAREZ, M.D. (1978). Attribution in the context of conflict and separation in close relationships. *In* "New Directions in Attribution Research, Vol. 2" (Eds. J.H. Harvey, W. Ickes and R.F. Kidd), Erlbaum, Hillsdale, New Jersey.

HATFIELD, E. and TRAUPMANN, J. (1981). Intimate relationships: a perspective from equity theory. *In* "Personal Relationships 1: Studying Personal Relationships" (Eds. S.W. Duck and R. Gilmour), Academic Press, London and New York.

HAWTON, K. (1980). Current trends in sex therapy. *In* "Current Trends in Psychiatric Treatment" (Ed. G. Tennent), Pitman Medical, London.

HAYDEN, B., NASBY, W. and DAVIDS, A. (1977). Interpersonal conceptual structures, predictive accuracy, and social adjustment of emotionally disturbed boys. *Journal of Abnormal Psychology*, **86**, 315-320.

HAYNES, S.N., FOLLINGSTAD, D.R. and SULLIVAN, J.C. (1979). Assessment of marital satisfaction and interaction. *Consulting and Clinical Psychology*, **47**, 789-791.

HEIBY, E.M. (1979). Conditions which occasion depression: A review of three behavioural models. *Psychological Reports*, **45**, 683-714.

HEIDER, F. (1958). "The Psychology of Interpersonal Relations", Wiley, New York.

HENDERSON, S., BYRNE, D.G., DUNCAN-JONES, P., ADCOCK, S., SCOTT, R. and STEELE, G.P. (1978). Social bonds in the epidemiology of neurosis: A preliminary communication. *British Journal of Psychiatry*, **3**, 463-466.

HERBERT, M. and IWANIEC, D. (1977). Children who are hard to love. *New Society*, **21**, 111-112.

HERMAN, S.J. (1977). Women, divorce, and suicide. *Journal of Divorce*, **1**, 107-117.

HERRMANN, J. (1978). An observational study of two children perceived as aggressive problems in playgroup. Supplementary report to Peter Appleton's 1977/78 report on Project No.15, financed by the East Anglian Regional Health Authority.

HERSEN, M. (1979). Modification of skill deficits in psychiatric patients. *In* "Research and Practice in Social Skills Training" (Eds. A.S. Bellack and M. Hersen), Plenum Press, New York.

HICKS, M.W. and PLATT, M. (1970). Marital happiness and stability: A review of the research in the sixties. *Journal of Marriage and the Family*, **32**, 553-574.

HILL, C.T., RUBIN, Z. and PEPLAU, L.A. (1976). Breakups before marriage: The end of 103 affairs. *Journal of Social Issues*, **32**, 147-168.

HINCHCLIFFE, M.K., HOOPER, D. and ROBERTS, F.J. (1978). "The Melancholy Marriage: Depression in Marriage and Psychosocial Approaches to Therapy", Wiley, New York.

HINCHCLIFFE, M.K., LANCASHIRE, M. and ROBERTS, F.J. (1970). Eye-contact and depression: a preliminary report. *British Journal of Psychiatry*, **117**, 571-572.

HINCHCLIFFE, M.K., LANCASHIRE, M. and ROBERTS, F.J. (1971a). Depression: defense mechanisms in speech. *British Journal of Psychiatry*, **118**, 471-472.

HINCHCLIFFE, M.K., LANCASHIRE, M. and ROBERTS, F.J. (1971b). A study of eye-contact in depressed and recovered psychiatric patients. *British Journal of Psychiatry*, **119**, 213-215.

HINDE, R.A. (1979). "Towards Understanding Relationships", Academic Press, London and New York.

HINDE, R.A. (1981). The bases of a science of interpersonal relationships. *In* "Personal Relationships 1: Studying Personal Relationships (Eds. S.W. Duck and R. Gilmour), Academic Press, London and New York.

HOFFMAN, S. (1977). Marital instability and the economic status of women. *Demography*, **14**, 67-76.

HOKANSON, J.E., SACCO, W.P., BLUMBERG, S.R. and LANDRUM, G.C. (1980). Interpersonal behaviour of depressive individuals in a mixed-motive game. *Journal of Abnormal Psychology*, **89**, 320-332.

HOLLANDSWORTH, J.G. (1977). Differentiating assertion and aggression: some behavioural guidelines. *Behaviour Therapy*, **8**, 347-352.

HOLMES, T.H. and RAHE, R.H. (1967). The social readjustment rating scale. *Journal of Psychosomatic Research*, **11**, 213-218.

HOLZMAN, P.S. and GRINKER, R.R. Sr. (1974). Schizophrenia in adolescence. *Journal of Youth and Adolescence*, **3**, 276-290.

HOME OFFICE (1961). "Murder", H.M.S.O., London.

HOME OFFICE (1975). "Homicide in England and Wales, 1967-1971", H.M.S.O., London.

HOOD, R. and SPARKS, R. (1970). "Key Issues in Criminology", Weidenfeld and Nicolson, London.

HOROWITZ, L.M., FRENCH, R. and ANDERSON, C. (In press). The prototype of a lonely person. *In* "Loneliness: A Sourcebook of Current Theory, Research and Therapy" (Eds. L.A. Peplau and D. Perlman), Wiley-Interscience, New York.

HOROWITZ, M.J. (1979). "States of Mind: Analysis of Change in Psychotherapy", Plenum Medical, New York.

HORROCKS, J.E. and BAKER, M.E. (1951). A study of friendship fluctuations of pre-adolescents. *Journal of Genetic Psychology*, **78**, 131-144.

HORROCKS, J.E. and THOMPSON, G.G. (1946). A study of the friendship fluctuations of rural boys and girls. *Journal of Genetic Psychology*, **69**, 189-198.

HOUSEKNECHT, S.K. (1979). Childlessness and marital adjustment. *Journal of Marriage and the Family*, **41**, 259-265.

HOWARD, J.W. and DAWES, R.M. (1976). Linear prediction of marital happiness. *Personality and Social Psychology Bulletin*, **2**, 478-480.

HOWELLS, K. (1976). Interpersonal aggression. *International Journal of Criminology and Penology*, **4**, 319-330.

HOWELLS, K. (1978). The meaning of poisoning to a person diagnosed as a psychopath. *Medicine, Science and the Law*, **8**, 179-184.

HOWELLS, K. (1981). Social construing and violent behaviour in mentally abnormal offenders. *In* "Dangerousness: Problems of Assessment and Prediction" (Ed. J. Hinton). George Allen and Unwin, London.

HOWES, M.J. and HOKANSON, J.E. (1979). Conversational and social responses to depressive interpersonal behaviour. *Journal of Abnormal Psychology*, **88**, 625-634.

HOY, E., WEISS, G., MINDE, K. and COHEN, N. (1978). The hyperactive child at adolescence: Cognitive, emotional and social functioning. *Journal of Abnormal Child Psychology*, **6**, 311-324.

HUESMANN, L.R. and LEVINGER, G. (1976). Incremental Exchange Theory: a formal model for progression in dyadic social interaction. *In* "Advances in Experimental Social Psychology, Vol. 9" (Eds. L. Berkowitz and E.H. Walster), Academic Press, New York and London.

HUSTON, T.L. and LEVINGER, G. (1978). Interpersonal attraction and relationships. *In* "Annual Review of Psychology, Vol. 29" (Eds. M.R. Rosenzweig and L. Porter), Annual Reviews, Palo Alto.

HUSTON, T.L., SURRA, C.A., FITZGERALD, N.M. and CATE, R.M. (1981). From courtship to marriage: Mate selection as an interpersonal process. *In* "Personal Relationships 2: Developing Personal Relationships" (Eds. S.W. Duck and R. Gilmour), Academic Press, London and New York.

INAMDAR, S.C., SIOMOPOULOS, G., OSBORN, M. and BIANCHI, E.C. (1979). Phenomenology associated with depressed moods in adolescents. *American Journal of Psychiatry*, **136**, 156-159.

IVEY, A.E. (1973). Media therapy: educational change planning for psychiatric patients. *Journal of Consulting Psychology*, **20**, 338-343.

JACOB, T. (1975). Family interaction in disturbed and normal families: A methodological and substantive review. *Psychological Bulletin*, **82**, 33-65.

JACOBSON, D.S. (1978a). The impact of marital separation/divorce on children: I. Parent-child separation and child adjustment. *Journal of Divorce*, **1**, 341-360.

JACOBSON, D.S (1978b). The impact of marital separation/divorce on children: II. Interparent hostility and child adjustment. *Journal of Divorce*, **2**, 3-19.

JACOBSON, D.S (1978c). The impact of marital separation/divorce on children: III. Parent-child communication and child adjustment, and regression analysis of findings from overall study. *Journal of Divorce*, **2**, 175-194.

JAFFE, D.T. and KANTER, R.M. (1979). Couple strains in communal households: A four-factor model of the separation process. *In* "Divorce and Separation" (Eds. G. Levinger and O.C. Moles), Basic Books, Inc., New York.

JEHU, D. (1979). "Sexual Dysfunction", Wiley, Chichester.

JOHNSON, R.E. (1970). Some correlates of extramarital coitus. *Journal of Marriage and the Family*, **32**, 449-456.

JONES, E.E. and NISBETT, R.E. (1971). "The Actor and the Observer: Divergent Perceptions of the Causes of Behaviour", General Learning Press, Morristown, New Jersey.

JONES, L. and COCHRANE, R. (1979). Stereotypes of mental illness: A test of the labelling hypothesis. Unpublished Manuscript., Birmingham University.

JONES, S.C. and PANITCH, D. (1971). The self-fulfilling prophecy and interpersonal attraction. *Journal of Experimental Social Psychology*, **7**, 356-66.

JONES, W.H. (in press). Loneliness and social behaviour. *In* "Loneliness: A Sourcebook of Current Theory, Research and Therapy" (Eds. L.A. Peplau and D. Perlman), Wiley-Interscience, New York.

JONES, W.H., FREEMON, J.E. and GOSWICK, R.A. (in press). The persistence of loneliness: Self and other determinants. *Journal of Personality*.

de JONG-GIERVELD, J. and RAADSCHELDERS, J. Types of loneliness. *In* "Loneliness: A Sourcebook of Current Theory, Research and Therapy" (Eds, L.A. Peplau and D. Perlman), Wiley-Interscience, New York.

JOURARD, S.M. (1965). "The Transparent Self", Van Nostrand, Princeton, New Jersey.

JOURARD, S.M. (1966). An exploratory study of body-accessibility. *British Journal of Social and Clinical Psychology*, 5, 221-231.

JUHASZ, A.M. (1979). A concept of divorce: Not busted bond but severed strand. *Alternative Lifestyles*, 2, 471-482.

KAPLAN, H.S. (1974). "The New Sex Therapy", Brunner/Mazel, New York.

KAPLAN, H.S. (1979). "Disorders of Sexual Desire and Other New Concepts and Techniques in Sex Therapy", Brunner/Mazel, New York.

KEGEL, A.H. (1952). Sexual function of the pubococcygeous muscle. *Western Journal of Obstetrics and Gynaecology*, 60, 521.

KELLEY, H.H. (1967). Attribution theory in social psychology. *In* "Nebraska Symposium on Motivation" (Vol. 15). (Ed. D. Levine), University of Nebraska Press, Lincoln.

KELLEY, H.H. (1973). The processes of causal attribution. *American Psychologist*, 28, 107-128.

KELLEY, H.H. (1979). "Personal Relationships: Their Structures and Processes", John Wiley and Sons, Inc., New York.

KELLEY, H.H. and STAHELSKI, A.J. (1970). The social interaction basis of co-operators' and competitors' beliefs about others. *Journal of Personality and Social Psychology*, 16, 66-91.

KELLY, G. (1955). "The Psychology of Personal Constructs", Vols. 1 and 2, W.W. Norton, New York.

KERCKHOFF, A.C. (1976). Patterns of marriage and family formation and dissolution. *Journal of Consumer Research*, 2, 261-275.

KIRCHNER, E.P., KENNEDY, R.E. and DRAGUNS, J.G. (1979). Assertion and aggression in adult offenders. *Behaviour Therapy*, 10, 452-471.

KIRKPATRICK, C. (1955). "The Family as Process and Institution", Ronald Press, New York.

KLEIN, H. and LA GAIPA, J.J. (1978). Causal explanations of interpersonal behaviour given by socially withdrawn children. Unpublished Manuscript.

KOHEN, J.A., BROWN, C.A. and FELDBERG, R. (1979). Divorced mothers: The costs and benefits of female family control. *In* "Divorce and Separation", (Eds. G. Levinger and O.C. Moles), Basic Books, Inc., New York.

KOHN, M.L. and CLAUSEN, J.A. (1955). Social isolation and schizophrenia. *American Sociological Review*, 20, 265-273.

KON, I.S. (1981). Adolescent friendship: Some unanswered questions for future research. *In* "Personal Relationships 2: Developing Personal Relationships" (Eds. S.W. Duck and R. Gilmour), Academic Press, London and New York.

KRANTZ, S. and HAMMEN, C.L. (1979). Assessment of cognitive bias in depression. *Journal of Abnormal Psychology*, 88, 611-619.

KRAUSE, M.S. (1978). Identifying improper persons. *Journal of the Theory of Social Behaviour*, 8, 285-296.

KUIPERS, L. (1979). Expressed emotion: A review. *British Journal of Social and Clinical Psychology*, 18, 237-244.

KURTH, S.B. (1970). Friendship and friendly relations. *In* "Social Relationships" (Eds. G.J. McCall *et al*), Aldine, Chicago.

LABOV, W. and FANSHEL, D. (1977). "Therapeutic Discourse", Academic Press, New York and London.

LA GAIPA, J.J. (1977a). Interpersonal attraction and social exchange. *In* "Theory and Practice in Interpersonal Attraction" (Ed. S.W. Duck), Academic Press, London and New York.

LA GAIPA, J.J. (1977b). Testing a multi-dimensional approach to friendship. *In* "Theory and Practice in Interpersonal Attraction", (Ed. S.W. Duck), Academic Press, London and New York.

LA GAIPA, J.J. (1979). A development study of the meaning of friendship in adolescence. *Journal of Adolescence*, **2**, 1-13.

LA GAIPA, J.J. (1981a). A systems approach to personal relationships. *In* "Personal Relationship 1: Studying Personal Relationships" (Eds. S.W. Duck and R. Gilmour), Academic Press, London and New York.

LA GAIPA, J.J. (1981b). Children's friendships. *In* "Personal Relationships 2: Developing Personal Relationships" (Eds. S.W. Duck and R. Gilmour), Academic Press, London and New York.

LA GAIPA, J.J. and ENGELHART, R.S. (1977). Extraversion-introversion, neuroticism and self disclosure in friendship. Paper read at meeting of the South-eastern Psychological Association, Hollywood, Florida.

LA GAIPA, J.J. and WOOD, H.D. (1973). The perception of friendship by socially accepted and rejected children. Paper read at meeting of the Eastern Psychological Association, Washington, D.C.

LA GAIPA, J.J. and WOOD, H.D. (1976). The development and validation of the Children's Friendship Expectancy Inventory. Unpublished Manuscript.

LANDIS, J.T. (1963). Social correlates of divorce or nondivorce among the unhappy married. *Marriage and Family Living*, **25**, 178-180.

LANER, M.R. (1978). Love's labours lost: A theory of marital dissolution. *Journal of Divorce*, **1**, 213-232.

LARSON, R., CSIKSZENTMIHALYI, M. and GRAEF, R. (In press). Time alone in daily experience. *In* "Loneliness: A Sourcebook of Current Theory, Research and Therapy" (Eds. L.A. Peplau and D. Perlman), Wiley-Interscience, New York.

LA RUSSO, L. (1978). Sensitivity of paranoid patients to nonverbal cues. *Journal of Abnormal Psychology*, **87**, 463-471.

LATHAM, J.D. and WHITE, G.D. (1978). Coping with homosexual expressions within heterosexual marriages: five case studies. *Journal of Sex and Marital Therapy*, **4**, 198-212.

LAWS, J.L. (1971). A feminist review of the marital adjustment literature: the rape of the Locke. *Journal of Marriage and the Family*, **33**, 383-516.

LAZARUS, A.A. (1976). "Multimodal Behaviour Therapy", Springer, New York.

LEARY, T. (1957). "Interpersonal Diagnoses of Personality: A Functional Theory and Methodology for Personality Evaluation", Ronald, New York.

LEIBLUM, S.L.R. and PERVIN, L.A. (Eds.) (1980). "Principles and Practice of Sex Therapy", Tavistock, London.

LERNER, M.J. (1970). The desire for justice and reactions to victims. *In* "Altruism and Helping Behaviour", (Eds. J. Macaulay and L. Berkowitz), Academic Press, New York and London.

LEVAY, A.N. and KAGLE, A. (1977). A study of treatment needs following sex therapy. *American Journal of Psychiatry*, **134**, 970-973.

LEVINGER, G. (1966). Sources of marital dissatisfaction among applicants for divorce. *American Journal of Orthopsychiatry*, **26**, 803-807.

LEVINGER, G. (1974). A three-level approach to attraction: toward an understanding of pair relatedness. *In* "Foundations of Interpersonal Attraction" (Ed. T.L. Huston), Academic Press, New York and London.

LEVINGER, G. (1976). A social psychological perspective on marital dissolution. *Journal of Social Issues*, **32**, 21-47.

LEVINGER, G. (1979a). A social psychological perspective on marital dissolution. *In* "Divorce and Separation" (Eds. G. Levinger and O.C. Moles), Basic Books, Inc., New York.

LEVINGER, G. (1979b). Marital cohesiveness at the brink: the fate of applications for divorce. *In* "Divorce and Separation" (Eds. G. Levinger and O.C. Moles), Basic Books, Inc., New York.

LEVINGER, G. (1979c). A social exchange view on the dissolution of pair relationships. *In* "Social Exchange in Developing Relationships", (Eds. R.L. Burgess and T.L. Huston), Academic Press, New York and London.

LEVINGER, G. and HUESMANN, L.R. (in press). An "incremental exchange" perspective on the pair relationship: interpersonal reward and level of involvement. *In* "Social Exchange: Advances in Theory and Research" (Eds. K.J. Gergen, M.S. Greenberg and R.H. Willis), Winston, New York.

LEVINGER, G. and MOLES, O.C. (1976). In conclusion: Threads in the fabric. *Journal of Social Issues*, **32**, 193-207.

LEVINGER, G. and SENN, D.J. (1967). Disclosure of feelings in marriage. *Merrill-Palmer Quarterly*, **13**, 237-249.

LEVINGER, G., SENN, D.J. and JORGENSEN, B.W. (1970). Progress toward permanence in courtship: a test of the Kerckhoff-Davis hypotheses. *Sociometry*, **33**, 427-443.

LEVY, R.I. (1973). "Tahitians: Mind and Experience in the Society Islands", University of Chicago Press, Chicago.

LEWINSOHN, P.M. (1974). A behavioural approach to depression. *In* "The Psychology of Depression: Contemporary Theory and Research", (Eds. R. Friedman and M. Katz), Wiley, New York.

LEWINSOHN, P.M., BIGLAN, A. and ZEISS. A.M. (1976). Behavioural treatment of depression. *In* "Behavioural Management of Anxiety, Depression and Pain", (Ed. P.O. Davidson), Brunner/Mazel, New York.

LEWINSOHN, P.M. and SHAW, D.A. (1969). Feedback about interpersonal behaviour as an agent of behaviour change: a case study in the treatment of depression. *Psychotherapy and Psychosomatics*, **17**, 82-88.

LIBET, J.M. and LEWINSOHN, P.M. (1973). Concept of social skill with special reference to the behaviour of depressed persons. *Journal of Consulting and Clinical Psychology*, **40**, 304-312.

LIBET, J.M., LEWINSOHN, P.M. and JOVEREK. F. (1973). The construct of social skill: an empirical study of several measures on temporal stability, internal structure, and situational generalizability. Unpublished manuscript, University of Oregon.

LIEM, J.H. and LIEM, R. (1976). Life events, social supports and physical and psychological well-being. Paper read at meeting of the American Psychological Association, Washington, D.C.

LIGHT, P. (1979). "The Development of Social Sensitivity: A Study of Social Aspects of Role-Taking in Young Children", Cambridge University Press, Cambridge.

LINEHAN, M.M. and EGAN, K.J. (1979). Assertion training for women. *In* "Research and Practice in Social Skills Training" (Eds. A.S. Bellack and M. Hersen), Plenum Press, New York.

LIVELY, E.L. (1969). Toward a concept clarification: The case of marital interaction. *Journal of Marriage and the Family*, **31**, 108-114.

LOCKE, H.J. and WALLACE, K.M. (1959). Short marital adjustment and prediction tests: Their reliability and validity. *Marriage and Family Living*, **21**, 251-255.

LOEW, C.A. (1967). Acquisition of a hostile attitude and its relationship to aggressive behaviour. *Journal of Personality and Social Psychology*, **5**, 335-341.

LONGFELLOW, C. (1979). Divorce in context: Its impact on children. *In* "Divorce and Separation" (Eds. G. Levinger and O.C. Moles), Basic Books, Inc., New York.

LOPATA, H.Z. (1969). Loneliness: Forms and components. *Social Problems*, **17**, 248-261.

LoPICCOLO, J. and HOGAN, D.R. (1979). Sexual Dysfunction. *In* "Behavioural Medicine: Theory and Practice" (Eds. J.P. Brady and O. Pomerleau), Williams and Wilkins, New York.

LOUCKS, S. (1974). The dimensions of loneliness: A psychological study of affect, self-concept and object relations. Doctoral dissertation, University of Tennessee.

LOWENTHAL, M.F. (1964). Social isolation and mental illness in old age. *American Sociological Review*, **29**, 54-70.

LUBORSKY, L.B. and SINGER, B. (1974). The fit of therapist's behaviour into patient's negative expectations: A study of transference-countertransference contagion. Unpublished Manuscript.

LUCKEY, E.B. and BAIN, J.K. (1970). Children: A factor in marital satisfaction. *Journal of Marriage and the Family*, **32**, 43-44.

LYNCH, J.J. (1977). "The Broken Heart: The Medical Consequences of Loneliness", Basic Books, New York.

Mc CALL, G.J. (1970). The social organisation of relationships. *In* "Social Relationships" (Eds. G.J. McCall *et al*), Aldine, Chicago.

McCARTHY, B. (1976). Agreement and friendship: Affective and cognitive responses to attitudinal similarity-dissimilarity among same sex friends. (Unpublished Ph.D. thesis, University of Lancaster, England).

McCARTHY, B. (1981). Studying personal relationships. *In* "Personal Relationships 1: Studying Personal Relationships" (Eds. S.W. Duck and R. Gilmour), Academic Press, London and New York.

Mc CARTHY, B. and DUCK, S.W. (1976). Friendship duration and responses to attitudinal agreement-disagreement. *British Journal of Social and Clinical Psychology*, **15**, 377-386.

McCLINTOCK, F.H. (1963). "Crimes of Violence", Macmillan, London.

McCORD, W., McCORD, J. and HOWARD, A. (1961). Familial correlates of agression in nondelinquent male children. *Journal of Abnormal and Social Psychology*, **62**, 79-63.

McGURK, B.J. (1978). Personality types among "normal" homicides. *British Journal of Criminology*, **18**, 146-161.

McGURK, B.J. and McGURK, R.E. (1979). Personality types among prisoners and prison officers. *British Journal of Criminology*, **19**, 31-49.

McLEAN, P. (1976). Therapeutic decision-making in the behavioural treatment of depression. *In* "Behavioural Management of Anxiety, Depression and Pain", (Ed. P.O. Davidson), Bruner/Mazel, New York.

McPARTLAND, T.S. and HORNSTRA, R.K. (1964). The depressive datum. *Comprehensive Psychiatry*, **5**, 253-261.

MAGNUSSON, D. and EKEHAMMAR, B. (1978). Similar situations — behaviours? A study of the intraindividual congruence between situation perception and situation reactions. *Journal of Research in Personality*, **12**, 41-48.

MALINOWSKI, B. (1972). Phatic communion. *In* "Communication in Face to Face Interaction" (Eds. J. Laver and S. Hutcheson), Penguin, Harmondsworth.

MANNING, M., HERON, J. and MARSHALL, T. (1978). Styles of hostility and social interactions at nursery, at school and at home. An extended study of children. *In* "Aggression and Anti-Social Behaviour in Childhood and Adolescence" (Eds. L.A. Hersov and M. Berger), Pergamon Press, Oxford.

MANNING, M. and SLUCKIN, A.M. (1979, 1980). A comparison of difficult and normal children in nursery schools. Unpublished reports to the Social Science Research Council (HR 6195).

MARINI, M.M. (1976). Dimensions of marital happiness: A research note. *Journal of Marriage and the Family*, **38**, 443-448.

MARKMAN, H.J. (1979). Applications of a behavioural model of marriage in predicting relationship satisfaction of couples planning marriage. *Journal of Consulting and Clinical Psychology*, **47**, 743-749.

MARKUS, H. (1977). Self-schemata and processing information about the self. *Journal of Personality and Social Psychology*, **35**, 63-78.

MARLOWE, D. and GERGEN, K.J. (1969). Personality and social interaction. *In* "*The Handbook of Social Psychology* (2nd Edn. Vol. 3)" (Eds. G. Lindzey and E. Aronson), Addison-Wesley, Reading, Mass.

MARRIOTT, S. and FOSTER, S.L. (1978). Functional effects of assertive communication styles: outcome and parameters. Paper presented at the meeting of the Association for the Advancement of Behaviour Therapy, Chicago, November 1978. (quoted by Linehan and Egan, 1979).

MARSH, P. (1978). "Aggro: The Illusion of Violence", J.M. Dent, London.

MARSH, P., ROSSER, E. and HARRÉ, R. (1978). "The Rules of Disorder", Routledge and Kegan Paul, London.

MASTERS, W.H. and JOHNSON, V. (1970). "Human Sexual Inadequacy", Little, Brown, Boston.

MATHEWS, A., BANCROFT, J., WHITEHEAD, A., HACKMA, A.K., JULIER, D., GATH, D., and SHAW, P. (1976). The behavioural treatment of sexual inadequacy: A comparative study. *Behaviour Research and Therapy*, **14**, 427-436.

MEAD, G.H. (1934). "Mind, Self and Society", University of Chicago Press, Chicago.

MEEKS, J.E. (1973). Nosology in adolescent psychiatry: An enigma wrapped in a whirlwind. *In* "Current Issues in Adolescent Psychiatry" (Ed. J.C. Schoolar), Brunner/Mazel, New York.

MEGARGEE, E.I. (1966). Undercontrolled and overcontrolled personality types in extreme antisocial aggression. *Psychological Monographs*, **80**, No. 611.

MEGARGEE, E.I. (1971). The role of inhibition in the assessment and understanding of violence. *In* "The Control of Aggression and Violence: Cognitive and Physiological Factors" (Ed. J.E. Singer), Academic Press, London and New York.

MEGARGEE, E.I. and COOK, P.E. (1975). Negative response bias and the M.M.P.I. overcontrolled-hostility scale: a response to Deiker. *Journal of Consulting and Clinical Psychology*, **43**, 725-729.

MEHRABIAN, A. and KZIONSKY, S. (1974). "A Theory of Affiliation", Lexington Press, Lexington.

MERTON, R.K. (1948). The self-fulfilling prophecy. *The Antioch Review*, **8**, 193-210.

MEYER, J.P. and PEPPER, S. (1977). Need compatibility and marital adjustment in young married couples. *Journal of Personality and Social Psychology*, **35**, 331-342.

MICHEL, A. (1971). Male and female roles in the family: Examination of classical theory. *Social Science Information*, **10**, 113-135.

MICHELA, J.L., PEPLAU, L.A. and WEEKS, D.C. (1980). Perceived dimensions and consequences of attributions for loneliness. Unpublished Manuscript, University of California, Los Angeles.

MIDDLEBROOK, P.N. (1974). "Social Psychology and Modern Life", Alfred A. Knopf, New York.

MIELL, D.E. (in preparation). Withdrawing from relationships.

MIELL, D.E., DUCK, S.W. and LA GAIPA, J.J. (1979). Some interactive effects of sex and timing in self disclosure. *British Journal of Social and Clinical Psychology*, **18**, 355-362.

MILLER, B.C. (1976). A multivariate development model of marital satisfaction. *Journal of Marriage and the Family*, **38**, 643-657.

MILLER, G.R. and PARKS, M. (in preparation). Communication in dissolving relationships. *In* "Personal Relationships 4: Dissolving Personal Relationships" (Ed. S.W. Duck), Academic Press, London and New York.

MINUCHIN, S. (1974). "Families and Family Therapy", Tavistock Publications, London.

MISCHEL, W. (1968). "Personality and Assessment", Wiley, New York.

MOLOF, M.J. (1967). Differences between assaultive and non-assaultive juvenile offenders in the California Youth Authority. California Dept. of Youth Authority, Division of Research, Report No. 41, Sacramento.

MONEY, J. (1980). "Love and Love-Sickness: The Science of Sex, Gender Difference, and Pair-Bonding", Johns Hopkins Press, Balitmore.

MONTAGNER, H. (1978). "L'enfant et la communication", Pernoud/Stock, Paris.

MONTEMAYOR, R. and EISEN, M. (1977). The development of self conceptions from childhood to adolescence. *Developmental Psychology*, **13**, 314-319.

MOOS, R.H. (1968). Situational analysis of a therapeutic community milieu. *Journal of Abnormal Psychology*, **73**, 49-61.

MOOS, R.H. and MOOS, B.S. (1976). A typology of family social environments. *Family Process*, **15**, 357-371.

MORGAN, D.H.J. (1977). Alternatives to the Family. *In* "Equalities and Inequalities in Family Life" (Eds. R. Chester and J. Peel), Academic Press, London and New York.

MORRIS, M. and GOULD, R. (1963). Role reversal: A necessary concept in dealing with the battered child syndrome. *American Journal of Orthopsychiatry*, **33**, 298-299.

MORTON, T.L. and DOUGLAS, M. (1981). Growth of relationships. *In* "Personal Relationships 2: Developing Personal Relationships" (Eds. S.W. Duck and R. Gilmour), Academic Press, London and New York.

MOTT, F.L. and MOORE, S.F. (1979). The causes of marital disruption among young American women: An inter-disciplinary perspective. *Journal of Marriage and the Family*, **41**, 335-365.

MOUSTAKAS, C.E. (1961). "Loneliness", Prentice-Hall, New York.

MULVIHILL, D.J., TUMIN, M.M. and CURTIS, L.A. (1969). "Crimes of Violence: a Staff Report to the National Commisson on the Causes and Prevention of Violence", Vols. 11, 12 and 13, U.S. Government Printing Office, Washington, D.C.

MURSTEIN, B.I. (1977). The Stimulus-Value-Role (SVR) Theory of dyadic relationships. *In* "Theory and Practice in Interpersonal Attraction" (Ed. S.W. Duck), Academic Press, London and New York.

MURSTEIN, B.I. and GLAUDIN, V. (1966). The relationship of marital adjustment to personality: A factor analysis of the Interpersonal Check List. *Journal of Marriage and the Family*, **28**, 37-43.

MURSTEIN, B.I. and GLAUDIN, V. (1968). The use of the MMPI in the determination of marital maladjustment. *Journal of Marriage and the Family*, **30**, 651-655.

NASBY, W., HAYDEN, B. and DePAULO, B.M. (1980). Attributional bias among aggressive boys to interpret unambiguous social stimuli as displays of hostility. *Journal of Abnormal Psychology*, **89**, 459-468.

NELSON, R.E. (1964). Irrational beliefs in depression. *Journal of Consulting and Clinical Psychology*, **45**, 1190-1191.

NELSON, R.E. and CRAIGHEAD, W.E. (1977). Selective recall of positive and negative feedback, self-control behaviours, and depression. *Journal of Abnormal Psychology*, **86**, 379-388.

NETTELBLADT, P. and UDDENBERG, N. (1979). Sexual dysfunction and sexual satisfaction in 58 married Swedish men. *Journal of Psychosomatic Research*, **23**, 141-147.

NEWCOMB, M.D. (1976). Based on unpublished analyses of data on divorced couples, UCLA.

NEWCOMB, M.D. (1981). Heterosexual cohabitation relationships. *In* "Personal Relationships 1: Studying Personal Relationships" (Eds. S.W. Duck and R. Gilmour), Academic Press, London and New York.

NEWCOMB, M.D. and BENTLER, P.M. (1980a). Cohabitation before marriage: A comparison of couples who did and did not cohabit. *Alternative Lifestyles*, **3**, 65-85.

NEWCOMB, M.D. and BENTLER, P.M. (1980b). Assessment of personality and demographic aspects of cohabitation and marital success. *Journal of Personality Assessment*, **44**, 11-24.

NICHOLS, K. (1980). Psychological Care for the Ill and Injured. *In* "Research in Psychology and Medicine, Volume 2" (Eds. D.J. Oborne, M.M. Gruneberg and J.R. Eiser), Academic Press, London and New York.

NICKEL, T.W. (1974). The attribution of intention as a critical factor in the relation between frustration and aggression. *Journal of Personality*, **42**, 482-492.

NORTON, A.J. and GLICK, P.C. (1979). Marital instability in America: Past, present and future. *In* "Divorce and Separation" (Eds. G. Levinger and O.C. Moles), Basic Books, Inc., New York.

NOVACO, R.W. (1975). "Anger Control: The Development and Evaluation of an Experimental Treatment", D.C. Heath, Lexington Books, Lexington, Mass.

NOVACO, R.W. (1976a). The functions and regulation of the arousal of anger. *American Journal of Psychiatry*, **133**, 1124-1128.

NOVACO, R.W. (1976b). Treatment of chronic anger through cognitive and relaxation controls. *Journal of Consulting and Clinical Psychology*, **44**, 681-687.

NOVACO, R.W. (1977a). Stress inoculation: a cognitive therapy for anger and its application to a case of depression. *Journal of Consulting and Clinical Psychology*, **45**, 600-608.

NOVACO, R.W. (1977b). A stress inoculation approach to anger management in the training of law enforcement officers. *American Journal of Community Psychology*, **5**, 327-346.

NOVACO, R.W. (1978). Anger and coping with stress. *In* "Cognitive Behaviour Therapy" (Eds. J.P. Foreyt and D.P. Rathjen), Plenum Press, New York.

NYE, F.I. and BERARDO, F. (1973). On the causes of divorce. *In* "The Family: Its Structures and Interaction" (Eds. F.I. Nye and F. Berardo), McMillan, New York.

OAKLEY, A. (1974). "The Sociology of Housework", Martin Robertson, London.

O'BANION, K. and ARKOWITZ, H. (1977). Social anxiety and selective memory for affective information about the self. *Social Behaviour and Personality* **5**, 321–328.

O'BRIEN, J.E. (1971). Violence in divorce-prone families. *Journal of Marriage and the Family*, **33**, 692-698.

O'BRIEN, J.E. (1972). Interrelationship of conflict and satisfaction in unstable marriages: A methodological analysis. Paper presented at the Annual Meeting of the American Sociological Association, New Orleans, August, 1972.

OLLENDICK, T.H. and HERSEN, M. (1979). Social skills training for juvenile delinquents. *Behaviour Research and Therapy*, **17**, 547-554.

OLSON, D.H. (1970). Marital and family therapy: Integrative review and critique. *Journal of Marriage and the Family*, **32**, 501-538.

OLSON, D.H., SPRENKLE, D.H. and RUSSELL, C. (1979). Circumplex model of marital family systems I. *Family Process*, **18**, 3-28.

ORDEN, S.R. and BRADBURN, N.M. (1968). Dimensions of marriage happiness. *American Journal of Sociology*, **73**, 715-731.

ORFORD, J. (1975). Alcoholism and marriage: The argument against specialism. *Journal of Studies on Alcohol*, **36**, 1537-1563.

ORFORD, J. (1980). The Domestic Context. *In* "Psychological Problems: The Social Context" (Eds. M.P. Feldman and J. Orford), Wiley, Chichester.

ORFORD, J., OPPENHEIMER, E., EGERT, S., HENSMAN, C. and GUTHRIE, S. (1976). The cohesiveness of alcoholism-complicated marriages and its influence on treatment outcome. *British Journal of Psychiatry*, **128**, 318-349.

ORFORD, J., OPPENHEIMER, E., EGERT, S. and HENSMAN, C. (1977). The role of excessive drinking in alcoholism-complicated marriages: A study of stability and change over a one-year period. *International Journal of Addictions*, **12**, 471-495.

ORVIS, B.R., KELLEY, H.H. and BUTLER, D. (1976). Attributional conflict in young couples. *In* "New Directions in Attribution Research: 1" (Eds. J.H. Harvey, W. Ickes and R.F. Kidd), Erlbaum, Hillsdale, New Jersey.

PAGE, R.A. and BALLOUN, J.L. (1978). The effect of voice volume on the perception of personality. *Journal of Social Psychology*, **105**, 65-72.

PAOLINO, T.J. and McCRADY, B.S. (1977). "The Alcoholic Marriage: Alternative Perspectives", Grune and Stratton, New York.

PARTEN, M.B. (1932). Social participation among pre-school children. *Journal of Abnormal and Social Psychology*, **27**, 243-269.

PAWLBY, S.J. (1981). Infant-Mother Relationships. *In* "Personal Relationships 2: Developing Personal Relationships" (Eds. S.W. Duck and R. Gilmour), Academic Press, London and New York.

PEARSON, W. and HENDRIX, L. (1979). Divorce and the status of women. *Journal of Marriage and the Family*, **41**, 375-385.

PEPLAU, L.A. and PERLMAN, D. (Eds.) (in press). "Loneliness: A Sourcebook of Current Theory, Research and Therapy", Wiley-Interscience, New York.

PEPLAU, L.A., RUSSELL, D. and HEIM, M. (1979). The experience of loneliness. *In* "New Approaches to Social Problems: Applications of Attribution Theory" (Eds. I.H. Frieze, D. Bar-Tal and J.S. Carroll), Jossey-Bass, San Francisco.

PERLMAN, D., GERSON, A.C. and SPINNER, B. (1978). Loneliness among senior citizens: An empirical report. *Essence*, **2**, 239-248.

PERLMAN, D., SHORE, M. and FLORENTINE, N. (1979). Egocentrism and evaluation in loneliness. Paper presented at the UCLA Research Conference on Loneliness, Los Angeles, May 1979.

PERRIN, F.A.C. (1921). Physical attractiveness and repulsiveness. *Journal of Experimental Psychology*, **4**, 203-217.

PETERSON, G.B., HEY, R.N. and PETERSON, L.R. (1979). Intersection of family development and moral stage frameworks: Implications for theory and research. *Journal of Marriage and the Family*, **41**, 229-235.

PETTIGREW, T.F. (1967). Social evaluation theory: Convergences and applications. *In* "Nebraska Symposium on Motivation" (Vol. 15) (Ed. D. Levine), University of Nebraska Press, Lincoln.

PIAGET, J. (1971). "Biology and Knowledge", Edinburgh University Press, Edinburgh.

PILKONIS, P.A. (1977). The behavioural consequences of shyness. *Journal of Personality*, **45**, 596-611.

PINEO, P.C. (1961). Disenchantment in the later years of marriage. *Marriage and Family Living*, **23**, 3-11.

POLAND, J.M. (1978). Subculture of violence: Youth offender value systems. *Criminal Justice and Behaviour*, **5**, 159-164.

POLLACK, J. and BJORK, D. (1978). Etiological family life factors leading to hospitalization of seriously disturbed adolescents. *Psychiatric Quarterly*, **50**, 30-36.

POND, D.A., RYLE, A. and HAMILTON, M. (1963). Marriage and neurosis in a working class population. *British Journal of Psychiatry*, **109**, 592-598.

POPE, H. and MUELLER, C.W. (1979). The intergenerational transmission of marital instability: Comparisons by race and class. *In* "Divorce and Separation" (Eds. G. Levinger and O.C. Moles), Basic Books, Inc., New York.

POSTER, M. (1978). "Critical Theory of the Family", Pluto Press, London.

PRKACHIN, K., CRAIG, K., PAPEGEORGES, D. and REITH, G. (1977). Non-verbal communication deficits and responses to performance feedback in depression. *Journal of Abnormal Psychology*, **86**, 224-234.

PRZYBYLA, D. and BYRNE, D. (1981). Sexual Relationships. *In* "Personal Relationships 1: Studying Personal Relationships" (Eds. S.W. Duck and R. Gilmour), Academic Press, London and New York.

QUALLS, C.B., WINCZE, J. and BARLOW, D.H. (1978). "The Prevention of Sexual Disorders: Issues and Approaches", Plenum Press, New York.

QUANTY, M.B. (1976). Aggression catharsis: experimental investigations and implications. *In* "Perspectives on Aggression" (Eds. R.G. Geen and E.C. O'Neal), Academic Press, London and New York.

QUINNEY, R. (1970). "The Social Reality of Crime", Little, Brown, Boston.

RAE, J.B. (1972). The influence of the wives on the treatment of alcoholics; Follow-up study at two-years. *British Journal of Psychiatry*, **120**, 601-613.

RAE, J.B. and DREWERY, J. (1972). Interpersonal patterns in alcoholic marriages. *British Journal of Psychiatry*, **120**, 615-621.

RAHAIM, S., LEFEBVRE, C. and JENKINS, J.O. (1980). The effects of social skills training on behavioural and cognitive components of anger management. *Journal of Behaviour Therapy and Experimental Psychiatry*, **11**, 3-8.

RASCHKE, H.J. (1977). The role of social participation in postseparation and postdivorce adjustment. *Journal of Divorce*, **1**, 129-140.

RASMUSSEN, P.K. and FERRARO, K.J. (1979). The divorce process. *Alternative Lifestyles*, **2**, 443-460.

RAUSH, H.L. (1965). Interaction sequences. *Journal of Personality and Social Psychology*, **2**, 487-499.

RAUSH, H.L., BARRY, W.A., HERTEL, R.K. and SWAIN, M.A. (1974). "Communication, Conflict and Marriage", Jossey-Bass, San Francisco.

REEVY, W.R. (1963). Vestured genital apposition and coitus. In "Advances in Sex Research" (Ed. H.G. Beigel), Harper and Row, New York.

REISMAN, J. (1981). Adult friendships. In "Personal Relationships 2: Developing Personal Relationships" (Eds. S.W. Duck and R. Gilmour), Academic Press, London and New York.

RENNE, K.S. (1970). Correlates of dissatisfaction in marriage. *Journal of Marriage and the Family*, **32**, 54-67.

RICE, J.K. (1978). Divorce and a return to school. *Journal of Divorce*, **1**, 247-257.

RICHMAN, N., STEVENSON, J.E. and GRAHAM, P.J. (1975). Prevalence of behaviour problems in three-year-old children: An epidemiological study in a London borough. *Journal of Child Psychology and Psychiatry*, **16**, 277-287.

RIESMAN, D., GLAZER, N. and DENNY, R. (1961). "The Lonely Crowd: A Study of the Changing America Character", Yale University Press, New Haven, Connecticut.

RIME, B., BOUVY, H. and ROUILLON, F. (1978). Psychopathy and nonverbal behaviour in an interpersonal situation. *Journal of Abnormal Psychology*, **87**, 636-643.

RIMM, D.C., HILL, G.A., BROWN, N.N. and STUART, J.E. (1974). Group-assertive training in treatment of expression of inappropriate anger. *Psychological Reports*, **34**, 791-798.

RISKIN, J. and FAUNCE, E. (1972). An evaluative review of family interaction research. *Family Process*, **11**, 365-455.

ROGERS, P.J. and ROGERS, T.B. (1979). Self-referent encoding in a middle aged group. Cited in Davis, H. (1979). Self-reference and the encoding of personal information in depression. *Journal of Cognitive Therapy and Research*, **3**, 97-110.

ROLLINS, B.C. and FELDMAN, H. (1970). Marital satisfaction over the lifecycle. *Journal of Marriage and the Family*, **32**, 20-28.

ROOK, K. and PEPLAU, L.A. (in press). Perspectives on helping the lonely. In "Loneliness: A Sourcebook of Current Theory, Research and Therapy" (Eds. L.A. Peplau and D. Perlman), Wiley-Interscience, New York.

ROPER, R. and HINDE, R.A. (1978). Social behaviour in a play group: consistency and complexity. *Child Development*, **49**, 570-579.

ROSENBERRY, C., WEISS, R.L. and LEWINSOHN, P.M. (1969). Frequency and skill of emitted and social reinforcement in depressed and non-depressed subjects. Paper presented at the meeting of the Western Psychological Association, Vancouver, Canada.

ROSENTHAL, R. (1973). On the social psychology of the self-fulfilling prophecy: Further evidence for Pygmalion effects and their mediating mechanisms. *MSS Modular Publications*, **53**, 1-28.

ROSS, D.M. and ROSS, S.A. (1976). "Hyperactivity: Research, Theory and Action", Wiley, New York.

ROTHBART, M. and BIRRELL, P. (1977). Attitude and the perception of faces. *Journal of Research in Personality*, **11**, 209-215.

ROTTER, J.B. (1966). Generalized expectancies for internal versus external control of reinforcement. *Psychological Monographs*, **80**, (Whole No, 609).

ROUNSAVILLE, B.J., WIESSMAN, M.M., PRUSOFF, B.A. and HERCEG-BARON, R.L. (1979). Marital disputes and treatment outcome in depressed women. *Comprehensive Psychiatry*, **20**, 483-490.

RUBENSTEIN, C.M. and SHAVER, P. (1980). Loneliness in two northeastern cities. *In* "The Anatomy of Loneliness" (Eds. J. Hartog, J.R. Audy and Y.A. Cohen), International Universities Press, New York.

RUBENSTEIN, C.M., SHAVER, P. and PEPLAU, L.A. (February 1979). Loneliness. *Human Nature*, 58-65.

RUBIN, Z. and PEPLAU, L.A. (1975). Who believes in a just world? *Journal of Social Issues*, **31** (3), 65-90.

RUBIN, Z., PEPLAU, L.A. and HILL, C.T. (in press). Loving and leaving: sex differences in romantic attachments. *Sex Roles*.

RULE, B.G. and NESDALE, A.R. (1976). Moral judgement of aggressive behaviour. *In* "Perspectives on Aggression" (Eds. R.G. Geen and E.C. O'Neal), Academic Press, London and New York.

RUSH, A.J., SHAW, B. and KHATAMI, M. (1980). Cognitive therapy of depression: Utilizing the couples system. *Cognitive Therapy and Research*, **4**, 103-113.

RUSSELL, C. (1979). Circumplex model of marital family systems III. *Family Process*, **18**, 29-46.

RUSSELL, D. (in press). The measurement of loneliness. *In* "Loneliness: A Sourcebook of Current Theory, Research and Therapy" (Eds. L.A. Peplau and D. Perlman), Wiley-Interscience, New York.

RUSSELL, D., PEPLAU. L.A. and FERGUSON, M.L. (1978). Developing a measure of loneliness. *Journal of Personality Assessment*, **42**, 290-294.

RUTTER, M. (1972). "Maternal Deprivation Reassessed", Penguin, Harmondsworth.

RUTTER, M., COX, A., TUPLING, C., BERGER, M. and YULE, W. (1975). Attainment and adjustment in two geographical areas - I. The prevalence of psychiatric disorder. *British Journal of Psychiatry*, **126**, 493-509.

SAFER, D. and ALLEN, R. (1976). "Hyperactive Children: Diagnosis and Management", University Park Press, Baltimore.

SAFILIOS-ROTHSCHILD, C. (1970). "The Sociology and Social Psychology of Disability and Rehabilitation", Random House, New York.

SARASON, I.G. (1978). A cognitive social learning approach to juvenile delinquency. *In* "Psychopathic Behaviour: Approaches to Research" (Eds. R.D. Hare and D. Schalling), Wiley, Chichester.

SARASON, I.G. and GANZER, V.J. (1973). Modelling and group discussion in the rehabilitation of juvenile delinquents. *Journal of Counseling Psychology*, **20**, 442-449.

SCANZONI, J. (1972). "Sexual Bargaining: Power Politics in the American Marriage", Prentice-Hall, Englewood Cliffs, New Jersey.

SCANZONI, J. (1979). A historical perspective on husband-wife bargaining power and marital dissolution. *In* "Divorce and Separation" (Eds. G. Levinger and O.C. Moles), Basic Books, Inc. New York.

SCHACHTER, S. (1959). "The Psychology of Affiliation", Stanford University Press, Stanford, California.

SCHAFFER, H.R. (1977). "Mothering", Fontana/Open Books, London.

SCHALLING, D. (1978). Psychopathy — related personality variables and the psychophysiology of socialization. *In* "Psychopathic Behaviour: Approaches to Research" (Eds. R.D. Hare and D. Schalling), Wiley, Chichester.

SCHEFF, T.J. (1966). "Being Mentally Ill: A Sociological Theory", Aldine Atherton, Chicago.

SCHULZ, R. (1976). Effects of control and predictabililty on the physical and psychological well-being of the institutionalized aged. *Journal of Personality and Social Psychology*, **33**, 563-573.

SCHWARTZ, R. and GOTTMAN, J. (1976). Towards a task analysis of assertive behaviour. *Journal of Consulting and Clinical Psychology*, **44**, 910-920.

SELIGMAN, M.E.P. (1975). "Helplessness", W.H. Freeman, San Francisco.

SERMAT, V. (1980). Some situational and personality correlates of loneliness. *In* "The Anatomy of Loneliness" (Eds. J. Hartog, J.R. Audy and Y.A. Cohen), International Universities Press, New York.

SHAFFER, M. and LEWINSOHN, P.M. (1971). Interpersonal behaviours in the home of depressed versus nondepressed psychiatric and normal controls: a test of several hypotheses. Paper presented at the meeting of the Western Psychological Association, San Francisco. USA.

SHEEHY, G. (1976). "Passages: Predictable Crises of Adult Life", Bantam, New York.

SHOPE, D.F. and BRODERICK, C.B. (1967). Level of sexual experience and predicted adjustment in marriage. *Journal of Marriage and the Family*, **29**, 424-427.

SHOTTER, J. (1974). The development of personal powers. *In* "The Integration of a Child into a Social World" (Ed. M.P.M. Richards), Cambridge University Press, Cambridge.

SILLER, J. (1976). Attitudes toward disability. *In* "Contemporary Vocational Rehabilitation" (Eds. H. Rusalem and D. Malikin), New York University Press, New York.

SIMMEL, G. (1950). "The Sociology of Georg Simmel" (Translated by K.H. Wolff), Free Press of Glencoe, New York.

SIOMOPOULOS, G. (1980). On a disturbance of affectivity in schizophrenic adolescents: Implications for affect theory. *Adolescence*, **15**, 123-141.

SKOREPA, C.A., HORROCKS, J.E. and THOMPSON, G.G. (1963). A study of friendship fluctuations of college students. *Journal of Genetic Psychology*, **102**, 151-157.

SLATER, P. (1970). "The Pursuit of Loneliness: American Culture at the Breaking Point", Beacon Press, Boston.

SLUCKIN, A. (1981). "Growing Up in the Playground: The Social Development of Children", Routledge and Kegan Paul, London.

SLUZKI, C.E. and RANSOM, D.C. (Eds), (1976). "Double Bind: The Foundation of the Communicational Approach to the Family", Grune and Stratton, New York.

SMALL, A.C., GROSS, R.B. and BATLIS, N.C. (1979). Sexual identity and personality variables in normal and disturbed adolescent girls. *Adolescence*, **14**, 31-44.

SMITH, P.K. (1973). Temporal clusters and individual differences in the behaviour of preschool children. *In* "Comparative Ecology and Behaviour of Primates" (Eds. R.P. Michael and J.H. Crook), Academic Press, New York and London.

SMITH, R.J. (1978). "The Psychopath in Society", Academic Press, London and New York.

SMITH-HANEN, S. (1976). Socialization of the physically handicapped. *Journal of Applied Rehabilitation Counseling*, **7**, 131-141.

SNYDER, M. (1974). Self-monitoring of expressive behaviour. *Journal of Personality and Social Psychology*, **30**, 526-537.

SNYDER, M. (1978). On the nature of social knowledge. Paper delivered at the Annual Meeting of the Midwestern Psychological Association, Chicago, U.S.A.

SNYDER, M. (in press). On the self perpetuating nature of social stereotypes. *In* "Cognitive Processes in Stereotyping and Intergroup Behaviour" (Ed. D.L. Hamilton), Erlbaum, Hillsdale, New Jersey.

SNYDER, M. and MONSON, T.C. (1975). Persons, situations and the control of social behaviour. *Journal of Personality and Social Psychology*, **32**, 637-644.

SNYDER, M., TANKE, E.D. and BERSCHEID, E. (1977). Social perception and interpersonal behaviour: On the self-fulfilling nature of social stereotypes. *Journal of Personality and Social Psychology*, **35**, 656-666.

SPANIER, G.B. (1976). Measuring dyadic adjustment: New scales for assessing the quality of marriage and similar dyads. *Journal of Marriage and the Family*, **38**, 15-28.

SPANIER, G.B. and ANDERSON, E.A. (1979). The impact of the legal system on adjustment to marital separation. *Journal of Marriage and the Family*, **41**, 603-613.

SPANIER, G.B. and CASTO, R.F. (1979). Adjustment to separation and divorce: A qualitative analysis. *In* "Divorce and Separation" (Eds. G.Levinger and O.C. Moles), Basic Books, Inc., New York.

STEINGLASS, P. (1981). The roles of alcohol in family systems. *In* "Alcohol and the Family" (Eds. J. Orford and J. Harwin), Croom Helm, London.

STEINGLASS, P., DAVIS, D.I. and BERENSON, D. (1977). Observations of conjointly hospitalized "alcoholic couples" during sobriety and intoxication: Implications for theory and therapy. *Family Process*, **16**, 1-16.

STORMS, M.D. and McCAUL, K.D. (1977). Attribution processes and emotional exacerbation of dysfunctional behaviour. *In* "New Directions in Attribution Research", Vol. 1, (Eds. J.H. Harvey, W.J. Ickes and R.F. Kidd), Erlbaum, Hillsdale, New Jersey.

STORR, A. (1978). Sadism and paranoia: cruelty as collective and individual response. *In* "Aggression and Anti-social Behaviour in Childhood and Adolescence" (Eds. L. Hersov, M. Berger and D. Shaffer), Pergamon Press, Oxford.

STROEBE, W. and STROEBE, M. (in preparation.) Growth and dissolution of close relationships. *In* "The Social Dimension: European Perspectives on Social Psychology" (Ed. H. Tajfel), Cambridge University Press, Cambridge.

STRYKER, S. (1964). The interactional and situational approaches. *In* "Handbook of Marriage and the Family" (Ed. H.T. Christensen), Rand, McNally, Chicago.

STUEVE, A. and GERSONS, K. (1977). Personal relationships across the life cycle. *In* "Networks and Places" (Ed. C.S. Fischer), Free Press, New York.

SULLIVAN, H.S. (1953). "The Interpersonal Theory of Psychiatry", W.W. Norton, New York.

SURTEES, P.G. (1980). Social support, residual adversity and depressive outcome. *Social Psychiatry*, **15**, 71-80.

SUTTLES, G.D. (1970). Friendship as a social institution. *In* "Social Relationships" (Ed. G.J. McCall *et al*), Aldine, Chicago.

TEDESCHI, J.T., SMITH, R.B. and BROWN, R.C. (1974). A re-interpretation of research on aggression. *Psychological Bulletin*, **81**, 540-562.

TERMAN, L.M. and ODEN, M.H. (1947). "The Gifted Child Grows Up: Twenty-five Years' Follow-Up of a Superior Group", Stanford University Press, Stanford, California.

THARP, B. (1963). Psychological patterning in marriage. *Psychological Bulletin*, **60**, 97-117.

THIBAUT, J.W. and KELLEY, H.H. (1959). "The Social Psychology of Groups", Wiley, New York.

THOMAS, A. and CHESS, S. (1977). "Temperament and Development", Brunner/Mazel, New York.

THOMAS, A., CHESS, S. and BIRCH, H.G. (1968). "Temperament and Behaviour Disorders in Children", New York University Press, New York.

TOCH, H. (1968). In report by Mulvihill *et al*. (1969).

TOCH, H. (1969). "Violent Men", Penguin, Harmondsworth.

TREVARTHEN, C. (1979). Instincts for human understanding and for cultural co-operation: their development in infancy. *In* "Human Ethology" (Eds. M. von Cranach, K. Foppa, W. Lepenies and D. Ploog), Cambridge University Press, Cambridge.

TREVARTHEN, C. and HUBLEY, P. (1978). Secondary intersubjectivity: confidence, confiding and acts of meaning in the first year. *In* "Action, Gesture and Symbol: The Emergence of Language" (Ed. A. Lock), Academic Press, London and New York.

TREVARTHEN, C., MURRAY, L. and HUBLEY, P. (1981). Infant psychology. *In* "Scientific Foundations of Clinical Pediatrics" (Eds. J. Davis and J. Dobbing), Heinemanns Medical Publishers, London.

TRILLING, L. (1953). "The Liberal Imagination", Doubleday Anchor, New York.

TROWER, P. (1979). Fundamentals of interpersonal behaviour: a social-psychological perspective. *In* "Research and Practice in Social Skills Training" (Eds. A.S. Bellack and M. Hersen), Plenum, New York.

TROWER, P. (1980). Situational analysis of the components and processes of behaviour of socially skilled and unskilled patients. *Journal of Consulting and Clinical Psychology*, **48**, 327-339.

TROWER, P., BRYANT, B. and ARGYLE, M. (1978). "Social Skills and Mental Health", Methuen, London.

TROWER, P. and O'MAHONY, J. (1978). Problems of social failure: Can social psychology help? Paper delivered at a one-day Conference of the British Psychological Society, March, 1978.

VALINS, S. and NISBETT, R.E. (1971). Attribution processes in the development and treatment of emotional disorders. *In* "Attribution: Perceiving the Cause of Behaviour" (Eds. E.E. Jones, D. Kanouse, H.H. Kelley, R.E. Nisbett, S. Valins and B. Weiner), General Learning Press, New York.

VAUGHAN, D. (1979). Uncoupling: The process of moving from one lifestyle to another. *Alternative Lifestyles*, **2**, 415-442.

VAUGHN, C.E. and LEFF, J.P. (1976). The influence of family and social factors on the course of psychiatric illness. *British Journal of Psychiatry*, **2**, 125-137.

VON BERTALANFFY, L. (1968). "General System Theory", Brajiller, New York.

VOSS, J.R. (1980). Sex Education: Evaluation and recommendations for future study. *Archives of Sexual Behaviour*, **9**, 37-59.

WACHTEL, P.L. (1977). "Psychoanalysis and Behaviour Therapy", Basic Books, New York.

WALSTER, E.H., WALSTER, G.W. and BERSCHIED, E. (1978). "Equity: Theory and Research", Allyn and Bacon, Boston.

WAXER, P. (1974). Nonverbal cues for depression. *Journal of Abnormal Psychology*, **53**, 318-322.

WEINER, B., RUSSELL, D. and LERMAN, D. (1978). Affective consequences of causal ascriptions. *In* "New Directions in Attribution Research" (Vol. 2) (Eds. J.H. Harvey, W.J. Ickes and R.F. Kidd), Erlbaum Press, Hillsdale, New Jersey.

WEISS, R.S. (1973). "Loneliness: The Experience of Emotional and Social Isolation", MIT Press, Cambridge, Mass.

WEISS, R.S. (1975). "Marital Separation", Basic Books, Inc., New York.

WEISS, R.S. (1979a). The emotional impact of marital separation. *In* "Divorce and Separation" (Eds. G. Levinger and O.C. Moles), Basic Books, Inc., New York.

WEISS, R.S. (1979b). Issues in the adjudication of custody when parents separate. *In* "Divorce and Separation" (Eds. G. Levinger and O.C. Moles), Basic Books, Inc., New York.

WEISSMAN, M.M. and KLERMAN, G.L. (1973). Psychotherapy with depressed women: an empirical study of content themes and reflection. *British Journal of Psychiatry*, **123**, 55-61.

WEISSMAN, M.M. and PAYKEL, E.S. (1974). "The Depressed Woman: A Study of Social Relationships", University of Chicago Press, Chicago.

WELLS, E.A. and DEZEN, A.E. (1978). The results of family therapy revisited: The non-behavioural methods. *Family Process*, **17**, 251-274.

WELLS, E.A., DILKES, T. and TRIVELLI, N. (1972). The results of family therapy: A critical review of the literature. *Family Process*, **11**, 189-207.

WENER, A.E. and REHM, A.P. (1975). Depressive affect: A test of behavioural hypotheses. *Journal of Abnormal Psychology*, **84**, 221-227.

WENZ, F.V. (1977). Seasonal suicide attempts and forms of loneliness. *Psychological Reports*, **40**, 807-810.

WERTHEIM, E.S. (1973). Family unit therapy and the science and typology of family systems. *Family Process*, **12**, 361-376.

WEST, D.J. (1965). "Murder Followed by Suicide", Heinemann, London.

WHEELER, L. and NEZLEK, J. (1977). Sex differences in social participation. *Journal of Personality and Social Psychology*, **35**, 742-754.

WIDOM, C.S. (1976a). Interpersonal and personal construct systems in psychopaths. *Journal of Consulting and Clinical Psychology*, **44**, 614-623.

WIDOM, C.S. (1976b). Interpersonal conflict and co-operation in psychopaths. *Journal of Abnormal Psychology*, **85**, 330-334.

WILLS, T.A., WEISS, R.L. and PATTERSON, G.R. (1974). A behavioural analysis of the determinants of marital satisfaction. *Journal of Consulting and Clinical Psychology*, **42**, 802-811.

WINCH, R.F. (1958). "Mate Selection: A Study of Complementary Needs", Harper, New York.

WOLFF, S. (1967). Behavioural characteristics of primary school children referred to a psychiatric department. *British Journal of Psychiatry*, **113**, 885-893.

WOLFGANG, M.E. (1958a). "Patterns in Criminal Homicide", University of Pennsylvania Press, Philadelphia.

WOLFGANG, M.E. (1958b). An analysis of homicide-suicide. *Journal of Clinical and Experimental Psychopathology*, **19**, 208-218.

WOLFGANG, M.E. (1978). Family violence and criminal behaviour. *In* "Violence and Responsibility" (Ed. R.L. Sadoff), Spectrum, London.

WOLFGANG, M.E. and FERRACUTI, F. (1976). "The Subculture of Violence", Tavistock, London.

WOLKIND, S.N. and EVERETT, B. (1974). A cluster analysis of the behavioural items in the preschool child. *Psychological Medicine*, **4**, 422-427.

WOLPE, J. (1954). Reciprocal inhibition as the main basis of psychotherapeutic effects. *Archives of Neurology and Psychiatry*, **72**, 205-226.

WOLPE, J. (1969). "The Practice of Behaviour Therapy", Pergamon Press, Oxford.

WOLPIN, M. (1969). Guided imagining to reduce avoidance behaviour. *Psychotherapy Research and Practice*, **6**, 122-124.

WOOD, H.D. (1972). The children's friendship expectancy inventory and the prediction of sociometric acceptability. Unpublished Masters thesis, University of Windsor.

WOOD, H.D. (1976). Predicting behavioural types in preadolescent girls from psycho-social development and friendship values. Unpublished Doctoral dissertation., University of Windsor.

WOOD, H.D. and LA GAIPA, J.J. (1978). Predicting behavioural types in preadolescent girls from psycho-social development and friendship values. Paper read at meeting of the Canadian Psychological Association, Toronto, Ontario.

WOOLFOLK, R.L. and DEVER, S. (1979). Perceptions of assertion: An empirical analysis. *Behaviour Therapy*, **10**, 404-411.

WORTMAN, C.B. and DUNKEL-SCHETTER, C. (1979). Interpersonal relationships and cancer: A theoretical analysis. *Journal of Social Issues*, **35**, 120-155.

WRIGHT, J., PERREAULT, R. and MATHIEU, M. (1979). The treatment of sexual dysfunction: A review. *Archives of General Psychiatry*, **34**, 881-890.

WYNNE, L., RYCKHOFF, I., DAY, J. and HIRSCH, S. (1958). Pseudo-mutuality in the family relations of schizophrenics. *Psychiatry*, **21**, 205-220.

YAFFÉ, M. (1980). Commentary paper on current trends in sex therapy. *In* "Current Trends in Psychiatric Treatment" (Ed. G. Tennent), Pitman Medical, London.

YAFFÉ, M. (1981). The assessment and treatment of paedophilia. *In* "Perspectives on Paedophilia" (Ed. B. Taylor), Concord/Batsford, London.

YOUNG, D.M. (1978a). The divorce experience workshop: A consumer evaluation. *Journal of Divorce*, **2**, 37-48.

YOUNG, D.M. (1978b). Consumer satisfaction with the divorce workshop: A follow-up report. *Journal of Divorce*, **2**, 49-53.

YOUNG, G.C.D. and TROWER, P.F. (in preparation.) Selective perception in the neurotic.

YOUNGREN, M.A. and LEWINSOHN, P.M. (1980). The functional relation between depression and problematic interpersonal behaviour. *Journal of Abnormal Psychology*, **89**, 333-341.

YULIS, S. (1976). Generalisation of therapeutic gain in the treatment of premature ejaculations. *Behaviour Therapy*, **7**, 355-358.

ZABLOCKI, B. (1973). Comparative study of west coast communes. Paper presented at the meeting of the American Orthopsychiatric Association, New York, 1973.

ZIGLER, E. and PHILLIPS, L. (1961). Psychiatric diagnosis and symptomatology. *Journal of Abnormal and Social Psychology*, **63**, 69-75.

ZILBERGELD, B. (1979). "Men and Sex: A Guide to Sexual Fulfilment", Souvenir Press, London.

ZILBERGELD, B. and EVANS, M. (1980). The inadequacy of Masters and Johnson. *Psychology Today*, August, 29-43.

ZILBOORG, G. (January, 1938). Loneliness. *Atlantic Monthly*, 45-54.

ZIMBARDO, P.G. (1977). "Shyness" Addison-Wesley, Reading, Mass.

Author Index

The numbers in italics indicate the pages on which the References appear

Subject Index

DATE DUE